More Liberty Means
Less Government

More Liberty Means Less Government

Our Founders Knew This Well

Walter E. Williams

HOOVER INSTITUTION PRESS

Stanford University   Stanford, California

www.hoover.org

Hoover Institution Press Publication No. 453
Copyright © 1999 by the Board of Trustees of the
Leland Stanford Junior University

First printing, 1999

15 14 13 12 11 10 09   15 14 13 12 11 10 9 8

Manufactured in the United States of America

The paper used in this publication meets the minimum requirements
of the American National Standard for Information Sciences—
Permanence of Paper for Printed Library Materials, ANSI Z39.48-1992. ∞

Library of Congress Cataloging-in-Publication Data
Williams, Walter E. (Walter Edward), 1936–
More liberty means less government : our Founders knew this well /
Walter E. Williams.
    p.   cm. — (Hoover Institution Press publication ; no. 453)
Includes bibliographical references and index.
ISBN-13: 978-0-8179-9612-3 (alk. paper)
ISBN-10: 0-8179-9612-5 (alk. paper)
    1. Liberty.   2. Natural law.   3. United States—Politics and government.
4. United States—Social conditions.   5. Bureaucracy—United States.
I. Title.
JC599.U5W55   1999
320.973—dc2   98-49950
                                                                  CIP

CONTENTS

PREFACE

When the Hoover Institution invited me to assemble this fourth collection of my newspaper columns syndicated nationally by the Los Angeles–based Creators Syndicate, I read through previous prefaces and asked myself what can I say in another preface without being too repetitious. After all, my core values have not changed, so why repeat the story. But then there are readers who are unfamiliar with that story and might be genuinely perplexed by my uncompromising posture regarding personal liberty and the principles laid out in our Declaration of Independence and Constitution. That being the case, a little reader preparation for what follows might be in order.

My core values derive from the principles of natural law, or what some might call God-given rights, expounded by philosophers like John Locke, Sir William Blackstone, and Edmund Burke. Their principles of natural law had a major influence on our Founding Fathers. We find those principles captured simply, elegantly, and compellingly in our Declaration of Independence by the words "We hold these truths to be self-evident; that all men are created equal; that they are endowed by their Creator with certain unalienable rights; that among these are life, liberty and the pursuit of happiness."

The initial premise of natural law is that each individual owns himself; he is his own private property. From that initial premise, certain forms of behavior are readily and easily deemed just or unjust. One of the best statements about what's just conduct was given to us by American philosopher-lawyer Lysander Spooner (1808–1887) who said, "Each man shall do, towards every other, all that justice requires him to do; as, for example, that he shall pay his debts, that he shall return borrowed or stolen property to its owner, and that he shall make reparation for any injury he may have done to the person or property of another. . . . Each man shall abstain from doing to another, anything which justice forbids him to do; as, for example, that he shall abstain from committing theft, robbery, arson, murder, or any other crime against the person or property of another."

Not everyone respects the natural rights of others; therefore, we form governments to enforce respect for private property rights. In the state of nature, prior to the formation of a government, each of us has the right to protect ourselves from predation. We have the right to be prosecutor, judge, jury, and, if needed, executioner. When we form a government, we delegate those particular rights to the state on the condition that the state will use its might to guarantee our rights. Thus, we give up a limited number of rights to guarantee security; however, if the state fails to provide security, we nonetheless retain the right to provide for our security.

Rights is a concept that is widely confused these days. We speak of "the right to affordable health care," "the right to housing," "welfare rights," and so forth. These notions are a gross corruption of the term *rights*. A right is something that is held simultaneously among people and imposes no burden on another. My right to free speech in no way diminishes another's right to free speech and imposes no burden on anyone beyond that of noninterference. A so-called right to food or housing is quite another matter. If we say that one person has a government-guaranteed right to food or housing, it means that another person must have less of something in order for government to make good on that "right." In other words, government does not have any resources of its own. For government to give one person something, it must first take it from another person, usually through taxes. Thus, one person's "right" to food and housing imposes a burden on another person requiring him to have less of something. If we applied this corrupt usage of rights to my free speech rights or my right to bear arms, it would mean that others would be required to provide me with a microphone or radio studio or they would be required to provide me with money to purchase a firearm. The more appropriate word for today's corrupted vision of rights is *wishes*. As such I am in agreement with most people, for I too wish every American had decent housing, plenty of food, and adequate health care.

A significant moral issue arises when government provides goods and services to others. By the democratic principles we espouse, government cannot have a right that citizens do not grant it. There are certain things that a person has no right to do. A person has no right to murder or rape another. Therefore, people cannot grant government authority to murder and rape. Similarly, no person has the right to forcibly take the property of one person in order to give it to another. Therefore, people cannot grant government authority to do the same thing. If I forcibly took property from one person, for any reason, most people would condemn it as theft, an immoral act. Theft or any other immoral act does not become moral because it is done by government acting on behalf of a consensus or majority vote just as murder or rape does not become a moral act simply because of a consensus or majority vote.

If there is a general theme to my columns, that theme is the attention I give to the proper role of government in a free society and the need for politicians to live up to their oath of office to uphold the U.S. Constitution. Today, little that Congress does is authorized by our Constitution. Most of what Congress is authorized to tax and spend money on is carefully enumerated in Article I, Section 8, of the U.S. Constitution. Even a casual observer would conclude that Congress has exceeded its authority by a wide margin. Close to two-thirds of the federal budget is spent on items like housing, education, farm and business subsidies, various domestic and international welfare programs, and Social Security. There is absolutely no constitutional grant of authority for Congress to make these expenditures. Debates in Congress on spending focus mostly on constitutionally irrelevant issues like whether the spending programs are effective or whether the nation can afford them. Save for a precious few members of Congress, the more important issue never surfaces, namely, are they *permissible* expenditures under the Constitution?

It is far too tempting for us to blame politicians for the virtual trashing of our Constitution. And, yes, I agree that they are culpable, but just a little bit. They are guilty of violating their oath of office, not being statesmen, and sacrificing principles as a means to election and reelection. But the bulk of the blame rests with you and me, the American people. Politicians are simply our agents doing precisely what we elect them to office to do, namely, to use the power of their office to take what rightfully belongs to one American to give to another American or confer a special privilege on one American that is denied another American or both.

This unflattering and immoral behavior can be readily demonstrated if the reader considers the following: Imagine there is a candidate from your state seeking election to the U.S. Congress. During his campaign, that candidate tells the electorate that he has read Article I, Section 8, of the United States Constitution enumerating the taxing and spending powers given to Congress. He says that if he is elected the people of his state cannot count on him to lobby or vote for aid to higher education, highway construction funds, ambulatory services for the elderly, higher Social Security and Medicare payments, more police to fight crime, not to mention midnight basketball. He tells the electorate that there is nothing in the Constitution that gives Congress the power to make these expenditures. If doubt is expressed about the constitutionality of congressional spending for the purposes of benevolence, the candidate might quote the words of James Madison, the acknowledged father of the Constitution, who said, "I cannot undertake to lay my finger on that article in the Constitution which granted a right to Congress of expending, on object of benevolence, the money of their constituents." If the candidate is challenged by someone arguing that the "general welfare" clause justifies social spending, the candidate might bring up Madison's warning, "With respect to the words general welfare, I have always regarded them as qualified by the detail of powers connected with them. To take them in a literal and unlimited sense would be a metamorphosis of the Constitution into a character which there is a host of proofs was not contemplated by its creators."

I guarantee that such a candidate would never be elected to the U.S. Congress. Respect for both the letter and the spirit of the Constitution would be an anathema to the electorate whose votes he hopes to win and would be political suicide. Why? Because he would not be promising voters what they want of him, namely, to use the power of his office to take the property of one American and give it to them and give them privileges denied other Americans.

The tragedy of such a voter calculation is that it makes a lot of sense from a private, rational, self-interested point of view. The reason is simple. If the candidate, who hopes to become a member of Congress or a senator representing, say, New York, does not bring back taxpayer-funded goodies for them, it does not mean that New Yorkers will pay lower federal taxes. All it means is that New Jersey citizens will get the goodies instead. Sometimes this situation is referred to as the tragedy of the commons, where once legalized theft begins, it pays for everyone to participate. Those not participating become losers.

While many of my columns discuss government, I also apply

economic analysis to issues involving race and sex discrimination, health and the environment, education, and international issues. My major objective in writing columns, and also in public speaking, is not necessarily to convert people to my way of thinking, although it would be great if such a conversion was forthcoming. My objective is to challenge conventional wisdom on a wide range of issues by offering an alternative outlook or way of analysis and allow people to reach their own conclusions their own way. That is precisely what I experienced as a Ph.D. student at the University of California at Los Angeles back in the 1960s. I thought various forms of government intervention made sense until various professors asked me, Have you looked at it this way? Have you considered its unanticipated effects? Is there a better way to achieve that objective?

ACKNOWLEDGMENTS

Credit, or some might prefer to call it blame, for my uncompromising commitment to liberty and literary iconoclasm belongs to the usual suspects. First, there is my mother, still going strong at eighty-seven years of age, who taught me values, discipline and self-respect. Complementing her efforts were primary and secondary school teachers who, in the face of my frequent resistance, insisted on academic excellence. The most memorable was Dr. Martin Rosenberg, my high school English teacher. During a time when there were not today's opportunities available for blacks, Dr. Rosenberg held high standards and ambition for his students. His frequent admonishment was, "One should always aim for the stars because should he fail, he'd fail in style." Looking back on my adolescence, my playful attitude must have been a source of great exasperation for Dr. Rosenberg—at least until that day he gave me a dressing-down I will never forget.

In 1960, I made the wisest decision of my life when I married Mrs. Williams. She became not only a good wife but a good partner and coach as well. She worked while I attended California State University at Los Angeles and later while I attended UCLA for my graduate degrees—giving me encouragement and moral support throughout. In 1975, she blessed me with the birth of my daughter, Devyn, whom I treasure dearly.

Finally, no one can write columns, have speaking engagements, teach classes, do academic research, chair a department without a superb assistant. For me, that's Kathy Spolarich, who is responsible for keeping my professional life in good order.

Race and Sex

Race issues have dogged our nation since its inception. Undeniably there has been racial injustice, not limited to blacks, but to other racial and ethnic groups as well. During the fervor of the 1960s civil rights movement, and the legislation, court decisions, and the huge spending programs that followed, even the most pessimistic person would have guessed that race problems would have been solved by the close of the century. Although there has been considerable progress, thorny problems remain.

I think we can safely say that America's civil rights struggle is over and won. At one time, black, Hispanic, and Asian Americans did not enjoy constitutional guarantees enjoyed by other Americans. Now we all do. There are no legal restrictions on where we may live, work, and eat. Once there were. In all public accommodations we must be treated like any other American. That means if we live in a particular neighborhood, we cannot be prevented from attending the public school or library in that neighborhood. We no longer have to search for a "colored" drinking fountain or restroom. If our children meet the academic standards, they can enroll at the same college that a white person attends. If our young men go to war for our nation, they are no longer restricted to serving in separate units, being cooks, chauffeurs, and quartermasters. Now they can be generals, aviators, and members of the special forces. Being sixty-two years of age, I can remember a time when none of this was true. Saying that the civil rights struggle is over and won is not the same as saying that all vestiges of discrimination are gone. It is to say codified and rampant discrimination is a thing of the past.

Because the civil rights struggle is over and won does not mean that there are not major problems that confront blacks as a group. Heading the list is the fraudulent education received by most black youngsters, rampant crime in many black neighborhoods, family breakdown (more properly described as families not forming in the first place), and unprecedented illegitimacy.

Most of the social pathology that characterizes a large percentage of the black community is entirely new in our history. At a time when there was far greater racial discrimination, and far fewer prospects for upward mobility, blacks who graduated from high school had a higher achievement level, black neighborhoods were safer, there was greater family stability, and illegitimacy was a tiny fraction of what it is today. If, as so many "experts" claim, discrimination and a legacy of slavery explain what we see today, a natural question is to ask, How come those conditions were not worse at a time when racial discrimination was rampant and codified?

I argue that whatever racial discrimination exists today has little or nothing to do with the most devastating problems that confront many blacks such as fraudulent education, rampant crime, family breakdown, and illegitimacy. These are not civil rights problems, and they won't be solved by civil rights strategy. The reason is that if discrimination cannot explain the problems blacks face, antidiscrimination measures are not likely to have a beneficial effect.

Some of these issues are discussed in the columns that follow. Also, there are columns about the increasingly contentious issue of sex equality. In an effort to promote sex equality, many people make the foolish argument that women are equal to men. Based on this argument, there have been calls to allow women to serve in combat units in the military and to serve as firefighters and police. Then when women have been allowed to serve in activities where physical strength and aggressiveness are important, there have been calls for different (lower) performance standards for women as opposed to their male counterparts. One result is a lowering of overall performance standards for both men and women. After all, is it not discriminatory to require that male cadets at a military academy run with heavy weapons, do full chin-ups, and rope climbs and not have identical requirements for women. The typical "solution" is to reduce standards for both men and women.

In the military, double standards not only threaten morale but can be mission- and life-threatening, as suggested by the finding at Parris Island that 45 percent of female marines couldn't throw a hand grenade far enough to avoid blowing themselves up or the case of U.S. Navy Lieutenant Kara Hultgreen, who was given preferential treatment in training and was eventually killed attempting to land her F-14 on an aircraft carrier.

I believe people argue that men and women are in fact equal because they errantly believe that in order to have equality before the law people must be in fact equal. Nothing is further from the truth. Equality before the law does not require that people be equal in fact. Being a human being is the only requirement.

People before Profits

October 25, 1995

Nation of Islam minister Louis Farrakhan says one of the demands of the million-man march on Washington is for the government to create an environment where "people are put before profits." Since profit demagoguery is a deceptive tool used by scoundrels all over the world, irrespective of ethnicity, let's demystify the concept of profits.

Let's get its definition out of the way first. Profits represent the residual claim earned by producers. It's what's left over after all other costs—wages, rent, interest—have been paid. Roughly six cents of each dollar taken in by companies represents after-tax profits. By far, wages paid are the largest part of that dollar, representing about sixty cents. Far more important than simple statistics is the social role played by profits: Profits guide resources to their highest valued uses as determined by people's wants and desires.

Remember when Coca-Cola introduced the "new" Coke™? People were outraged. Who do you think made them bring back the old Coke? Was it Health and Human Services secretary Donna Shalala? Sorry. It was the specter of negative profits (losses). Profits make sure producers correct mistakes and find out what most consumers want.

After Hurricane Andrew's destruction, people in the Miami area wanted more plywood. What made lumber mills increase production and lumber yards get the trucks out and head south? Again, the specter of profits—this time the windfall variety. All that plywood heading south meant plywood prices rose in other locations, perhaps discouraging less-valued uses of plywood such as home improvement projects. That's wonderful. After all, rebuilding and repairing homes after a hurricane is a more highly valued use of plywood.

Profits also force producers to behave themselves. If producers waste input, their production costs will be higher and they'll charge prices higher than what consumers are willing to pay. Therefore, the company will make losses (negative profits) and go out of business. As a result the company's resources become available to someone who'll put them to a better use. That's if there's no government bailout, as in the case of Chrysler Corporation, enabling the company to continue squandering resources.

If we care about people's wants, rather than beating up on profit we should beat up on nonprofit makers. Government schools fit the latter category. They squander resources and produce a shoddy product while administrators, teachers, and staff earn higher pay and perks with customers (taxpayers) picking up the tab. Unlike other producers, educationists don't face the rigors of the profit discipline and, hence, they're on easy street.

How about the U.S. Postal Service? It provides shoddy and surly services, but the management and workers receive increasingly higher wages while customers pay higher and higher prices. Again, wishes of customers can be safely ignored because there's no bottom-line discipline of profits.

Without any question the major problem of people in general, and blacks in particular, is the nonprofit-making sector of our economy. In any poor neighborhood, you'll see some nice cars, some nice clothing, and some nice food but no nice schools.

Here's Williams' law: Whenever the profit incentive is missing, the probability that people's wants can be safely ignored is the greatest. It's not just the post office and schools but delivery of police services and garbage collection as well. More than anybody, poor blacks should know this well.

White People Are Divine

January 10, 1996

You've really got to hand it to white people, particularly white men. Ask any race expert why do blacks, as a group, earn less income than white people. Five will get you ten, the answer will be racism. Given black history and the everlasting "legacy of slavery," racism is a plausible answer. But racism doesn't affect all blacks the same way. The fact that white people exempt some blacks from the burdens of racism, and do it in ingenious ways, leads me to the conclusion that they have divine powers. "Williams," you say, "we proudly accept your divinity conclusion, but how do you reach it?"

According to one study, as far back as 1969, black males who grew up in homes where there were magazines, books, and library cards had incomes identical to whites from similar homes and education. The obvious conclusion is that whites discriminate against blacks from homes without magazines, books, and library cards. How they do it is a mystery to me. I haven't seen any white people—at least not that many—peeking into the windows of black houses to see who had books, magazines, and library cards.

Another study points out that in the 1970s, black husband-and-wife families outside the South earned as much as white husband-and-wife families outside the South. Then, by 1981, black husband-and-wife families, in which both had a college degree, earned slightly more than identical white husband-and-wife families, and that was true nationwide. I can understand how God might know that a black man is married to a woman with a college degree, but it's mind-boggling how white employers would have the same information.

Racism is a two-way street and blacks are also guilty. You ask, what's the evidence? Race experts teach us wherever there's disparity there's racism. Look at the announcement and photos of the starting lineup of any professional football or basketball game. It's so much of a tragedy that, cherishing equality of opportunity, I become ecstatic when a photo of a white player comes up on the screen. What else, other than racism, can explain how blacks, who are 13 percent of the population, are 66 percent of professional football players and 80 percent of basketball players? Some people might try genetic explanations like white men can't jump or black guys run like monkeys. I don't buy it; it's racism.

You never see Chinese and Japanese football and basketball players, at least not in the starting lineups. Again, a disparity and, again, racism. Initially, one might think of it as an injustice; but it just as soon could be payback. Everybody knows that blacks have a higher infant mortality rate than whites, and it is caused by racism. It turns out that whites have a higher infant mortality rate than Chinese, Japanese, or Filipinos. This can only be chalked up to some mysterious Far Eastern form of racism, particularly when coupled with the fact that Asians receive less prenatal care than whites. Another disparity is seen in the fact that the proportion of Asian American students who score over 700 on the math portion of the Scholastic Aptitude Test is double the number of whites.

There are many racially rooted disparities resulting from one form or another of group wonderfulness, but the most bothersome one to me is a sex disparity. Men are 50 percent of the population, but men are struck by lightning six times as often as women. I want to know what whoever is in charge of lightning strikes has against men.

Mortgage Racism Revisited

June 12, 1996

In last year's column titled "Myth, Lies and Propaganda," I exposed as a hoax the study by Alicia Munnell, the Federal Reserve of Boston's research economist, that alleged massive bank mortgage discrimination against blacks.

Of course the national media flooded our living rooms portraying the study as controlled and definitive and begging for government attention. I pointed out that Munnell's study failed to take into account significant black/white differences in net worth, credit histories, existing debt, and the size of the loan sought as a percentage of the value of the property. When these factors were taken into account, racial differences in mortgage approvals virtually disappear.

On May 10, 1996, the *New York Times* carried a story by Peter Passell titled "Race, Mortgages and Statistics," which showed that the mortgage discrimination debate is far from over.

David Horne of the Federal Deposit Insurance Corporation (FDIC) obtained records from seventy banks accounting for half of the loan applications in the Munnell study and found serious inconsistencies. For example, several cases of affluent minority loan applicants were rejected because their income status made them ineligible for the government-subsidized mortgage they sought. It had nothing to do with race; they were ineligible, just as a white would be under similar circumstances.

Horne also pointed out that minority-owned banks, specializing in lending in black neighborhoods, were responsible for half of all minority loan rejections in the FDIC sample. Could those minority-owned banks also be motivated by racial discrimination?

Ted Day and Stan Liebowitz, professors of economics at University of Texas, Dallas, also uncovered flaws in Munnell's study in that the interest rates for a large number of applicants were below the market rate. Eliminating those cases from the sample sharply reduced differences in loan rejections by race. They also found that by using the individual bank's method of determining applicant creditworthiness, rather than the Boston Federal Reserve's standard, eliminated racial discrimination as a factor in loan rejections.

Alicia Munnell's flawed study created a witch hunt. The Justice Department brought suit against Shawmut National Corporation, New England's third-largest bank, but dropped it after the bank agreed to pay $960,000 to black and Hispanic applicants who were denied loans. The Justice Department forced a Washington bank that had only a few black applicants to open a branch in a black neighborhood.

Peter Passell did a reasonably good job of reporting on the new evidence about the mortgage discrimination controversy, but he loses it when he says, "Flawed or not, the Boston Fed's investigation had a noble purpose: leveling the mortgage playing field for minorities."

That's the kind of fuzzy thinking that has created one social disaster after another for blacks: Noble purposes or intentions do not necessarily lead to noble results. We see that with well-intentioned increases in minimum wages that have resulted in unprecedented unemployment among black teens. Welfare programs had a noble antipoverty purpose but they've virtually destroyed the black family in a way slavery and racism could not have ever done. The noble purpose of judicial leniency, guided by the desire to rehabilitate criminals, has resulted in many black neighborhoods becoming mini-Beiruts.

No one wants to argue that every vestige of racial discrimination has been eliminated. The important, policy-relevant question is, How much of what we see is caused by discrimination, and how much is caused by other factors? If we don't ask that question, and instead chalk every black/white difference up to discrimination, the policy results will have the greatest negative impact on blacks, not whites.

God and the Underclass

January 1, 1997

Robert Rector, Senior Policy Analyst at the Heritage Foundation, wrote "God and the Underclass" that appeared in the July 1996 issue of *National Review*.

It starts off with stunning snippets of what's daily fare in predominantly black cities: In Queens, New York, a heroin-addicted mother murders her four-year old daughter, stuffs the body in a bag, and tosses it into the East River. In Detroit, a five-year old is thrown from the 14th floor because he refuses to steal. In Chicago, police raided an apartment of five welfare sisters that was swarming with roaches and whose floor was covered with garbage and feces. Inside, they found nineteen cold and hungry children sharing food in a dog bowl with several dogs. Dazed, one kid asked a police woman, "Can you be my mommy?"

In the nation's capital, a gunman empties a semiautomatic into a swimming pool crowded with children. In Cleveland, black illegitimacy is 85 percent; in Washington, nearly half of all young black men are either in jail, on parole, or under arrest. Young men in Harlem are more likely to die of violence than were soldiers in Vietnam.

White people might give a sigh of relief and say, "That's a black thing; thank God it's not us." American Enterprise scholar Charles Murray warned against such complacency in his *Wall Street Journal* article (10/29/93) "The Coming White Underclass." Illegitimacy among whites approaches 25 percent. That's what it was among blacks during the mid-1960s when now-Senator Daniel Patrick Moynihan issued his first prophetic warnings about black family collapse.

Illegitimacy is the harbinger of just about all underclass problems. Boys growing up without fathers are less likely to become civilized. The values in communities without fathers are adolescent values: predatory sex, violence, and self-destructive behavior. Our welfare system produces what is known in the insurance industry as "moral hazard." Young women who lose self-control, are promiscuous, and engage in early sex activity are rewarded with welfare benefits. Welfare rewards self-destructive behavior.

Rector says that "religion is a social penicillin, lethal against a wide array of behavioral pathogens." He cites a study of black inner-city youth by Harvard University's Richard Freeman: Boys who regularly attend church are 50 percent less likely to commit crimes. They are 54 percent less likely to use drugs and 47 percent less likely to drop out of school. In Rector's own studies, he finds that church-going boys and girls are two-thirds less likely to engage in teen sex. Regular church attendance halves the chances a woman will have a child out of wedlock.

These statistics confirm my long-held belief that, contrary to what liberals preach, the solutions to the devastating problems of black communities lie neither in Washington nor at state capitals but in our own communities. Think about it. Helping people requires that you be a part of their solution. Someone has to be there, nearly on a day-to-day basis, to suggest, encourage, threaten, scold, and praise. Can that be done by a politician or a welfare bureaucrat?

Black people have come a long way since slavery. Most of that progress has been the direct result of strong families, traditional values, and community organizations such as churches, sororities, fraternities, and clubs. There would be much greater dispersion of the benefits of that progress if we hadn't bought into the bankrupt idea that government programs can be a substitute for local institutions. The good news is that more and more black people are coming to the realization that only we can solve our problems.

Cosmic Justice

January 29, 1997

Thomas Sowell, Hoover Institution's distinguished senior fellow, delivered a lecture in New Zealand last year titled "The Quest for Cosmic Justice." He discussed how often we observe tragic differences in the lives of people. Some live in luxury; others live in squalor; some people have food to throw away while others are close to starvation. The most tragic inequalities occur in other countries. Albeit on a much smaller scale, there are also inequalities in the United States. These inequalities, we're told, represent social injustices that beg for a remedy.

"Social justice" is an elusive term at best, but most people demanding social justice are really demanding what Sowell calls "cosmic justice," a process that seeks to put "particular segments of society in the position they would have been in but for some undeserved misfortune." Pursuit of cosmic justice requires the pretense of knowledge and the wholesale dismissal of issues of cost.

Sowell briefly discussed a minor example of cosmic justice from a San Francisco incident. A relative of a city supervisor called for pizza delivery. The company told him they didn't make deliveries where he lived, a high-crime area. After much moral posturing, the city passed a law requiring that any company making public deliveries must make deliveries all over the city.

The supervisor's relative, like the thousands of his honest neighbors, did nothing to deserve the company's decision not to deliver in their neighborhood. However, the public response shouldn't be simply "do something" unless we, like the San Francisco supervisors, disdain the costs of that something. In other words, the San Francisco city supervisors shouldn't be indifferent to the question, How many pizza deliveries are worth how many dead or injured truck drivers?

Undeserved inequalities go beyond prejudicial decisions; they encompass biological, geographic, and cultural differences as well. Though no fault of their own, whites don't excel in basketball and football to the degree blacks do. Through no fault of their own, blacks don't excel on academic achievement tests as well as whites do. These inequalities and their effects are often seen as social injustices begging for a remedy.

Anyone questioning the costs of the liberal cosmic justice remedy is seen as "mean spirited." Thus, the military gives preferential treatment to women without regard to what the costs of significant strength and stamina differences between men and women might mean in a combat situation. College admission offices admit black students with test scores well below the campus median, ignoring that policy's costs to both black and white students. The only reason the elite haven't mandated quotas for women, Japanese, and other underrepresented groups in the NBA and the NFL is because the folly and costs of their cosmic justice vision would be exposed.

Nobel laureate economist Milton Friedman said that "a society that puts equality—in the sense of equality of outcome—ahead of freedom will end up with neither equality nor freedom." The only equality consistent with freedom is equality before the law. Sowell says the only clear-cut winners in the quest for cosmic justice are those who believe they are morally and intellectually superior to the rest of us. They gain greater power. Among this century's most notable winners in the struggle for cosmic justice were Adolf Hitler, Joseph Stalin, Mao Tse-tung, and Pol Pot.

Proposition 209—The Messenger

June 11, 1997

California voters passed the California Civil Rights Initiative of 1996, more popularly known as Proposition 209, which says, "The state shall not discriminate against, or grant preferential treatment to, any individual or group on the basis of race, sex, color, ethnicity, or national origin in the operation of public employment, public education, or public contracting."

The spirit of Proposition 209 is identical to the Civil Rights Act of 1964: "No person in the United States shall, on the grounds of race, color, or national origin, be excluded from participation in, be denied the benefits of, or be subject to discrimination under any program or activity receiving federal financial assistance."

Through logical contortionism, liberals and the civil rights establishment praise the Civil Rights Act of 1964 and condemn Proposition 209 as racist and unconstitutional. Let's look at some of Proposition 209's initial results.

Recently released acceptance figures by the University of California at Los Angeles School of Law show that only 21 black applicants were accepted, down 80 percent from the 104 accepted the previous year. At the University of California at Berkeley's law school, of the 792 students accepted this year, there were only 14 blacks, compared to 75 last year. There were also declines in the number of Mexican American students accepted. At each school, the number of white and Asian students accepted rose.

How should people concerned with the upward mobility of blacks and Mexican Americans respond? One strategy is to try to overturn Proposition 209. The first attempt to do so failed when the Ninth Circuit Court of Appeals overruled a lower court's preliminary injunction.

Another strategy is to support President Clinton's legal manipulation to "mend not end" affirmative action. A far superior strategy emerges if we ask why blacks need preferential treatment in the first place. We darn sure don't need preferential treatment to be in, and in fact dominate, the National Basketball Association or the National Football League.

It all has to do with excellence. If blacks graduated from college with the same grade-point averages and Law School Admission Test scores, there'd be no question—they'd be admitted to law schools at the same rate as whites and Asians.

Nobody has claimed that law schools are turning away blacks with academic credentials equal to and higher than whites and Asians. The truth of the matter is that too many blacks receive twelve years of fraudulent primary and secondary education that cannot be overcome by four years of college. Unfortunately, liberals and civil rights organizations add to that disaster by giving unquestioned support to a corrupt education establishment that produces the fraud. Any kind of effective education reform, including educational vouchers, tuition tax credits, and even private voucher programs, is fought tooth and nail.

I reject the notion that blacks need preferential treatment. What's needed is more of what my friend Alfred Jenkins, a retired Los Angeles Assistant District Attorney, is doing.

Al is concerned about the problems blacks have passing the bar examination, but he doesn't charge the exam as racist or culturally biased. He conducts a free intensive tutorial program.

To give you a flavor of his approach, he asks students, "How many hours can you study for the bar each day?" Students might respond with six hours, ten hours, and so forth. Then Al asks, "If I had an Uzi pointed at your head, how long could you study?" Then he says, "Tell your friends and family goodbye, eliminate any other distractions, and pretend there's an Uzi pointed at your head."

Jenkins has chalked up a phenomenal success record. Unlike white liberals and the civil rights establishment, Al and I have confidence in black abilities.

Silencing Dissent

June 25, 1997

After years of procrastination, I finally got around to reading Yale University law professor Stephen L. Carter's book, *Reflections of an Affirmative Action Baby*. Carter writes engagingly about race issues like affirmative action, racial stereotypes, and the civil rights movement. Particularly interesting was a group of chapters titled "On Being a Black Dissenter."

During the 1970s and 1980s, Thomas Sowell and I came under scurrilous attacks for our departures from the conventional wisdom on race by the news media, campus intellectuals, and members of the civil rights establishment. To give a sample of the viciousness of the attacks, Carl Rowan said, in his nationally syndicated column, "Vidkum Quisling, in his collaboration with the

Nazis, surely did not do as much damage to the Norwegians as Sowell is doing to the most helpless of black Americans. Sowell is giving aid and comfort to America's racists."

Not long after, a black reporter for the *Cleveland Plain Dealer* found Rowan's column so compelling that he plagiarized it, simply substituting my name in place of Sowell's, to attack me. Both during and after confirmation hearings, and right up to today, Supreme Court justice Clarence Thomas has been called "Uncle Tom," "Oreo," "race traitor" and caricatured in cartoons in national publications in most unflattering ways.

Other targets of these attacks have included California San Jose State University professor Shelby Steele; Robert Woodson, director of the National Center for Neighborhood Enterprises; and University of Massachusetts professor Julius Lester.

Carter points out that these attacks and the stifling of dissent is not new among blacks. When W.E.B. Du Bois criticized Marcus Garvey's back-to-Africa movement, Garvey dismissed him as "purely and simply a white man's nigger."

Du Bois responded in kind, blasting Garvey as "without a doubt the most dangerous enemy of the Negro race in America and the world." There were attacks and counterattacks between Booker T. Washington and Du Bois.

Carter adds, "Many a great thinker in our history, from Arna Bontemps to Ida B. Wells to James Weldon Johnson to Paul Robeson, has chafed under the pressure to conform or be ostracized. Black intellectuals had no monopoly on being attacked for straying away from the conventional wisdom."

In a 1960 speech to the Nation Association of Manufacturers, S. B. Fuller, founder of Fuller Brush, opined, "Even more than racial barriers, it is a lack of understanding of the capitalist system that keeps blacks from making progress." Fuller was echoing Booker T. Washington's argument that racial progress came from having something to sell. For that sin, black leaders led a boycott against

Fuller Brush, causing him $8 million in losses and nearly bank-
rupting him.

Carter says, and I agree, "We as a people should have learned a
lesson about the importance of permitting, encouraging, even
cherishing, critical thinking. By encouraging open and robust debate about the problems confronting our community, we can
march upward toward a better tomorrow. If instead we choose to
stifle the voices of dissent, it is hard to see how we will get anyplace
at all."

No people, particularly black people, can afford a monopoly on
ideas. Only in an unfettered marketplace of ideas will better ideas
emerge. And black Americans need better ideas. After all who in
their right mind can say that after years and trillions of dollars
spent on government programs like urban renewal, Head Start,
and War on Poverty there's no more urban blight, black kids can
read and write as well as white kids, and poverty has been eliminated?

Sacrificing Blacks

September 3, 1997

Pretend that I was Evander Holyfield's coach back when he was
beginning his boxing career. A fight promoter approaches me saying, "There's a big payday if you'll let your man get into the ring
with Larry Holmes." What would I do if I cared about Holyfield's
long-run interests? I'd recognize he had champion potential, but
if he's put in the ring with Holmes, he's going to get his brains beat
out before he learns to bob and weave. His career would be over.

That's an example of what might be applied to so many black youngsters who've become sacrificial lambs to diversity.

Opponents of California's Proposition 209, outlawing the use of racial preferences in college admissions, hysterically point to this year's declining black enrollment at the prestigious University of California at Berkeley. President Clinton echoed this hysteria saying, "I don't know why the people who promoted this in California think it's a good thing to have a segregated set of professional schools."

How about some facts? At Berkeley, black student average Scholastic Aptitude Test scores (952) were higher than the nationwide average (900) for all students. However, 70 percent of black students fail to graduate. In 1987, greater numbers of black students were admitted to Berkeley; however, fewer actually graduated than in 1976. What was the problem? While black student average SAT scores were 952, the rest of Berkeley's students averaged nearly 1,200. Just like in the Holmes/Holyfield fight example, they weren't "qualified" or "unqualified" in any absolute sense; they were mismatched.

That situation is not unique to Berkeley. At Massachusetts Institute of Technology (MIT), the average black student scored in the top 10 percent nationwide on the math portion of the SAT. Other MIT students scored in the top one percent. That meant that black students were in MIT's bottom 10 percent. Nearly, one-fourth of these students didn't graduate, and those that did had significantly lower grade-point averages. These black students could have been successes at most colleges, but in the name of affirmative action they were turned into artificial failures.

I think having black students actually graduate from college is far better than having blacks students be used as affirmative action tokens. College administrators have a different agenda. Black students on campus, whether they graduate or not, allow administrators to gush about diversity, keep their hands in the federal till, and avoid flack from the affirmative action lady.

Blacks not admitted to Berkeley will not evaporate; there are three thousand other colleges they can attend. Eliminating racial preferences that lead to academic mismatches will lead to increased black graduation rates. If a black student with a SAT of 952 attends, for example, California State University at Los Angeles, where he is admitted on merit, instead of Berkeley, where he's admitted on racial preferences, there's a greater probability he'll graduate.

Black parents must be more diligent in college selection. Yes, it's flattering to have a son or daughter recruited by prestigious universities like Berkeley, Harvard, and MIT. But there can be a difference between what's in the best interest of their kid and what's in the best interest of the university. So here's Williams's suggestion: Don't enroll your kid in a college where its student average SAT score is 100 points or so higher than his. Graduating from a less prestigious university is better than flunking out of a prestigious one, not only for your kid but for blacks as a group and the nation as a whole.

Blacks and Crime

September 24, 1997

Professors Stephan and Abigail Thernstrom have just published *America in Black and White*. Its discussion of race is far more level-headed and useful than anything the president or his recently appointed commission on race has said or is likely to say. The Thernstroms' seven-hundred-page volume covers race from the Jim Crow days right up to California's Proposition 209, but I want to highlight their chapter on crime.

Most violent crime in our country is committed by blacks. According to U.S. Department of Justice statistics, blacks commit 54 percent of murders, 42 percent of forcible rapes, 59 percent of robberies, and 38 percent of aggravated assaults. For the most part, the victims are black. Ninety-three percent of murdered blacks were murdered by a black.

In fact, most victims of violent crimes report having been victimized by a member of their own race. However, in the case of interracial violent crime, blacks are fifty times more likely to commit violent crimes against whites than whites against blacks. Bureau of Justice victimization reports show that 89 percent of interracial crimes involved black perpetrators and white victims.

Crime is a major problem and lies at the heart of other major problems faced by blacks. High crime translates into low rates of businesses formation in black neighborhoods. That translates into fewer resident employment and shopping opportunities. Unsafe schools compromise black education; it creates incentives for the best teachers and students to go elsewhere. Crime drives upwardly mobile residents out and the neighborhood loses stabilizing influences.

During the 1980s, for example, 50,000 blacks left Washington, D.C. Nationally, for at least two decades, black suburban migration rate has been higher than that of whites. As middle-class people and businesses leave, cities lose their tax base.

Experts love to blame crime on poverty. That's nonsense! From 1900 to 1929, the nation's murder rate rose from 1.2 per 100,000 of the population to 8.4. However, during parts of the 1930s, when the unemployment rate stood at 37 percent, the murder rate fell to 6.3 per 100,000 and to 4.7 per 100,000 by 1960. After 1960, violent crime rates shot up. By 1993, the murder rate was 9.5 per 100,000, falling to 8.2 in 1995. Rather than poverty causing crime, one might more easily make the case that crime causes poverty.

Survey polls show a high degree of black fear of crime. However, crime is an uncomfortable subject for black people. Given our history, this is understandably so. But when crime puts progress on hold for a third of the black population, we can no longer be silent and deny its widespread, devastating effects. We have to do something about it.

Part of doing something requires the recognition that politicians, black elite and civil rights organizations are virtually useless. If anything, their excuse-making gives aid and comfort to criminals.

Citizens in high-crime neighborhoods must adopt a zero tolerance of crime. They must privately organize and send a message to criminals: Crime is hazardous to your health in this neighborhood. If school authorities can't prevent students who are alien and hostile to the education process from making education impossible for everyone else, black parents should privately organize and show up on the school premises to create order.

Defending oneself, one's family, and one's communities against predators is a natural or God-given right. Just because those to whom we've delegated authority to defend us are derelict does not mean we don't have the right to defense. Most Americans wouldn't begin to tolerate the horror that's daily fare in black communities— why should blacks?

Race Hustlers

December 24, 1997

With President Clinton's appointment of a race commission, and his selection of Bill Lann Lee as acting head of the Justice Department's civil rights division, America's race hustlers are having a bit of a field day. But what beneficial effect will any of these initiatives have on black Americans, especially those for whom there appears to be little hope?

Let's start by asking what are the most pressing problems for the black underclass for whom the race hustlers pretend to speak. On the short list are family breakdown (maybe more descriptive: families not forming in the first place), high illegitimacy rates, crime, and poor education. There's no question that these sociological factors produce devastating effects, but can they be attributed to racial discrimination or, as the race experts say, the "legacy of slavery"? Let's look at it.

A hundred years ago, when blacks were just one generation out of slavery, census data shows that a slightly higher percentage of black adults had married than white adults. This fact remained true in every census from 1890 to 1940.

Today, black family stability is a mere skeleton of its past. As recently as 1960 only 21 percent of black children grew up in female-headed households. By 1991, only 37 percent of black children lived in two-parent households compared to 77 percent for whites. Black illegitimacy rate in 1940 was 19 percent; by 1965, it had grown to 28 percent. Today, black illegitimacy stands around 66 percent. Does anyone want to explain yesteryear's black family stability by saying there was less discrimination back then?

One of today's racial hot buttons is racial preferences in college admissions. There is no evidence that colleges are discriminating by denying blacks admission who score 1,000 on the SAT. The fact of business is relatively few blacks score that high. Why? By and large, it's the grossly fraudulent education blacks receive from the government schools (education received by whites is nothing to write home about).

It's pretty hard to make a case that the poor education is a result of racism. Some of the worst education is in cities where the mayor is black, there's significant black representation on the city council, there have been black school superintendents, and the highest per capita education expenditures are made. Washington, D.C., is a prime example.

There is nothing to say that black academic excellence is inherently impossible. Check out Marcus Garvey School in Los Angeles, Marva Collins Schools in Chicago and Cincinnati, and Ivy Leaf School in Philadelphia. These are black-founded, -owned, and -operated schools. Nearly 100 percent of their students from low- and moderate-income families are at, and up to four years above, grade level. I have personally toured and sat in on classes at these schools and there's no magic—unless you call student discipline and teacher competence and dedication magic.

Crime takes a devastating toll on black communities. People live in constant fear. Criminals, not the Klan, have turned many communities into economic wastelands where there's reduced employment and shopping opportunities.

Nobody can say that there's no racial discrimination or that it has no effect. However, the major problems for many blacks have nothing to do with racial discrimination. That being the case, President Clinton going around the country making touchy-feely statements about race will make little or no contribution to solutions.

Ordinary black people must wake up to the fact that white people, including Clinton, government, and race hustlers, cannot solve our problems; but they can sabotage and thwart meaningful solutions. Only we can solve our problems.

Feminization of the Military

September 10, 1997

"Boy, what's that @#&*! growing under your nose? It looks like a &@*@#. You'd better get that &@*#! off your face by the next formation."

It was July 1959. With about sixty other recruits, I was being welcomed to basic training at Fort Jackson, South Carolina. According to John Leo's "A Kinder, Gentler Army" (in *U.S. News & World Report* on August 8, 1997), such a welcome is now out. Today's Army manual dictates, "Stress created by physical or verbal abuse is nonproductive and prohibited." Forget whether traditional adversarial training produced a first-class military throughout our history.

Why the changes? Partly, it's because today's youth are unaccustomed to discipline and authority, but mainly it's because our lovelies want to be fighting persons. To accommodate them means the military must lower standards. Carrying a stretcher used to be a two-man job, now it's a four-person job. The navy finds that very few of its females can manage shipboard emergency tasks such as hefting fire hoses or carrying wounded personnel up a ladder on a stretcher.

Females pass physical training because of gender norming. Yellow lines are put on climbing ropes. Male trainees have to climb to the top, but for our lovelies the yellow line will do. As for those awful push-ups, men have to do twenty and women just six. Then there's the "confidence course," called obstacle course in the pre–political correctness days. At Quantico's marine training facility, a visitor noticed a footstool placed in front of an eight-foot wall so no trainee would fail to climb over it.

There's one male/female strength difference quite worrisome. At Parris Island, it was discovered that 45 percent of female marines were unable to throw a hand grenade far enough to avoid blowing themselves up. Translated in Williams's terms: If I were in a foxhole with a woman about to toss a hand grenade, I'd consider her the enemy.

The movie *G.I. Jane* is a clever Hollywood propaganda ploy to generate public support for women in combat. Actress Demi Moore joins the Navy Seals and eschews all sex-based considerations and competes on the same basis as the males.

Of course, if women were ever admitted to the Seals, training standards would be lowered. Navy Seals undergo the military's most strenuous training. A woman has as much of a chance of successfully completing the Navy Seal program as she would of being a successful linebacker in the National Football League. Two-thirds of well-conditioned men who qualify for Seals training flunk out.

Double standards in the military understandably foster resentment between men and women. Men see female soldiers, who are incapable of performing tasks men are required to perform, get the same rank and pay as they do. They see their lives unnecessarily threatened in combat.

Imagine your ship is hit by a torpedo and your shipmate can't heft and control a fire hose or, if you're injured, carry you to safety—or worse yet, is pregnant and completely out of action. I'm not at all surprised by resentment that often manifests itself as "sexual harassment." In fact, a Government Accounting Office report says that male complaints about double standards are the first or second most common form of verbal sexual harassment. Sex double standards in the military, like race double standards on college campuses, produce resentment.

I may be unnecessarily alarmed about sex double standards. Maybe future adversaries like Russia, China, and Iran are feminizing their defense forces and using double standards, too. If they are then it's no big thing—unless their lovelies are not as lovely as ours.

Black English?

November 1, 1995

Y'awl might axin me why Ah be writin dis way. Y'awl might tink ma fambly didn't gib me a gud upbringin. Y'awl might say Ah be a no-count, woebegone yaller dawg fit for nothin but taters and chittlins. What be wrong wid yo innards and book-learning, y'awl might be axing?

Run that paragraph by your intellectual multiculturist at one of our universities. Ask him to comment on the language or dialect. Five will get you ten he'll perk up and say, "Why that's black English; I'd know it anywhere!" But it ain't. It is as white an English as you can get.

According to David H. Fischer's book *Albion Seed*, in 1773 Philip Fithian, from New Jersey, went to Richmond, Virginia, to teach at Nomini Hall. In his journal, he told how Northerners said, "I am," "You are," "She isn't," and "I haven't," whereas Virginians, "even if high rank," preferred to say "I be," "You be," "She ain't," and "I hain't." The Virginian dialect, Fithian discovered, even had its own vocabulary: afeared for afraid, cater-cornered for crooked, chomp for chew, disremember for forget, and a host of similar substitutions.

Virginians tended to add syllables to words and embellish vowels such as ha-alf for half, puriddy for pretty, and wah-a-tah-mill-i-an for watermelon. They also had a way of softening consonants: sebem for seven, chimbly for chimney, mo for more, and wid for with.

These Virginia speech patterns were not invented in America. They were derived from a family of regional dialects spoken throughout the south and west of England during the seventeenth century in the counties such as Sussex, Surrey, Hampshire, Dorset, Devon, Wiltshire, Oxford, and Gloucester. By the late eighteenth century, these words had all but disappeared from polite usage. Fischer says, "In the twentieth century, words like dis or dat were rarely heard in any part of rural England, but they persisted among poor whites and blacks in the American South."

According to Fischer, a few Africanisms crept into the English language, even words of African origin; however, "The major features of the Virginia accent, however, were established before African slaves could possibly have had much impact on language."

The bottom line is the language we often hear spoken among blacks has little or nothing to do with Africa. They're speaking like purebred Englishmen of yesteryear from the South and West counties of Britain. The question you may ask is, How come Englishmen from those regions don't speak like that today? The answer's easy. They have benefited from being educated to speak more correctly. The next question is, How come this English dialect continues to be spoken among some black people? Again, an easy answer with a minor side complexity. Those blacks have not benefited from being educated to speak correctly. The side complexity that distinguishes them from the English is that blacks have had multicultural intellectuals to convince them that "I be" talk is a part of their heritage and roots. Bad-talking Englishmen suffered through the brutal "insensitivity" of having someone telling them they were wrong, at the same time demanding proper grammar and pronunciation.

The bottom line is so-called black English is nonsense and an attempted coverup of government school corruption and capitulation to mediocrity. It's not simply a matter of "black English" being hard on the ears. Poor command of language is devastating to learning potential and reasoning skills. After all language is how we transmit knowledge and experiences.

But don't take my word. Just ax yourself: How many successful blacks be talkin' black English?

Gender-Norming Update

April 9, 1997

In October 1994, Lieutenant Kara Hultgreen was killed during an attempted landing of her F-14 on the aircraft carrier *Abraham Lincoln*. Fem-feared (afraid of feminists) navy officials first reported that engine failure caused the death of the navy's first female F-14 pilot. That was a deliberate lie and coverup as later revealed in a leaked Mishap Investigation Report and the navy's Judge Advocate General's report.

After three requests, under the Freedom of Information Act, the Center for Military Readiness obtained a 1995 report written by Admiral Lyle G. Bien. It confirms special treatment for female F-14 pilots. It also notes that Hultgren was retained in the F-14 training program and graduated to the fleet despite low scores and four major errors (downs), two of which were similar to those made the day she died. Just one or two major downs have been enough to send men packing.

Then there's Lieutenant Carey Lohrenz, who was washed out of the F-14 program, who's brought suit against Elaine Donnelly, director of the Center for Military Readiness, and several newspapers. Lt. Lohrenz claims public release of her training records violated her privacy. Claiming sex discrimination, she's demanding reinstatement. Her training records are reported as being "the lowest night grades in the history of the FRS [Pacific F-14 Fleet Replacement Squadron]. . . . No pilot in the history of the FRS was allowed to attempt requalification with grades as low as hers."

Aircraft carrier maneuvers are error-unforgiving. Pilot incompetency jeopardizes not only the life of the pilot but also the crew members and the ship's mission. Case in point: During refueling, Lohrenz failed to secure the F-14's right engine so as not to suck approaching crew members into a turning engine. Since there is so much noise on deck, deckhands can't tell whether an engine is off—it's the pilot's responsibility.

Because of the alertness of the flight instructor a catastrophe was averted. Lt. Lohrenz was given the minor demerit, signal of difficulty (SOD), instead of a more serious down. Other concessions included no downs for serious violations such as not engaging automatic maneuvering devices in air combat engagements. Officers who insist that females be held accountable to the same high standards as males are seen by higher brass as obstructionist, and risk their careers.

Double standards to accommodate women have compromised military effectiveness. Women are three to four times as nondeployable as men, as we learned during Desert Storm. Despite relentless sex education and condom distribution, pregnancy rates average 8 to 10 percent and are much higher in some enlisted units. Fighting ships compromise their missions to insure the safety of pregnant females. Training standards have been lowered to accommodate lower strength and stamina of women.

The General Office of Accounting reports that annual surveys done at service academies since 1992 show that complaints about double standards have been identified as the first or second most common form of verbal sexual harassment. Male resentment against double standards is sometimes expressed in inappropriate ways that have been featured in news stories of sexual harassment, intimidation, and rape at military posts.

Physical differences between the sexes affect combat readiness, but those differences do not deny a role for women in the nation's defense. Women were indispensable and served honorably in World War II. The fem-fearing military leadership does not have the guts to recognize sex differences and are willing to risk national security to appease radical feminists.

Of Rats and Women

September 18, 1996

Tulane University professor Wilfred M. Clay penned an interesting article in *Commentary* (September 1996) titled "Of Rats and Women." It's about the Supreme Court's order that Virginia Military Institute (VMI) admit women. The fact that its freshmen are known as rats is enough to suggest VMI is not a place for women nor the weak and timid. VMI uses the "adversative method" designed to build moral character and physical and mental discipline.

"What's the adversative method, Williams?" you say. It's especially tough on rats and includes complete absence of privacy, shaved heads, uniformity of standards, as many as 300 sit-ups in a day, and upperclassmen talking to you as if you're something that crawled out not from under a rock but out of a cesspool. Barracks are barren, no closets, no air-conditioning, no radio or TV. The only luxury afforded a rat is a photo in his room. Rats can be awakened at night for grueling exercise known as "sweat parties." There are five-mile runs, obstacle courses, and fighting with pugil sticks. Up to 20 percent of "weenie" rats drop out in their first year.

However we might judge VMI's adversative method, it has produced some our nation's finest men, including the likes of General George C. Marshall. Superintendent Major General Josiah Bunting vows the school will continue its mission but I'm not optimistic. Admission of women will destroy VMI's high standards just as they've been destroyed at West Point and the Naval Academy.

Supreme Court justice Ruth Ginsberg, who wrote the Court's majority opinion, laid out the prescription for that destruction. Ginsberg said, "VMI's implementing methodology is not inherently unsuitable to women." Continuing, she said, "Some women are capable of all the individual activities required of cadets, and can meet the physical standards VMI now imposes upon men." Then she totally contradicts herself, saying admitting women to VMI "would undoubtedly require alterations necessary to afford members of each sex privacy from the other sex in living arrangements and to adjust aspects of the physical training programs."

If Ginsberg contends that women require privacy, then she's saying VMI's program is unsuitable to women. What she means by adjusting aspects of physical training is VMI must, like Annapolis and West Point, lower physical training standards. If VMI does not lower them, they will be sued by feminist outfits who claim women are equal to men. If VMI lowers standards for female cadets, they must lower them for male cadets less they get sued for sex discrimination by men. The bottom line is VMI will become feminized. Justice Ginsberg, and the majority who voted with her, have little understanding and great power to do harm.

The Court would have been on sounder moral grounds if it had ruled that publicly supported colleges cannot employ any discriminatory admissions criteria. Parents of children with IQs of 70 pay taxes, so their kids shouldn't be barred admission from any state-supported colleges. People who can't read or write pay taxes—what's fair in denying them admission? To force people to pay taxes for something, yet require them to meet some arbitrary criteria to use the service is unfair. It differs little from taxing a person to pay for supermarket products and then requiring him meet some requirement in order to use those products. The fair way is for those who benefit from a college, supermarket, or anything else is for them to pay for it. In a word, colleges ought to be privatized. That way they could have any admissions criteria they wish. But, I'm afraid, that solution is too liberty oriented both for the Court and a society hell-bent on socialism.

Costly Affirmative Action

May 31, 1995

Remember navy Lieutenant Kara Hultgreen, who was killed while attempting to land her $38 million F-14A Tomcat fighter on the USS *Abraham Lincoln*? The navy's official public report was the crash "was precipitated by a malfunction of the left engine." Questions about pilot error were greeted with charges of sexism. ABC's

Peter Jennings said there had been a "vicious campaign against allowing women to serve in combat."

According to John Corry's summary in the *American Spectator* (June 1995) and a report of the Center for Military Readiness (CMR), the government and media version of Hultgreen's accident is part of the continuing saga of government deceit and media complicity. But here's what really happened.

On approach to the USS *Abraham Lincoln*, Hultgreen made five major errors and ignored repeated wave-off signals by ship's landing officer. One of those errors caused the F-14A's left engine to stall, sending the plane out of control, because Hultgreen mistakenly jammed on the rudder. In the twenty years of F-14A's service, no pilot had ever stalled an engine this way. In an effort to back up their lie that the crash was due to engine failure, the navy selected nine male pilots to "fly" through Hultgreen's precrash conditions in a ground simulator.

Chief of Naval Operations admiral Jeremy M. Boorda reported, "The situation was recreated in an F-14 flight simulator. Eight of nine pilots in the simulator were unable to fly the plane out of the replicated regime." What Admiral Boorda failed to say was that the male pilots had been ordered not to execute the F-14A manual's so-called Bold Face Instructions, the critical things a pilot must do to fly through an emergency similar to Hultgreen's.

Documents obtained by Elaine Donnelly, director of CMR, shows that Hultgreen not only had subpar performance on several phases of her training but had four downs (major errors), just one or two of which are sufficient to justify the dismissal of a trainee. The White House and Congress's political pressure to get more women in combat is the direct cause of Hultgreen's death. But the story doesn't end there. A second female F-14A pilot, identified by Elaine Donnelly only as Pilot B, has been allowed to continue training despite marginal scores and seven downs—the last of which was not recorded so she could pass the final stages of training.

These double standards are destructive in several important ways. They risk the lives not only of young women like Hultgreen and Pilot B but the lives of fellow military men and women. They dumb down aviation standards. After all, what do we do when a male F-14A trainee, washed out because he had four downs and subpar performance, accuses the navy of sex discrimination? In the name of sex equality, do we lower standards for males? Finally, special concessions for female pilots undermine military morale and respect.

The Hultgreen incident demands several responses. The first is courts-martial of the navy officers who deliberately submitted false and misleading reports about the incident. Second, Senator Strom Thurmond, chairman of the Armed Services Committee, and Senator Sam Nunn, its ranking member, must call hearings. If the navy establishes double standards for female aviation trainees, families of those exposed to unnecessary death should be informed and the nation should debate the wisdom of the navy's affirmative action policy. Then there's the pure military mission question: How much military efficiency are we prepared to sacrifice to promote the leftist quota vision?

Liberty's Only Equality

August 30, 1995

Merely to ask certain questions is to invite scorn and ridicule, but what the heck. Bothering me for some time is the question, In what sense are women equal to men? Here's why I ask. I've never seen sexually integrated professional boxing matches, football games, basketball games, 100-yard dashes, or ice hockey games. Is that because male chauvinists deny women the chance to compete?

The military response to the conspicuous absence of women in male-dominated areas suggests a remedy for professional sports. Army fitness standards call for eighty push ups for men and fifty-six for women. Male soldiers ages seventeen to twenty-five must run two miles in 17 minutes and 55 seconds. Females are given 22 minutes and 14 seconds. Male marine trainees must climb twenty feet of rope in 30 seconds; women are given 50 seconds.

The military's "gender norming" might be implemented in sports. In football, new rules might allow the offensive team's female pass receiver to take up an uncovered position half the distance to the goal behind the defensive team's line. In the 100-yard dash women could get a 25-yard head start. In baseball, a midfield hit might count as a home run. I'm at a loss for what can be done to gender norm boxing. All that I come up with to level the playing field between a woman and George Foreman or Mike Tyson is to give the woman a gun.

Some might be offended by these musings, but I ask, Why? If gender-norming tactics are acceptable for something as critical as national defense, why not obtain their benefits for less important activities? Feminists themselves wouldn't want sports desegregated and gender normed. The folly and disastrous consequences would be obvious to all. For them gender norming is best left to areas where its effects are more readily concealed.

The fact of business is that we humans are not equal. Some of us are women and some are men. Some are smart and some are not so smart. Some are colored, others are uncolored. Some are tall and some are short. Some of us are poor and others wealthy.

The differences—inequalities—are endless.

Equality before the general rules of law is the only kind of equality conducive to liberty that can be secured without destroying liberty. It is an equality that neither requires nor assumes people are in fact equal. Our attempt to make people equal in fact by rigging law to produce equal results destroys civility and generalized respect for the law. Government cannot create an advantage for one person without simultaneously creating a disadvantage for another.

Unfairness to women and minorities is a part of our history, but we shouldn't make the cure more destructive than the disease. We should use common sense. Take the trucking industry as an example. For decades minorities and women were conspicuously absent. It was a result of a government-sponsored transportation collusion managed by the Interstate Commerce Commission. Greater fairness came when trucking was deregulated. Afterward, the number of minority and women-owned trucking firms exploded.

Few Americans are even aware of the progress. It occurred without the rancor, conflict, and bitterness that would have resulted had quotas and set-asides been employed to address the unfairness. We simply eliminated the government-sponsored unfairness and allowed each person to compete.

This is the kind of inequality—privilege granting—to which we should give greater attention. Government agencies have no right telling one American he or she can go into a business and another, who is just as able, that he or she cannot.

Black Confederate Soldiers

August 21, 1996

Most historical accounts portray Southern blacks as anxiously awaiting President Abraham Lincoln's "liberty-dispensing troops" marching South in the war between the states. But there's more to the story; let's look at it.

Black Confederate military units, both as freemen and slaves, fought federal troops. Louisiana free blacks gave their reason for fighting in a letter written to New Orleans's *Daily Delta*: "The free colored population love their home, their property, their own slaves . . . and recognize no other country than Louisiana, and are ready to shed their blood for her defense. They have no sympathy for Abolitionism; no love for the North, but they have plenty for Louisiana. They will fight for her in 1861 as they fought in 1814–15." As to bravery, one black scolded the commanding general of the state militia, saying, "Pardon me, general, but the only cowardly blood we have got in our veins is the white blood."

General Nathan Bedford Forrest had slaves and freemen serving in units under his command. After the war, Forrest said of the black men who served under him, "These boys stayed with me . . . and better Confederates did not live." Articles in *Black Southerners in Gray*, edited by Richard Rollins, gives numerous accounts of blacks serving as fighting men or servants in every battle from Gettysburg to Vicksburg.

Professor Ed Smith, director of American Studies at American University, says Stonewall Jackson had 3,000 fully equipped black troops scattered throughout his corps at Antietam—the war's bloodiest battle. Smith calculates that between 60,000 and 93,000 blacks served the Confederacy in some capacity. They fought for the same reason they fought in previous wars and wars afterward: "to position themselves. They had to prove they were patriots in the hope the future would be better . . . they hoped to be rewarded."

Many knew Lincoln had little love for enslaved blacks and didn't wage war against the South for their benefit. Lincoln made that plain, saying, "I will say, then, that I am not, nor have ever been in favor of bringing about in any way the social and political equality of the white and black races. . . . [I am] in favor of having the superior position assigned to the white race." The very words of his 1863 Emancipation Proclamation revealed his deceit and cunning; it freed those slaves held "within any State or designated part of a State the people whereof shall then be in rebellion against the United States." It didn't apply to slaves in West Virginia and areas and states not in rebellion. Like General Ulysses Grant's slaves, they had to wait for the Thirteenth Amendment. Grant explained why he didn't free his slaves earlier, saying, "Good help is so hard to come by these days."

Lincoln waged war to "preserve the union." The 1783 peace agreement with England (Treaty of Paris) left thirteen sovereign nations. They came together in 1787, as principals, to create a federal government, as their agent, giving it specific delegated authority—specified in our Constitution. Principals always retain the right to fire their agent. The South acted on that right when it seceded. Its firing on Fort Sumter, federal property, gave Lincoln the pretext needed for the war.

The war between the states, through force of arms, settled the question of secession, enabling the federal government to run roughshod over states' rights specified by the Constitution's Tenth Amendment.

Sons of Confederate Veterans is a group dedicated to giving a truer account of the war between the states. I'd like to see it erect a statue of one of the thousands of black Confederate soldiers on Richmond, Virginia's, Monument Avenue.

We Are Not Bright

February 8, 1995

Much of what's wrong in our country is the result of our heeding the advice of "experts" and "intellectuals" that defy every notion of common sense. Take the skyrocketing black illegitimacy. But first let's put it into perspective. In 1940, black illegitimacy was 19 percent. Today, it's 68 percent and estimated to be 75 percent by the year 2000. As early as the 1870s, up to 80 percent of black kids lived in two-parent families. Between 1905 and 1925, 85 percent of Harlem youngsters lived in two-parent families. Today, less than 40 percent of black kids live in two-parent families. The black family could survive slavery and Jim Crowism but not the welfare state.

During the 1960s, now-Senator Daniel Patrick Moynihan wrote a report concluding, "At the heart of the deterioration of the fabric of Negro society is the deterioration of the Negro family." At that time black illegitimacy was 30 percent. Liberals attacked the report. Civil rights leader Bayard Rustin said, "What may be a disease to the white middle class may be a healthy adaptation to the Negro lower class." Floyd McKissick, director of the Congress of Racial Equality, echoed that sentiment, saying, "Just because Moynihan believes in middle class values doesn't mean they are the best for everyone in America."

Those sentiments were supported by many, including supposed

intellectuals. Andrew Cherlin, a Johns Hopkins professor and sociologist, argued that it had yet to be shown that the "absence of a father was directly responsible for any of the supposed deficiencies of broken homes." Cherlin concluded that the real issue "is not the lack of male presence but the lack of male income." In other words, fathers can be replaced by a monthly welfare check. That's a stupid idea, but we bought it.

When Moynihan completed his report, according to Rowland Evans and Robert Novak, attempts were made to suppress its release. Professors Lee Rainwater and William Yancey suggested "it would have been well to reduce the discussion of illegitimacy because of the inflammatory nature of the issue with its inevitable overtones of immorality."

According to William Bennett writing in the *American Enterprise* (January/February 1995), "More than 70 percent of black children will have been supported by Aid to Families with Dependent Children payments at one point or another during childhood." He adds, "The most serious problems afflicting our society today are manifestly moral, behavioral, and spiritual, and therefore remarkably resistant to government cures." That recognition is thankfully slowly dawning on us after years of listening to experts and their destructive nonsense.

But the experts are doing their level best to keep us befuddled. They continue to preach nonsense like crime, and other forms of antisocial behavior, are caused by poverty. The truth of the matter is that the causal direction may be the other way around: Poverty is caused by crime and antisocial behavior. After all poverty is the likely result when a person does not respect the rights and property of others, and ignores the values of hard work, sacrifice, and deferment of gratification.

Congress has put welfare reform high on its agenda. In seeking advice on what to do, they should summarily disqualify all the experts whose advice we've listened to in the past that has resulted in today's calamity. If I had my way, there'd be a blanket exclusion of anyone from any government agency dealing with poverty who has received a government grant to do research on poverty.

Free Markets and Blacks

April 5, 1995

Just about the most devastating idea many black Americans have bought into is socialism is a friend and free markets the foe. Let's look at it, but first let's define terms. Socialism is government ownership and/or control over the means of production. Capitalism is private ownership and/or control over the means of production. Most societies are neither pure socialist nor capitalist but constitute a mixture of various proportions.

If you are a discriminated-against minority, what scenario would you like to confront as a condition for going into business? The first option is where incumbents and bureaucrats determine the conditions you must meet before being allowed to enter. Or would you prefer the second where there's unrestricted entry and your diligence and ability to satisfy customers determine whether you stay in business?

If you are a discriminated-against minority with just one ounce of brains, you'd probably opt for the second. The fact the free market befriends outsiders and discriminated-against people is why there's been so much hostility toward it. Just a cursory reading of black history shows how people used the political mechanism to acquire advantages unattainable through the voluntary exchange of free markets. Practices such as licensing laws, minimum wage laws, and often outright prohibitions were used to limit black earning opportunities.

Often the stated motivation behind many regulatory laws was to exclude blacks. Today that is no longer the case but many of the same laws are on the books. Broadening opportunities, not only for blacks but for all Americans, requires efforts to repeal laws written in the interests of incumbents that have the effect of keeping people out who can be generally described as outsiders, discriminated against, and lacking political clout.

The Washington-based Institute for Justice is doing just that. After testimony by the Institute's director, Chip Mellor, Cincinnati removed its cap on the number of cabs allowed to operate in the city. Cincinnati mayor Roxanne Qualls and the city council said existing cab companies could no longer block new entrants by stating the new companies would hurt their business. Last year the Institute for Justice forced the Colorado Public Utility Commission to relax taxi entry conditions in Denver and they also assisted in bringing suit to lift Houston's ban on jitney services.

Literally hundreds of regulations block upward mobility and are supported by black politicians and civil rights organizations. It's hard for me to decide whether these people are simply uninformed or pursuing their own personal agendas. They support the Davis-Bacon Act setting minimum wages in federally financed construction projects. This 1930s law was enacted to get blacks out of the construction industry. Today its supportive rhetoric is not racist but its effect reduces opportunities for black construction workers and contractors. But there's hope for change. The Institute for Justice has brought a suit challenging the act's constitutionality.

Setting minimum wages is one of the most effective tools in the arsenal of racists everywhere. South Africa's racist Mine Workers Union discovered that years ago, saying, "When the minimum wage is introduced we believe that most of the difficulties in regard to the colored question will automatically drop out." Of course the motivation for the minimum wage in the U.S. is different but effects are identical—unemployment for the least skilled and least preferred worker.

Any way we cut it, the free market is a friend to discriminated-against people and socialism is the foe. One of the smartest things blacks can do in today's changed political scene is to demand that Republicans link welfare reform to the elimination of government-sponsored collusion.

Affirmative Action in the Skies

May 24, 1995

Let's review the legislative debate surrounding the Civil Rights Act of 1964. In shepherding the act through Congress, Senator Hubert Humphrey said that, "contrary to the allegations of some opponents of this title, there is nothing in it that will give any power to the commission or to the court to require hiring, firing, or promotion of employees, in order to meet a racial quota or to achieve a certain racial balance," adding later, "in fact, the title would prohibit preferential treatment for any particular group."

Representative Emanuel Celler pronounced, "Even . . . the court could not order that any preference be given to any particular race, religion, color or other group." Senators Clark and Case decreed that "any deliberate attempt to maintain a racial balance, whatever such a balance may be, would involve a violation of Title VII."

With assurances like these, coupled with support of the nation, the Civil Rights Act of 1964 passed. People who saw the Civil Rights

Act as a "bait-and-switch" tactic for quotas later on were portrayed as either racists or obstructionists.

The gross betrayal of both the spirit and the letter of the Civil Rights Act is now obvious to the nation. Nonetheless, affirmative action defenders protest they're not for quotas but for "level playing fields." They lie through their teeth and when they're confronted with something indefensible they say, "That was just an aberration."

Let's look at another one of their "aberrations." In 1976, a consent decree was reached between the Equal Opportunity Commission (EEOC) and United Airlines. The U.S. District Court for the Northern District of Illinois ordered: "United will be considered to be in compliance with the interim incumbency goals for management positions if on an annual basis 50 percent of the initial entrants into management positions are minorities and/or females."

That's the management quota. Turning to pilots the Court ordered, "For the first 1,200 pilots hired by United, when pilot hiring resumes, United will maintain a goal of hiring minority and female pilots at a rate of two times the percentage of minority and female pilot applicants, respectively, who meet the basic qualifications."

Let's look at qualifications. According to a *USA Today* article (9/26/89), the Federal Aviation Administration required 250 hours of flight time to get a commercial pilot's license and 1,500 hours to be a captain. Major airlines usually require much more experience. In 1989, new hires for major airlines had flying time that ranged from 650 hours to 17,500 with an average of 3,910 hours. *USA Today* reported that a woman with only 500 hours flying was hired and was training to be second officer on a Boeing 747. The woman said, "Even though I might not have as much experience as people in my class, I have confidence I'll be just as good."

There's no way for us to know whether female pilots are hired and assigned on merits or hired and assigned as a result of EEOC decrees. To doubt the credentials of an authentic female pilot is unfair to that pilot, but given our quota agenda, how do we know? If airlines are caving in to EEOC pressure, fairness to passengers might require a departure announcement such as, "Affirmative action flight 99 to Los Angeles; all optimists aboard." That way passengers can decide whether they are for or against affirmative action.

The nondiscriminatory vision of the Civil Rights Act of 1964 is what America is all about. The system of racial and sexual quotas is offensive. Calling them goals and timetables doesn't make them less offensive. Quotas have heard their death knell. That's good for America and the alleged beneficiaries.

Will We Ever Learn?

June 21, 1995

The nation's capital provides one of the best examples of the destructiveness of liberal ideas. Washington used to be a thriving city where free persons of color and freed slaves established flourishing family businesses that covered the gamut from taxicabs and small stores to hotels and restaurants. Plus, there were well-educated descendants of freed slaves.

As early as 1899, the black students of Washington's Paul Lawrence Dunbar High School scored higher than any of the white schools in the District of Columbia. From 1870 to 1955, most Dunbar graduates went to college, including schools like Oberlin, Harvard, Amherst, Williams, and Wesleyan. Washington was home to a broad upwardly mobile black middle class.

All that has changed. According to Philip Murphy in an article in *Policy Review*, Washington has "the highest per capita murder and violent crime rates, the highest percentage of residents on public assistance, the highest-paid school board, the lowest SAT scores, the most single-parent families, and the most lawyers per capita." Neighborhoods, once bustling and serene, are now economic wastelands where law-abiding residents live in daily terror.

People are fleeing Washington in droves. It's not white flight but black flight to the suburbs. During the second half of the 1980s alone, over 157,000, or one fifth of Washington's population, moved. This exodus disproportionately consisted of black households earning between $30,000 and $50,000 a year. Today, Washington's population is 578,000, down from a peak of 800,000.

Can we blame racism for Washington's emergence into a bankrupted Third World type of city? To do so requires a lot of imagination. Washington is a city where the mayor is black, the chief of police is black, the superintendent of schools is black, and most of the city council is black. Can we blame poor revenue sources? According to Murphy the city takes in an astonishing $8,950 in revenue for every man, woman and child in its jurisdiction. That's to be compared to $4,000 and $3,700 in nearby Maryland and Virginia, respectively. Nonetheless, the city is in receivership; its bonds have achieved junk status because it manages to spend $1,000 more per person than it receives in revenue. The city's deficit is approaching $1 billion.

Washington's story can be told in varying degrees in other predominantly black cities. That story is a monument to the failure of the liberal ideas of Democrats, black politicians, and civil rights organizations. Liberals have convinced blacks that we deal with crime not by arresting and locking up criminals but by searching for crime's original causes. That gives criminals carte blanche to prey on law-abiding citizens. Liberals have convinced blacks that we deal with educational fraud by spending more money to create programs that fall just short of lunacy. Liberals don't expose their children to this nonsense—they enroll their children in private schools, as does Franklin Smith, Washington's Superintendent of Public Schools.

Victims of the liberals are mostly poor black people who have few options—such as Sheila Stamps, a widowed mother of five living in a housing project. She complains, "You can't let the children out by themselves, and the playground is littered with intravenous needles." Like most black parents, Stamps wants school choice, saying: "Any child in this city should be able to go to the best schools; if they meet the criteria, let them go." But her liberal "benefactors" say no.

When black Americans finally come to the full realization of what liberals have done to us, it's going to make last November's [1994] political revolution look like a Girl Scout outing.

Recapturing the Can-Do Spirit

August 9, 1995

With disbelief and sometimes sorrow, I listen to poor blacks and their welfare state advocates give one excuse after another for dependency.

During the boom of the 1980s, some said they knew where work was available but complained it took too much commute time, or they had no one to take care of their kids or it was a low-pay dead-end job. Life doesn't always deal a fair hand but you just don't sit, surrender, and rest on excuses. The unfairest hand was dealt to our enslaved ancestors. But let's look at some of their responses, with an eye toward asking, How much sympathy should we have for those among their descendants who whine and make excuses?

Historian Loren Schweninger's book *Black Property Owners in the South: 1790–1915* gives numerous stories such as "Two ambitious Charles Town bricklayers, Tony and Primus, who spent their days building a church under the supervision of their master, secretly rented themselves to local builders at night and on weekends."

Several of plantation owner John Liddell's slaves worked all day in the field. Under the cover of darkness, they'd steal away to work for wages, returning to the field the next morning to put in another day's work. When Liddell discovered this, he sought legal action, telling his lawyer, "I request that you would forthwith proceed to prosecute John S. Sullivan of Troy, Parish of Catahoula, for hiring four of my Negro men, secretly, and without my knowledge or permission, at midnight on the 12th of August last 1849 (or between midnight and day)."

In Tennessee it was illegal for a slave to practice medicine; however, a slave called Doctor Jack practiced with "great & unparalleled success" even though he was forced to give a sizable portion of his earnings to his owner. After his owner's death, Doctor Jack set up practice in Nashville. White patients valued his services so much they petitioned the state legislature, saying, "The undersigned citizens of Tennessee respectfully petition the Honourable Legislature of the State to repeal, amend or so modify the Act of 1831, which prohibits Slaves from practicing medicine, as to exempt from its operation a Slave named Jack the property of William H. Macon, Esq., of Fayette County."

Many women were found among slave entrepreneurs. They established stalls and small stores. They managed tiny businesses as seamstresses, laundresses and weavers. A Maryland slave recalled that, "after my father was sold, my master gave my mother permission to work for herself, provided she gave him one half [of the profits]." She ran two businesses—a coffee shop at an army garrison and a secondhand store selling trousers, shoes, caps, and other items. In the face of protests by poor whites she "made quite a respectable living."

So prevalent was the practice of slaves illegally working and in business the term *quasi-free Negroes* emerged.

Sometimes whites didn't play fair in business but whining was out and acumen in. Take Robert Gordon, who purchased his freedom and moved to Cincinnati where he invested $15,000 in a coal yard and a private dock on the waterfront. White competitors tried to run him out of business through ruthless price-cutting. Gordon simply hired fair-complexioned mulattoes to purchase coal from price-cutting competitors to fill his own customer's orders.

Black history is full of examples of people making a bad situation better. But compare the message then with today's. An 1848 black convention in New York resolved: "To be dependent is to be degraded. Men may pity us, but they cannot respect us." And in 1853, Frederick Douglass warned "Learn trades or starve!" Today, it's handouts, reparations, and society owes us something.

Government

Thomas Paine said, "Government, even in its best state, is but a necessary evil; in its worst state, an intolerable one." Paine, like so many others, recognized that the essence of government is coercion. However, we need government and its coercive powers to protect our natural rights to life, liberty, and property. Protecting these rights is the legitimate and moral role of government in a free society. But as Thomas Jefferson warned, "The natural progress of things is for government to gain ground and for liberty to yield."

Jefferson was absolutely right. Today the average worker pays close to 40 percent of his yearly earnings to federal, state, and local governments. Additionally, there is little that a person can do that is not regulated by some government edict, be it mowing our lawn, riding a bike, flushing our toilets, taking a shower, hiring a gardener, and many other day-to-day activities that used to be considered strictly personal and private.

It's tempting to blame our politicians for an increasingly meddlesome and oppressive government. Yes, we can blame them a tiny bit for not being statesmen, being contemptuous of our Constitution, and dishonest. But the bulk of the blame lies with the American people. Politicians tend to do precisely what we elect them to office to do. We Americans elect politicians to office on their promise to take what belongs to some Americans and give it to other Americans to whom it does not belong. Or we elect them *to give some Americans special privileges that are denied other Americans.*

Such descriptions may not be flattering to most Americans so let me give a few examples. Welfare is one example where politicians, through the tax code, take the earnings of one American and give them to another. But there are many other examples of this practice: farm subsidies, business subsidies and bailouts, foreign aid expenditures through the International Monetary Fund and the World Bank and the Agency for International Development. Indeed, more than two-thirds of the federal budget is spent for programs that fit the category of legalized theft.

Then there are special privileges: The government tells one North Carolina landowner that he may plant and sell peanuts and another that he may not. It tells one group of Americans that they can receive a government check for not raising pigs or cows and the rest of Americans that they are not eligible to receive money for not raising pigs and cows. Government tells one group of industries that they are eligible for subsidized loans and loan guarantees, through the Export-Import Bank, and another group of industries that no such subsidies are available. Plus, special privileges are doled out by race and sex.

A senatorial or congressional candidate who tells the electorate that if he wins office he will vote for only those expenditures authorized in Article I, Section 8, of the Constitution would go down to blazing political defeat. It is unreasonable to expect a politician to do something, such as respect the Constitution, when doing so is the equivalent of committing political suicide.

Thus, in the task of restoring moral and constitutional government, we shouldn't focus our energies on trying to change the hearts and minds of politicians. We should try to change the hearts and minds of our fellow Americans. We must sell our fellow Americans on the idea that the legitimate and moral role of government is to protect those unalienable rights to life, liberty, and property.

States Rebellion Update

February 1, 1995

The founders petitioned and pleaded with King George to get his boot off their throats. He ignored their petition and, rightfully, they declared a unilateral declaration of independence and went to war. Today it's the same story, but it's Congressional usurpations against the rights of the people and the states that make King George's actions look like child's play. Our constitutional ignorance, coupled with the fact that we've become a nation of wimps, sissies, and supplicants, has made us easy prey for Washington's tyrannical forces.

But that might be changing. There is a long overdue reemergence of American's characteristic spirit of rebellion. Coloradans have been a leading player. Last year, their state legislature passed a concurrent resolution ordering the federal government to obey the Tenth Amendment and cease and desist unconstitutional mandates and the commandeering of its state legislature. Subsequently, a number of other states have passed, or are now in the process of passing, a similar resolution. An arrogant Congress and their minions, like King George's parliament, have little respect for toothless resolutions. But teeth might be emerging.

Colorado Senator Charles Duke, one of the authors of Colorado's Tenth Amendment Resolution, has introduced a bill called the "State Sovereignty Act." If it passes the legislature, it would require all persons liable for any federal tax that's a component of the highway users fund to remit those taxes directly to the Colorado State Department of Revenue. The money would be deposited in an escrow account called the "Federal Tax Fund" and remitted monthly to the IRS along with a list of payees and respective amounts paid.

If the federal government imposes sanctions on Colorado for failing to carry out an unconstitutional mandate and penalizes the state by withholding funds due, say, for highway construction, the State Sovereignty Act prohibits the State Treasurer from remitting any funds in the escrow account to the IRS. Instead, Colorado would impose a surcharge on the account to continue the highway construction.

Further west, the rebellion spreads. The federal government lays claim to 85 percent of Nevada's territory. There is no similar land grab in any of the states east of the Mississippi. Therefore, according to the *Elko Daily*, citizens are petitioning the federal government to abandon all claims to land within the boundaries of the state of Nevada. They're asserting an "equal footing" claim that they had the right to be admitted to the union on the same basis as other states.

For sissies a petition is fine. But if Nevadans had the character and courage of the Founders, they'd send a unilateral declaration to Congress asserting that, from this day forward, all land within the state boundaries belongs to the people of the State of Nevada, except as permitted by Article I, Section 8, of our Constitution, which grants the federal government the right to exercise "authority over all places purchased by the consent of the legislature of the state . . . for the erection of forts, magazines, arsenals, dock-yards, and other needful buildings."

Some might say, "Williams, it's not for you or the people to interpret the Constitution; that's the job of those nine cats on the U.S. Supreme Court!" I say nonsense. Our Constitution is not written in hieroglyphics. The Constitution is easy to understand. Nevadans can easily establish where the federal government has jurisdiction in their state simply by walking around and picking out forts, magazines, arsenals, and dock-yards.

It's high time Washington gets the clear constitutional message that the federal government is a creature of the states—not the other way around.

Where to Cut Spending

March 22, 1995

Republicans have a chance to rise above political expediency and become a party of principle. They are absolutely right in pushing for welfare reform. Welfare and liberal visions of the War on Poverty haven't simply been failures. They've made whole classes of Americans indolent, dependent, and immune to the traditional cure for poverty—a growing economy. But how about other welfare recipients?

This year, Congress plans to hand out $431 million to IBM, Hewlett-Packard, and Eastman Kodak to develop new computer storage systems. Over the last decade, Congress has given wine-grower Ernest & Julio Gallo $15.9 million for overseas advertisement. Sunkist latched on to the same handout agenda for $66.9 million, and Clinton friend Tyson Foods got $9.9 million.

According to a story in *Reason* magazine (March 1995), Congress has given General Motors, Ford, and Chrysler $250 million to develop better cars. In order to promote corporate equality of opportunity to raid taxpayer pockets, $587 million is going to AT&T, Rockwell International, and Xerox to support their flat-panel research. The Export-Import Bank and the Overseas Private Investment Corporation give out close to $1 billion in credit loans, loan guarantees, and grants to U.S. businesses trying to sell overseas. The recent bailout money for Mexico is essentially a handout to American banks stupid enough to toss good money after bad at the Mexican government.

There is neither moral nor constitutional justification for government handouts to corporate welfare queens. Moreover, there's no public support for these handouts. So if Republicans moved to eliminate them, they wouldn't face irate voters. However, they would face an outraged corporate lobbyist community that makes large contributions to their campaign coffers. But we should press Republicans with this question: How can you possibly talk about slamming the handout door on a poor, lazy, good-for-nothing welfare recipient while at the same time sponsoring handouts for members of America's Fortune 500?

The Washington-based Heritage Foundation has come up with forty independent federal agencies ripe for the cutting block at a saving of $2 billion a year. Included among them are the Corporation for Public Broadcasting (PBS), the Legal Services Corporation, the National Endowment for the Arts, and the National Endowment for the Humanities. Other independent agencies you've never heard of, but your paycheck has, that should be eliminated are the Christopher Columbus Foundation, the Appalachian Regional Commission, the Commission on National Community Service, and the State Justice Institute.

Liberals protest, asking, how can PBS and the educational programs it airs exist without handouts? As for their existence argument, Bell Atlantic recently offered to buy PBS outright. Programming such as the Arts and Entertainment Network, the Learning Channel, the Discovery Channel, and National Empowerment Television gives lie to claims that educational/cultural shows require taxpayer subsidies. The people at PBS simply want the luxury of reduced accountability and the right to live at the expense of taxpayers.

Congress can cut much more spending and enhance productivity by selling government albatrosses such as the Tennessee Valley Authority, the Power Marketing Administration, Amtrak, and billions of dollars' worth of government real estate holdings. The U.S. Postal Service ought to be privatized simply by giving all of its assets to its employees.

Republicans would be on far greater moral, persuasive, and principled footing if their version of welfare reform included government corporate handouts. Contrary to Labor secretary Robert Reich's claim, allowing corporations to keep more of their earnings through tax cuts is not corporate welfare. Giveaways are.

Minimum Wage, Maximum Folly

April 19, 1995

Economic theory is quite simple but yields powerful predictions. You don't have to be an economist to understand economics. It's easy. Say you commissioned me to do a study to make recommendations on how to eliminate Haitian poverty. Upon completion of the study, I tell you what's needed is for the Haitian legislature to enact a $7.00-an-hour minimum wage law. That way, Haitians would no longer be poor. President Clinton and Department of Labor secretary Robert Reich would probably compliment me on my findings, but you'd probably say, "Williams, you are a fool." You'd be right. If higher miminum wages were an effective anti-poverty device world poverty would have been eliminated ages ago.

Minimum-wage proponents say higher minimum wages won't cause unemployment. The first fundamental law of demand, to which there are no exceptions, says when prices rise, people tend to buy less, and when they fall, people tend to buy more. When beef prices rise, we buy less beef. When interest rates rise, we take out fewer mortgages. After all, if people didn't respond that way, sellers could charge any price they wanted and we'd still buy it. Labor services are no different. When labor's price exceeds its value—what it can produce—employers will buy less of it and seek substitutes. Among those substitutes are automation, moving to a lower-wage country, and customer self-service.

"Williams," you say, "but what can be done to raise people's wages?" Low wages are more a result of people being underproductive than being underpaid. They simply do not have the skills to produce and do things their fellow man highly values. Seldom do we find poor highly productive individuals or nations. Those who earn low wages tend to have low skills and education. Our challenge is this: How can we make these people more productive? Raising minimum wages will not raise worker productivity; however, it can sabotage worker potential to acquire higher productivity.

Put yourself in the place of an employer and ask, If I must pay Clinton's minimum wage of $5.15 per hour, does it pay me to hire a worker so unfortunate as to have skills enabling him to produce only $3 an hour's worth of value? Most employers would see that as a losing economic proposition and wouldn't hire such a worker. Therefore, a major impact of the minimum-wage law is to discriminate against the employment of low-skilled workers. The denial of a job makes the disadvantages of low-skilled workers more permanent. After all, one of the most important means to higher skills is to be employed in the first place and receive on-the-job training and learn about other opportunities.

Among academic economists, there is little or no debate over the unemployment effects of minimum wages. Our only debate is on the magnitude of unemployment. Close to 90 percent of academic economists agree minimum wages cause unemployment, especially for teenagers, particularly black teenagers. Check it out yourself: Introductory college textbooks in most sciences represent a distillation of what constitutes a broad consensus in the field. Virtually all economics textbooks that say something about minimum wages conclude that they cause unemployment.

People working at or near the minimum wage are exercising their best known alternative. Even though their income is meager we shouldn't destroy that alternative just so we can feel good. The minimum wage and other regulations help explain why today's underclass has taken on a permanency not typical of yesteryear. I'm with House majority leader Dick Armey. The minimum-wage law is evil legislation and deserving of repeal altogether.

More Guns Reduce Crime

July 5, 1995

Liberals produce one specious argument after another to foster greater government control over our lives. One of them is their seemingly plausible argument that gun control and outright ban of certain weapons will reduce crime. T. Marcus Funk exposes some of that nonsense in his article "Gun Control and Economic Discrimination" in the *Journal of Criminal Law and Criminology* (winter 1995).

Funk points out that murder rates in "gun-controlled" areas such as Mexico and South Africa are more than twice as high as those in the United States. Countries such as New Zealand, Israel, and Switzerland have household gun ownership rates comparable to ours yet have much lower rates of crime and violence than we do. Among the six million Swiss there are an estimated two million guns, including 600,000 fully automatic assault rifles, and their murder rate is 15 percent of ours.

Liberals tell us registration and waiting periods will reduce crime. According to Justice Department and Bureau of Alcohol, Tobacco and Firearms estimates, 90 percent of violent crimes are committed without a handgun. Of those committed with a handgun, 93 percent of the guns used were obtained through unlawful means. Registration and waiting periods are of little value in deterring criminals. What's more, a 1986 study revealed that 20 percent of the guns seized by Washington, D.C., policemen were homemade.

The liberal vision sees the world in reverse, and the gun issue is no exception. It is estimated that there are 2.5 million instances where guns are used for self-defense and stop a crime. In most of these cases, gun owners fired warning shots or threatened perpetrators by pointing or referring to their guns. In 1980, there were an estimated 8,700 to 16,600 nonfatal, justifiable woundings of criminals by civilians. In 1981, there were 1,266 justifiable homicides by civilians using guns against criminals. By comparison, police officers killed only 388 felons in 1981.

Nearly 60 percent of convicted felons surveyed said, "A criminal is not going to mess around with a victim he knows is armed with a gun." Seventy-four percent of convicted burglars said the reason they avoid burglarizing houses when people are home is because they fear being shot. In Orlando, Florida, after its police department set up a program to teach women how to use firearms, the rape rate dropped 88 percent. In Kennesaw, Georgia, the city passed an ordinance requiring households to have a gun. Within seven months the burglary rate fell 89 percent.

As a result of liberal laws and court decisions the police cannot and will not protect us. People have a natural, or God-given, right to protect themselves. Americans know this and that's why a 1979 survey revealed that 73 percent of Americans said they'd refuse to comply with handgun prohibition.

Protection against criminals wasn't exactly what the Framers had in mind when they gave us the Second Amendment. Their vision of a citizen militia was "the able-bodied men in a township or country," such as today's Michigan Militia. In Virginia's ratifying convention, George Mason warned that if government ever controlled the militia, the government could "gradually increase its power by totally disusing and neglecting the militia." And Patrick Henry repeated this fear, saying, "The militia, sir, is our ultimate safety.... The great object is that every man be armed.... Everyone who is able may have a gun."

While criminals endanger our liberties, the greatest threat comes from the organized power of the U.S. Congress and their minions—this the Framers knew well.

The Lame Game

August 2, 1995

James Bovard has an article about the lunacy of the Americans with Disabilities Act (ADA) in the *American Spectator* (July 1995) that will make your day. In August 1993, the Equal Employment Opportunity Commission announced that obesity is a protected disability. Therefore, a three-hundred-pound woman who was turned away as a nurse's aide could sue the hospital. A 360-pound woman brought a $1.5 million suit against a Memphis theater for her emotional distress when she found out she couldn't fit into any of the theater's seats. Not to be outdone, a 410-pound man, denied a promotion from cleaner to train operator, sued the New York Transit Authority for discrimination.

A Santa Monica, California, deaf woman sued Burger King, claiming its drive-through windows illegally discriminated against deaf people. Burger King settled the lawsuit by agreeing to install visual electronic ordering devices at ten restaurants. In March 1993, a federal judge ruled that the District of Columbia's practice of excluding blind people from jury duty was a violation of ADA.

The Americans with Disabilities Act also has been a godsend to dumb college students. Thousands have successfully dodged required courses by getting a shrink to certify them as "math disabled." A Tufts University student claimed that under ADA the university was obliged to accommodate her aversion to test-taking. The president of Boston University said ADA lawsuits and threats have resulted in demands to "accommodate foreign-language majors who have foreign-language phobia [and] to comfort physics students who suffer from dyscalculia, the learning disability that prevents one from learning math."

University professors also benefit from ADA. A Suffolk University professor sued the law school, claiming she was denied tenure because she had a disease that results in lethargy and lower productivity. Professor Donald Winston, an English instructor at Central Maine Technical College, was fired for kissing students and having sex with them. Winston sued the college claiming discrimination against the handicapped. Two doctors at his trial testified the professor suffered from "sexual addiction."

Some attempts at blatant extortion and special privilege have been thrown out of court. Others have cost companies millions of dollars. Even when a case is thrown out, companies spend thousands of dollars defending themselves against frivolous suits. And who pays? You and I, through higher product prices or less convenience. But lawyers love it. In fact, in some quarters ADA is taken to stand for "Attorney's Dream Answered."

We can't blame ADA on mush-headed liberals. It was passed at President Bush's urging in 1990 along with those other Bush economy-crippling favorites such as the Clean Water Act and the 1990 Civil Rights Act. What Bush did, and Clinton is trying to perfect, is producing an economic nightmare for local jurisdictions as well. According to the National Association of Counties, county governments will be forced to spend almost $3 billion by 1998 to comply with ADA mandates. Cities are ordered to put wheelchair curb cuts at intersections where even an Olympic-class sprinter might not hazard crossing.

What's Williams's solution to ADA mandates? I'm not smart. I depend on our Constitution for guidance. Amendment 10 says, "The powers not delegated to the United States by the Constitution, nor prohibited by it to the States, are reserved to the States respectively, or to the people." Then I checked Article I, Section 8, and found no authorization for ADA. That being the case, the solution is a broad-based refusal to comply with ADA mandates. After all neither the states, nor the people, have a moral duty to obey unconstitutional acts of Congress.

A Better Agenda

August 23, 1995

There are two questions, easily answered, to determine whether or not the new Republican majority will become big-government Democrats in elephant garb.

The first is, From whence comes the money the federal government spends on welfare, food stamps, school lunches, and other entitlements? If you said, It's taken from the earnings of people like you and me, who pay tribute to Washington, go to the head of the class.

The next question is, What's one of our constitutional guarantees? Article IV, Section 4, says in part, "The United States Shall guarantee to every State in this Union a Republican Form of Government." That means the people and their states are sovereign but bound together with common interests as principals who delegate certain powers to their agent—the central government.

With those two basic questions answered, let's evaluate the Republican cutting-down-the-size-of-government agenda.

Block-granting entitlement programs is the Republican newspeak. Instead of Congress and its Washington bureaucrats dictating to the states how welfare, food stamps, school lunches, and other federal programs are run, Republicans propose sending the money to the states in the form of block grants. With strings attached, governors and mayors will be permitted to experiment and design programs they think work best in their states and local communities.

Aside from Democrats, disgruntled federal bureaucrats, handout advocates, and lobbyists who see their empires crumbling, there is fairly widespread support, particularly from governors and mayors, who want the handout power and who'd like their states to function as "fifty laboratories."

Block grants are an improvement over the status quo, but, like other Republican proposals for greater federalism and more constitutional government, they're timid and not likely to have long-run success. After all, a future Congress can increase the strings and control. Republicans are simply talking clipping noxious weeds when, as every homeowner knows, getting rid of weeds requires uprooting and killing. If they're simply clipped, bureaucracies, like weeds, will grow back stronger and healthier.

If the new Republican Congress had more character and foresight, it would work on getting Washington out of the handout picture altogether. Here's a rough guide of what it might do.

First, figure out federal spending on the programs it proposes to block grant. Then, enact personal income tax reductions of an equivalent amount. Then, Brother Newt can tell governors and mayors that the money the fed used to take from the citizens of your state is now back in their pockets. If you think a particular entitlement program is important for your state, then you enact state and local taxes to get the money.

Of course governors and local officials would go ape for a very simple reason. No politician likes to be known for raising taxes. Moreover, social activists would have far less success getting governors and local politicians to raise taxes to support their socialist agenda.

Citizens could make a more direct comparison between the value of the programs and their pocketbooks. It's much easier for social activists to get remote politicians in Washington to impose burdens on states and local communities. After all, for example, if House minority leader Richard Gephart shepherds a tax increase through Congress, what does he care about the anger and resentment of the citizens of Atlanta, Georgia? Georgia's governor and Atlanta's mayor would be far more sensitive to their feelings and opinions.

If Republicans really respect the Constitution, and its guarantee of a republic, they'll stop this block-grant talk and replace it with entitlement-program elimination and tax cuts. Or is that too much to expect?

Political Arrogance

September 20, 1995

Let's begin with a problem that Hoover Institution's visiting scholar Paul Romer might pose: Imagine a simple manufacturing process that requires attaching 20 different parts to a frame. They may be attached in any order: part 1 first, then part 8, part 14, and so on. Or you can first attach part 18, part 11 next, then part 3, and so on. The number of possible sequences for attaching those 20 parts to the frame totals 10^{18} That's a pretty large number, roughly the number of seconds since the big bang.

Now think a moment about the thousands of parts involved in automobile manufacturing. Japanese assembly-line workers are allowed to experiment with slightly different ways of doing their jobs. They may, for example, put the rearview mirror on the door before attaching the door to the car, or they may do it the other way around. That way, the company can discover which is the more efficient method.

These two manufacturing problems aren't important in and of themselves. What's important is there are literally trillions of ways of doing even the simplest task. That being the case, what would you think of a person, a committee, or a bureaucrat who said, "I (we) know which is the single most efficient way of doing a particular task." Unless that person has tried the trillions of ways of doing that task, how can he know? You'd probably call him a fool. And if he was a politician and mandated one way of doing the task, and outlawed all others, you'd probably call him an arrogant fool.

That is precisely the description we can give politicians who want to micromanage our lives. How can Bill Clinton and Hillary

Clinton know, as they pretended last year in their attempt to nationalize our health-care system, what is the best use of a person's earnings? Jennifer might be a healthy twenty-five-year-old who chooses to risk being uninsured so that she can save that money to purchase high-tech computer equipment to research and develop an idea she has on DNA. Or she might want to save the money to start a landscaping business. What the Clintons and their minions were in effect saying was, "Of the millions of possible uses for that $3,000 Jennifer earned, its best use is to purchase health insurance."

How can they possibly know that? They don't even know Jennifer. I'm not saying Jennifer can predict her future perfectly or knows what best serves her long-term interest. But who's in the best position to make the choice about her earnings, the Clintons or Jennifer? And how arrogant and brutal it is when they tell Jennifer, "Even if you swear not to take a single taxpayer dollar should you get sick, we're going to make you buy health insurance whether you want to or not. If you resist, we'll put you in jail."

Fortunately, Clinton was unsuccessful in nationalizing healthcare, but think about the thousands upon thousands of regulations mandating the way we do things, as if bureaucrats knew the most efficient method of getting things done. Republican efforts toward regulatory reform should take this information and knowledge into account. For example, instead of the Environmental Protection Agency's mandating antipollution methods, there should be reasonable pollution targets, like industries can emit only so many tons of pollutants into the air. This would permit companies and local communities to develop and experiment to meet the target, so the best means can be discovered.

Far more wisdom can be found among millions of individuals acting privately to discover the best ways of doing things than a room full of bureaucrats.

Mankind's Most Brutal Institution

August 16, 1995

Generically, what's the most brutal institution on the face of the earth? If you said government, go to the head of the class. If anyone is in doubt of that fact, they only need to read *Death by Government*, recently published by Professor R. J. Rummel of the University of Hawaii's political science department.

This century, so far, international wars and civil wars have taken about thirty-nine million lives. But that's small in comparison to deliberate government murder. Since the beginning of this century, governments have murdered 170 million people, mostly their own citizens.

The top government murderers are those most adored by America's campus leftists and their counterparts in the media and the political arena: the former Soviet Union and the People's Republic of China. Between 1917 and 1987, the Soviet Union, where even our president traveled to protest against our involvement in Vietnam, murdered 62 million of their own citizens. Between 1949 and 1987, mostly under that leftist favorite Mao Tse-tung's rule, thirty-five million Chinese citizens were murdered by their own government.

Hitler's Nazis were pikers by comparison to the Communists. They managed to exterminate about twenty-one million Jews, Slavs, Serbs, Czechs, Poles, Ukrainians, and people they deemed misfits, such as homosexuals and the mentally ill.

Trailing badly behind the USSR, China, and the Nazis, Japan murdered six million unarmed citizens in Asian countries they conquered during World War II. Many of the deaths included unspeakable barbarities like soldiers tossing an infant in the air so a comrade could catch it on his bayonet.

Lesser-known murdering governments include Turkey who between 1909 and 1918 murdered close to two million Armenians; the Khmer Rouge in Cambodia, which caused two million Cambodians to lose their lives; Pakistan's government, which murdered 1.5 million people; and Tito's Yugoslavian government, which murdered a million citizens. It might surprise us to know that our southern neighbor, Mexico, had a hand in these barbarities, murdering about 1.5 million of its citizens between 1900 and 1920.

Professor Rummel estimates that pre-twentieth-century government murder, from the Christian Crusades, slavery of Africans, to witch hunts and other episodes, totals about 133 million. Therefore, our century is clearly mankind's most brutal and we might ask why.

Rummel gives the answer in his book's very first sentence, "Power kills; absolute Power kills absolutely. . . . The more power a government has, the more it can act arbitrarily according to the whims and desires of the elite, and the more it will make war on others and murder its foreign and domestic subjects." That's the long, tragic, ugly story of government: the elite's use of government to forcibly impose their will on the masses.

You say, "Williams, you're not suggesting that the United States government has anything in common with these murderous regimes, are you?"

The answer is a clear no. Nothing in our history is even remotely similar to these murderous governments.

But the note of caution surfaces if you ask, Which way are we headed tiny steps at a time: toward more liberty or toward more government restrictions on our liberty.

The unambiguous answer is toward more government restrictions of our liberties.

Our government has massive power to do evil. Murderers like Josef Stalin, Adolf Hitler, Mao Tse-tung, and Pol Pot would have loved to have the kind of information about its citizens that agencies like the Internal Revenue Service and the Bureau of Alcohol, Tobacco and Firearms have.

We should view our government the way we would a friendly, cuddly lion. Just because he's friendly and cuddly shouldn't blind us to the fact that he's still got teeth and claws.

Hating Government

December 6, 1995

At the time of the Oklahoma City bombing, Bill Clinton chastised those Americans who loved their country but hated their government. That's a morally blind statement at best. After all, would Clinton have said that to Germans who loved their country but hated the Nazi regime or the Russians who loved their country but hated Moscow?

It is both possible, and moral, to love one's country and hate its government. Our government is not like Germany's or Russia's, but if we ask whether we're heading toward more liberty or more totalitarianism, it's clearly toward the latter—tiny steps at a time.

Northern California's Fred and Nancy Cline might be among the rising numbers of Americans who hate Washington. According to *Reader's Digest* (November 1995), the Clines bought their 350-acre farm in 1989 to grow grapes, raise cattle, and bring up their five children. That year, the Clines plowed up 190 acres of it for oats and cattle grazing, as had the previous owner.

In August 1990, the U.S. Army Corps of Engineers slapped them with a "cease and desist" order, accusing them of destroying wetlands and thereby polluting the "navigable waters of the United States." The order threatened the Clines with a one-year prison term and/or $25,000 fine for each day of the violation. The Clines immediately stopped their leveling of the field but continued plowing.

The Clines secured records to show their land had been continuously farmed for decades, contrary to the U.S. Army Corps of Engineers' claim it hadn't. Then, their case took an ominous turn: FBI and Environmental Protection Agency agents began interviewing their business associates, friends, and neighbors. A federal grand jury subpoenaed their business and tax records. Army helicopters started surveillance of their property, hovering for minutes over various structures.

By an act of extraordinary luck, Bernie Goode, former chief of the Army Corp's regulatory branch in Washington, heard about the Clines' case and visited their farm. He found no evidence of Clean Water Act violations, saying, "Everything you did clearly qualified for the agricultural exemptions written into the law." The U.S. Justice Department decided not to file criminal charges against the Clines, but the "cease and desist" order remains in effect, denying the Clines use of most of their farm.

Given the Clines' experience and others more brutal, one can only marvel at the level of civility toward government bureaucrats. Put yourself in the place of the Clines. You take out a mortgage and plow your life's savings into a farm that you have every reasonable expectation to fully use. A bureaucrat, acting on behalf of environmental wackos, orders you not to use half of it. What has happened to the Clines, and thousands of other Americans, not only offends basic decency but violates the Constitution's Fifth Amendment so vital to our liberty.

There may be a compelling case, though hard to imagine, for

the government's denying the Clines the use of 190 acres of their property. The solution envisioned by the Framers is for the government to purchase the Clines' property or otherwise compensate them for the loss in its value. But Washington's tyrants, like tyrants anywhere, view abrogation and confiscation as the preferred alternative.

Most Americans could care less about the Clineses of our country who face increasing government abuse of basic constitutional and moral principles, but we do so at our peril. When Washington's Huns and Vandals are finished with the Clineses of our country, they're coming after you and me. That, by the way, is why statist liberals want gun control; it will make their job easier.

The Flat Tax's Enemies

February 7, 1996

Most Americans view our current tax code as complicated, abusive, and unfair, but politicians love it, hence the attack on presidential candidate Steve Forbes for his advocacy of the flat tax proposed by Representative Dick Armey and Senator Richard Shelby. The proposal calls for a tax rate of 17 percent on all income. It contains a $13,000 individual deduction, $17,200 for a single head of household, $26,200 for a married couple, and a $5,300 deduction per child. A family of four wouldn't pay taxes on income under $36,800. To achieve this low rate, most deductions would be eliminated, including mortgage and charitable deductions.

The flat tax would instantly increase our gross national product. Americans spend six billion hours annually simply complying with the tax code: record keeping, tax planning, preparing tax returns, audits, and court appearances. Those hours, spent productively, would produce the annual outputs of our auto, truck, and aircraft industries.

Presidential candidate Lamar Alexander, probably assisted by the real estate and building lobby, is one of Forbes' attackers. He's telling people that, if there's a flat tax, the value of their homes and farms will decrease. That's a fear-mongering lie. Yes, loss of interest deduction has the effect of reducing housing and land values, but a flat tax will more than compensate. First, the flat tax is estimated to reduce interest rates by 25 percent. A $50,000-a-year family currently averages a $3,834 mortgage deduction yielding a tax saving of $575. But a 25 percent drop in interest rates would yield a yearly saving of $959 for a net gain of $384. Second, since lenders wouldn't have to pay taxes on interest income, they'd charge lower rates. Finally, there'd be benefits from lower tax compliance costs and higher economic growth.

The flat tax has a two-to-one support in opinion polls so the big question is, Why are politicians and some lobby groups against it? The answer is easy and it's the same old story: Politicians love power. Congress's most powerful committee is the Ways and Means Committee, whose former boss was Dan Rostenkowski and which is now headed by Bill Archer. It's also the committee whose members have the fattest political war chests. Getting on the Ways and Means Committee is a major goal for many members of Congress because it's in charge of tax favors. Among its largest clients are the real estate and building industries. Washington's big-time lobbyists attend every public meeting to protect and advocate their special interests. With a flat tax, members of Congress wouldn't have anything to sell in exchange for votes and campaign contributions (read: extortion).

As Bill Simon, former Treasury secretary, asks, "Now that Republicans control the levers of power, will they suddenly decide that big government is not so bad after all and decide to preserve the status quo?" I'm sorry to say that with the exception of those freshmen congressmen who've earned the zealot label for having voiced respect for the Constitution, there's probably an affirmative answer to Simon's question.

To be fair, the new Ways and Means Committee chairman Bill Archer wants to scrap the income tax altogether and replace it with a national sales tax. Getting rid of the income tax would be a national blessing but collection of a 30 percent sales tax, needed to raise today's revenues, would require an agency more abusive than the Internal Revenue Service. An idea better than either the flat tax or national sales tax would be to get federal spending back to its historic levels of 3 percent to 4 percent of our gross national product. That way, we could live with any tax collection system.

Ending Ignorance

October 16, 1996

The average worker has no idea what he pays for government. The Mackinac Center for Public Policy, based in Midland, Michigan, has come up with a wonderful idea it calls the "Right To Know Payroll Form." It proposes that each pay period employers supply workers with a detailed estimate of visible and concealed taxes. If workers are better informed about government costs, they might make different political choices.

The Mackinac Center uses a hypothetical scenario where Acme Manufacturing Company hires John Doe and pays him $916.67 every two weeks. The company's cost to hire him is much more.

Employee costs the company must bear in addition to salary include: employer's share of Medicare ($13.29), employer's share of Social Security ($56.83), worker's compensation ($9.46), unemployment insurance ($10.66), mandated program administration costs, that is, Americans with Disabilities Act, Family and Medical Leave Act, and affirmative action ($4.25). Finally, the company has to administer John Doe's federal, state, and local taxes ($15.43).

Subtracted from John Doe's gross pay of $916.67 are federal income tax ($105), state income tax ($36.45), employee's share of Social Security ($56.83), employee's share of Medicare ($13.29), and city income tax ($18.43). John Doe takes home $686.67. Even some of that will go for taxes such as sales taxes on gasoline, clothing, and telephone service.

If we asked John Doe how much he paid in taxes every two weeks, he might be able to come up with the answer $230—the amount deducted from his gross paycheck. But he's really paying much more. We see that by asking the question, If it cost Acme Manufacturing Company $1,026.59 to hire John Doe, how much value must he add to the company's bottom line in order for the company to remain profitable? If you said at least $1,026.59, go to the head of the class. So who really pays the so-called employer's share of Social Security ($56.83), Medicare ($13.29), unemployment insurance ($10.66), and other so-called employer costs? If you said John Doe, again, go to the head of the class. No employer who expects to stay in business will hire a person who costs him $1,026.59 bimonthly but who can only produce $916.67 bimonthly (John Doe's gross pay).

The reason Congress created the fiction of "employer's share" of Social Security and Medicare, and require employers to "pay" worker's compensation and unemployment compensation, is purely for purposes of worker deception. They figure, and probably correctly so, there would be political hell to pay if John Doe knew that Social Security really costs him $113.66 every two weeks and

Medicare cost him $26.58. There'd be even more political hell to pay if John Doe was under forty years old and knew that he'd be paying that money into Social Security and that the system will be bankrupt when he retires because it is an unfunded Ponzi scheme. Directors of a private retirement program, having any characteristic of Social Security, would be put in jail at best—or more properly executed.

I hope America's CEO's see the merit of the Mackinac Center for Public Policy's "Right To Know Payroll Form" and include it with employee pay statements. But there are two things that might stop them. First, the IRS might deny companies the right to do so. Second, and probably a more important hurdle, is that CEO's, for the most part, are cowards. They are so dependent on being in the good graces of government officials they wouldn't want to do anything that might anger politicians and bureaucrats.

Proof of Washington Rot

March 19, 1997

The nation's response to the scandal-a-day revelations about money funneled into Clinton's reelection and the Democratic party's fund-raising is entirely misfocused. Campaign finance reform measures such as full disclosure and dollar limits do not address the political rot and cancer underlying the scandals.

Let's begin by asking why would a person or corporation fork over thousands of dollars for a politician's campaign? I doubt whether they do it so that Clinton or a member of Congress will guarantee them the rights to free speech, freedom of religious expression, or the right to peaceably assemble.

I also doubt they spend the money so Congress and Clinton will give them national defense. They don't make big money contributions for any constitutional guarantee. After all every American gets constitutional guarantees without spending a dime in political contributions.

What has far greater explanatory value for political contributions is the expectation that Congress or the White House will grant the contributor a right or privilege that other Americans don't get. It might be changes in the tax code that benefit one class of Americans at the expense of another, business or farm subsidies, the favorable location of an airport, or restrictions on imports that compete with a corporation's product. In other words, big campaign contributors want a special privilege—mostly a monopoly privilege—given to them but denied to other Americans.

What do we need? First, we have to recognize that politicians are selling favors. Campaign finance reform measures such as full disclosure and spending limits do not alter the fact that politicians sell favors; it just focuses on the method of payment. If politicians are in the business of selling favors, we can bet the rent money that people will find some way to purchase them.

The solution lies in our finding a way to take the White House and Congress out of the privilege-granting business. That's a tall order because most Americans think privilege granting is a perfectly legitimate government function, though they may occasionally disagree with who's getting what favor.

If you share my value of equality before the law, we should demand that if Congress enacts a privilege for one American that privilege should be available to all Americans. For example, if Congress makes payments to one American for not raising pigs, that law should apply to all Americans who are not raising pigs. If Congress enables peanut growers to charge higher prices by limiting who can be in the peanut business, it ought to give me a similar right to monopoly income by limiting the number of economists.

Some might argue that certain monopolistic laws are vital to national interests and that enrichment of the few at the expense of the many is a secondary effect. No problem. For example, if sugar import restrictions are vital to the national interest, Congress could simply pass a law taxing away the higher wages and profits resulting from the restrictions—call it a national interest tax.

The bottom line is that as long as Americans permit politicians to give special favors and privileges, there are going to be people willing to buy them. We must reform Washington and true reform is a no-brainer. The framers put their hope and faith in the Constitution because they knew politicians were untrustworthy. That's what you and I must do—demand obedience to both the letter and spirit of the Constitution. But in order to do that, we must know what's in the document. Unfortunately, most Americans don't.

The Coming Social Security Disaster

April 16, 1997

The most recent report from Social Security's Board of Trustees' predicts the system will be insolvent by the year 2029; it had been predicting insolvency in 2030.

By 2010, the Social Security system will be running deficits, the year when the Social Security trust funds go to zip. What needs to be done? Earlier this year, Federal Reserve Board chairman Alan Greenspan recommended higher taxes and reduced benefits as a solution.

But wait: Thirteen years ago, Alan Greenspan headed a commission, named after him, whose 1983 report assured the American people that Social Security had been "fixed" through higher taxes and that it would be sound until at least 2058.

Let's face it—there is no government solution that can fix what is an inherent contradiction and a Ponzi scheme.

You say, "Williams, there's nothing wrong with Social Security; after all there's a big trust fund cushion." There is no trust fund. The actual money earmarked for the trust fund is used to finance today's spending, thereby understating the true federal deficit. What politicians call the trust fund is simply a bunch of IOU's. When 2010 comes, and payouts are larger than payins, government has three options. They can make good on the IOU's by increasing taxes, borrowing money, or cutting spending. This is exactly what they'd have to do if there were no trust fund.

Social Security is not only a corrupt system, it's a bad deal as well. According to "Social Security Privatization," a publication of the Washington-based Cato Institute, and written by Harvard professor Martin Felstein, Social Security privatization would not only make retirees richer, it would raise annual GNP by at least 5 percent.

Social Security's rate of return is 2.9 percent compared with 9.3 percent in the private market. Simplified that means a fifty-year-old person has to fork over $1,000 to get $1,900 worth of benefits at age 75. In a private market, that person would only have to pay $206 to get the same benefits.

Since most payments into Social Security go to pay today's recipients, there's reduced national savings. With privatization, retirement money would be saved and made available for investment. Investment is what makes for a higher GNP and greater national wealth.

"But Williams," you say, "the Social Security Advisory Council is way ahead of you. They're talking about putting our Social Security money in the stock market." I can't think of much that's more sinister than the government buying and selling stocks. I can see congressmen threatening companies telling them if you don't have an affirmative action program, you won't be on the list of "approved" companies. Or the White House saying, "If you don't come to our coffee hour, and make a contribution, the Social Security Administration is going to sell the stock in your company."

How about the liberty-oriented solution to Social Security: Let people take care of their own retirement. After all, aren't we emancipated adults? Under what moral principle or constitutional authority has the government the right to threaten a person with the proposition that if he does not pay into the government's retirement program, they will seize his property, impose fines, jail him and, if he is too resolute in insisting on his liberty, possibly kill him?

Ed Crane, the President of the Cato Institute, has it right when he says, "Privatization of Social Security may well be the most important issue confronting our nation." We've listened to the fine-tuners long enough. It's time to listen to our common sense.

Air Bag Update

April 30, 1997

Not long ago, I wrote about the National Highway Traffic Safety Administration's (NHTSA) air bag safety coverup and the fifty-two lives (thirty-two were children) lost caused by 200-mph deploying air bags.

Then there were air bag lies. In 1977, the Transportation Department claimed that air bags "protect automobile occupants from collision injuries, without the need to fasten seatbelts or take any other action." The 1979 head of the NHTSA, Joan Claybrook, said, "It was possible to design air bags that will meet the performance criteria and will provide a high level of protection for children whether they are seated properly or not."

I ended the column suggesting that Americans ought to be free to choose to have air bags or not. After all the additional safety benefit air bags provide, for seat belt–wearing passengers, is virtually zero.

Acting under the assumption of being an emancipated adult, living in a free country, I wrote the following letter to Mr. John Womack, Acting Chief Counsel of the U.S. Department of Transportation: "Dear Mr. Womack: I am very concerned for my safety in light of a number of recent reports about air bags going off and killing people. I herein request permission to have the air bag in my car deactivated. Thank you for your assistance."

More than a month later, I received an answer from Mr. James R. Hackney, Director of the Office of Crashworthiness Standards, that in part read: "In your letter, you request approval to disconnect one or both of the air bags in your vehicle. I regret to inform you that, at this time, we cannot grant your request to authorize your auto dealer or repair shop to disconnect your air bags."

Then he went on to talk about NHTSA plans to mandate "smart air bags" in 1999: "That will stop air bags from deploying under unsafe conditions or effectively tailor the speed of the deployment to match the size of the occupant and the crash circumstances."

How do you like that for elitist bureaucratic arrogance? Mr. Hackney implicitly concedes there's a safety issue with air bags deploying "under unsafe conditions" and deployment speed not matching occupant size and crash circumstances. But, more importantly, who in the world does he think he is to tell me that he's not granting me permission to take a measure that might save my life?

Moreover, I'd like to know what specific article in the U.S. Constitution authorizes the NHTSA to command Americans to suffer the indignities of paternalism and the additional risks of air bags. Or, does the NHTSA share my mother's attitude when I was a child? "There's no Constitution in this house; you do what I say!"

Whether air bags are safe or unsafe is not the real issue. The real issue is whether Americans shall be free to choose. The elitist arrogance demonstrated by the NHTSA's letter is a direct result of an American general willingness to sacrifice liberty for safety.

The elitist response to calls for liberty might be, "Williams, if you don't have an air bag in your car, or wear a seat belt, you might become a burden on society if you're injured and can't take care of yourself."

That's not a problem of liberty; it's a problem of socialism. In a free society, another can't be compelled to take care of me for any reason. Under socialism, you are compelled to take care of me and—like my mother—you have the right to control my life.

As for me, I'll take liberty over nannyism.

Should Laws Be Obeyed?

July 2, 1997

Should we obey laws? It all depends; some laws aren't worthy of obedience.

"There you go again, Williams," you say. "What kind of society would there be if people decided which laws they'd obey or disobey?"

That might be a problem, but let's look at it. During several visits to South Africa, during its apartheid era, one of my many remarkable discoveries was the widespread disobedience and contravention of its apartheid laws. Whites rented to blacks in open violation of the Groups Areas Act. Whites hired blacks in defiance of job-reservation laws that set aside certain jobs for whites. Would you have insisted that whites obey apartheid law?

In Nazi Germany, it was illegal to conceal Jews or assist them in escape. Some Germans violated the law; would you have prosecuted them? In our country, the Fugitive Slave Act (1850) forbade and set penalties for anyone aiding, abetting, concealing a runaway slave or interfering with his capture.

Once again, how many Americans think that those assisting runaway slaves should have been prosecuted? For decent people, laws shouldn't be blindly obeyed. They should ask not whether the law has majority support, or even whether it's constitutional (apartheid laws were part of South Africa's constitution); instead they should ask whether the law is moral.

Morality can be a contentious issue but there are some broad guides for deciding what laws and government actions have moral sanction. Lysander S. Spooner, one of America's great nineteenth-century thinkers, put it this way: No person or group of persons can "authorize government to destroy or take away from men their natural rights; for natural rights are inalienable, and can no more be surrendered to government—which is but an association of individuals—than to a single individual."

French economist-philosopher Frederic Bastiat's test for immoral government acts is, "See if the law benefits one citizen at the expense of another by doing what the citizen himself cannot do without committing a crime."

By these criteria, most acts of Congress do not have moral sanction, which is not to say Congress doesn't possess the brute force to command obedience. Most of what's enacted by Congress consists of various ways of taking from one American to give to another. That's a criminal act—theft—if done by a private person.

The moral principle undergirding our Declaration of Independence is natural law. The essence of natural law (those "unalienable rights") is that each person owns himself. Accepting that principle, what's moral and immoral is simplified. Murder, rape, theft, done privately or collectively, is immoral—it violates self-ownership rights.

By the same token, seemingly innocent acts like the government's forcing people to protect themselves is immoral. Take the minor examples of speed limits and seat belt laws. Driving at inappropriate speeds places others at risk. Not wearing a seatbelt places a driver at risk. We have rights to take risks with our own lives but not that of others; therefore, speed laws have moral sanction, whereas seat belt laws don't.

Slowly but surely, liberty-minded Americans are increasingly faced with the dilemma of either obeying their moral consciences or obeying the law. It's a hard decision because doing what's moral and exercising one's natural rights can lead to fines, loss of property, imprisonment, and possibly death at the hands of the agents of Congress.

But most of my heroes are those men brave enough to risk all and opt for the more moral. We'll be celebrating some of these men July 4th. But unfortunately Americans will give our founder's values and sacrifices lip service, not commitment.

How versus How Much We're Taxed

October 8, 1997

Horror stories about the outrageous, criminal behavior of Internal Revenue Service (IRS) agents have brought new debate on taxation, but I think the discussion misses the main issue.

Representative Dick Armey (R-Texas) has proposed a broad-based flat tax of 17 percent. Representative Bill Archer (R-Texas) has suggested a national sales tax, along with the abolition of the IRS and hopefully repeal of the Sixteenth Amendment. Comparing the benefits of the flat tax versus the national sales tax is really a debate about which is the better way for government to subjugate its citizens.

I seriously doubt we'd be having this argument if the federal government was spending what it was historically—4 percent of the GNP. If that was the case, any method of taxation would be OK, even the current complex code. However, when spending is close to 30 percent of the GNP, as it is today, Americans are in bondage whether we're taxed by a flat income tax or a national sales tax.

To me, the debate is analogous to my being sentenced to crucifixion and given the option, "You can carry the cross on your back to the crucifixion site, or we can spare you the burden by having it set up, waiting for you." Of course, I'd opt for having it ready and waiting.

To think clearly about taxation, we have to recognize what it is. Taxes represent government claims on private property. If taxes were 100 percent, there'd be no private property and we'd be serfs. Government is necessary. For government to do its job, it has to collect taxes.

What's government's job? Our government's job is laid out in Article I, Section 8, of the U.S. Constitution. It grants Congress authority to lay and collect taxes to provide for roughly nineteen enumerated functions like common defense, coinage of money, and establishment of post offices and courts. If members of Congress obeyed their oath of office and did only what the Constitution permitted, I doubt whether federal spending would be even 10 percent of the GNP.

I'm sure there's an idiot congressman who'd respond, "Williams, you forgot about promoting 'the general welfare' clause of the Constitution. That authorizes us to tax and spend for Medicare, food stamps, crop subsidies, and other handouts." Balderdash! If the framers of the Constitution had that vision, they could have spared themselves the contentious debates they had writing and ratifying the Constitution. They could have simply written, "Congress has the power to lay and collect taxes to provide for all those things Americans would like to have but are unable or unwilling to pay for."

They didn't do any thing like that. They rightfully understood and feared the oppressive powers of government and sought to limit government threats to liberty by specific enumeration of what Congress can do.

Don't get me wrong. I think that a flat tax or a national sales tax is a major important improvement over the status quo. Either would reduce the power of Congress to play favorites and engage in social engineering.

But I think there's a more important debate on which Congress should conduct hearings, namely, should one American, or group of Americans, have the right to use Congress to force one American to toil for another's benefit? What Congress is doing violates all principles of moral conduct, not to mention the Thirteenth Amendment, which reads, "Neither slavery nor involuntary servitude . . . shall exist within the United States."

Social Security Rip-Off

October 15, 1997

Politicians demagogue so much about children that if Samuel Johnson, who told us that "patriotism is the last refuge of a scoundrel," was alive today, he'd probably change patriotism to children.

Let's pretend that politicians and other elite really care about children, then how about a few Social Security facts (available from the Social Security Administration)?

When infants who are born today enter the labor force in 2020, they will face a 24 percent payroll tax to finance Social Security checks and Medicare payments. Toward the end of their work lives (2065), the payroll tax will be 35 percent. That's the more optimistic scenario. According to the Social Security Administration's "pessimistic assumptions," which many investigators believe are far more realistic, it's worse. In 2020, the Social Security plus Medicare payroll tax will be 32 percent, and by 2065 it will be 59 percent to honor today's promises. These tax bites do not include federal income taxes.

Those are the projections. We won't see 32 and 59 percent payroll taxes. I cannot imagine future generations giving up a third to almost two-thirds of their earnings to take care of a bunch of old people. The Social Security system will have collapsed long before. In fact, Social Security is projected to start coming apart by 2011 or so. Not to worry—people receiving, or about to receive, Social Security checks, like I am, shouldn't be alarmed. We'll rip off young people and be dead or comatose when the disaster strikes our children and grandchildren. We will have ridden their backs, and the worst they can do to us is curse our memory.

There's little evidence that Americans, particularly politicians and retirees, have the courage and willingness to talk and think reasonably about our pending Social Security disaster. Barry Goldwater sounded a warning in 1964, and it probably cost him the presidency. In 1985, Ronald Reagan suffered political heat for merely mentioning the problem. Steve Forbes risks his presidential aspirations for being open and honest about Social Security.

In order to avoid economic chaos we must own up to the fact that Social Security cannot be fixed. Other countries such as Chile, Australia, the United Kingdom, and Singapore recognized this and switched from their government-run Ponzi schemes to private savings programs that provide pensioners with a safer and wealthier retirement.

While each program differs, and are in different stages of transition, their structures are quite similar. Workers put a percentage of their earnings in private pension funds that in turn are invested in stocks, bonds, real estate, and other income-producing assets. When workers retire, they use all or part of their accumulated wealth to purchase annuities that guarantee them an income, for the rest of their lives, up to three times the former government program. These countries have "safety net" retirement programs for the few workers who have inconsistent work records and very low wages.

Several national think tanks have developed sound analyses and proposals for avoiding the coming crisis. Among them are the Washington-based Cato Institute and the Heritage Foundation, along with the Dallas-based National Center for Policy Analysis. Highly respected scholars have done the idea work but it's going to take pressure from the people to get Congress off its duff.

The bottom line is if people care about children as much as they pretend, they'll support the few politicians, like Steve Forbes, who have the courage to openly acknowledge that Social Security needs to be scrapped and retirement privatized.

Campaign Finance Reform

October 22, 1997

Campaign finance sleaze will not end, no matter what laws are enacted, until we Americans own up to a simple fact: Whenever there's a seller, there's going to be a buyer. It makes no difference whether Republicans or Democrats control the White House or Congress. The problem is that we have a democratic process that confers an aura of respectability on clearly totalitarian acts. Let's use a minor example to make the point.

Flo-Sun, a huge sugar company in Florida, contributed at least $3 million to both political parties since 1979. Question: Are we to believe that Flo-Sun's executives forked over this cash out of a civic concern for America's democratic process of electing public officials?

Before you reach a conclusion, how about some facts? This year, Congress voted again to renew the 1981 law that subsidizes the sugar industry through a combination of price supports, special loans, and restrictions on imported sugar. Those measures boost domestic sugar prices to 21 cents a pound, about double the world price. According to General Accounting Office (GAO) estimates, in one year alone the subsidy yielded $65 million in additional revenues for Flo-Sun. That's a nice return for Flo-Sun. What about you and me? Sugar subsidies translate into consumers' paying $1 billion dollars more each year for the sugar we buy.

Consumers don't like higher sugar prices—so how can Congress get away with ripping us off? It's the political problem economists refer to as narrow, well-defined benefits versus widely dispersed low costs. It pays sugar companies to organize, hire Washington lobbyists to watch Congress and the White House, and fatten politicians' pockets so they'll vote for sugar subsidies.

That's the benefit side. On the cost side, you and I may pay $10 or so more for the sugar we buy each year. Who among us is willing to incur the costs of organizing and the expense of going to Washington to try to unseat congressmen whose vote cost us $10 more for our sugar? We're better off just paying the $10 and forgetting it. Also, since we consumers are a diverse group with diverse interests, it would be difficult to organize us to fight Congress and the sugar industry.

Washington is loaded with lobbyists who represent every industry, labor union, and other special interest groups. Most of their agenda is to spread money around to get Congress or the White House to rig the economic or political game in their favor. If politicians don't cave to that agenda, they'll find money being funneled into their districts to help their opponents unseat them.

Campaign finance sleaze will not end until we, the American people, reduce Congress's ability to sell favors. The term *favors* is a charitable description. What Congress actually does is use its brutal force to enable one American to live at the expense of another. Congress stops me from buying sugar from a cheaper foreign producer and forces me to buy sugar from Flo-Sun or some other American company at higher prices. That's not only immoral, but it seems to be a violation of the Fifth Amendment's prohibition against taking property.

There might be a reason, which I can't fathom, for Congress to funnel my money to the sugar industry. If there's a reason the handout should be honest, aboveboard, and visible. If Florida's congressional delegation thinks Flo-Sun needs help, it should write a bill titled "Aid to Dependent Florida Sugar Companies" and put it to a vote.

Bill Gates and the Justice Department

November 26, 1997

Here's my complaint and I want to know what you think.

I enjoy reading the *Washington Times* but they won't sell it to me without advertisements. In effect they tell me, "Williams, if you want our newspaper, take our product as we configure it or take your business elsewhere."

I know what the average uncaring person would advise, "Williams, if you don't like the way the *Washington Times* packages its product, buy another newspaper!" But I'm not going to accept that kind of insensitivity; I'm going to the Justice Department's assistant attorney general Joe Klein in the hope that he'll initiate an antitrust investigation of the *Washington Times*.

"Williams," you say, "have you lost your marbles?" I say no, and the Justice Department's actions against Microsoft support my reasoning. Bill Gates's computer operating system, Microsoft Windows 95, includes Internet Explorer, which can connect users to the Internet. As a part of the licensing agreement, computer manufacturers who purchase Windows 95 must install the entire program on their computers, including Internet Explorer.

According to Joe Klein, consumers "who take the machines and the browser given to them are obviously being force-fed a Microsoft product." Therefore, Joe Klein seeks to stop Microsoft from requiring that computer manufacturers include the Internet Explorer when they install Windows 95; make Microsoft notify users that they are not required to use its browser; and instruct users how to remove the Explorer icon from the software.

Let's look at Joe Klein's nonsensical statement. First, are machines and browsers given or did customers purchase them? I suspect they're purchased. If they're purchased, consumers made a voluntary choice among an array of products. Nobody forced them to purchase a particular computer or a particular operating system.

Microsoft Windows has about 85 percent of the operating systems market so obviously millions of customers view Windows as superior to their next best alternative. What about being "force-fed" a Microsoft product? I own Windows 95, but I don't use its Internet Explorer—I use another service.

A partial explanation for Klein's attack is that Microsoft's competitors, such as Netscape, are complaining about the possibility of stiff browser competition and seek to use government restrictions to achieve what they cannot achieve through the free market.

That's just one more reason why Washington is a town of sleaze. Companies who can't compete use government to stymy the competitiveness of their competitors. Their techniques include antitrust allegations, complaints that their competitor's products are unsafe, sell for too low a price, or are pollution-causing. They also lobby for tariffs, sales quotas, and marketing agreements.

Ralph Nader, always at the center of corporate-bashing, said Microsoft's Internet Explorer is a "classic definition of predatory pricing. Once they [Microsoft] get rid of Netscape, you'll see the difference." Nonsense! Any modern industrial organization economist will tell you there isn't much evidence anywhere suggesting that predatory pricing (driving your competition out of business and then jacking up prices) is either an intelligent or a widely practiced strategy to achieve monopoly wealth.

Here's my suggestion for Klein. Bring antitrust charges against the U.S. Postal Service. That's a monopoly that bans any competition in the delivery of first-class mail. Year after year, they gouge consumers by charging higher prices and providing shoddier services.

Then, after Klein breaks the U.S. Postal Service monopoly, he can focus on my issue: How I can buy the *Washington Times* without the advertisements. Hopefully, he'll order them to instruct me that I am not required to read the ads and give instructions on how to remove them.

Ignorance Is Bliss

December 17, 1997

Last September, the National Constitution Center conducted a survey to determine just how much Americans know about our Constitution. The news wasn't good. It turned out that only 5 percent of Americans could correctly answer ten simple questions about the Constitution. For example, only 6 percent could name all four rights guaranteed by the First Amendment (freedom of speech, religion, press, and assembly). Almost one-quarter could not name a single First Amendment right. The survey uncovered some strange beliefs like: the Constitution was written in France, one of the rights guaranteed by the First Amendment is "freedom from fear," the first ten amendments to the Constitution are called the Pledge of Allegiance, and the Commander-in-Chief is Norman Schwarzkopf. Despite gross ignorance, 91 percent of Americans surveyed said the Constitution is important to them.

My question is, How can the Constitution be important to us while at the same time we're so ignorant of it? As a college undergraduate, I majored in social psychology before I discovered it was a vacuous science and switched my major to economics. Anyway, I retain enough social psychology knowledge to render an expert opinion on why Americans are ignorant about our Constitution. Simply put, it's the way we avoid cognitive dissonance. To maintain sanity, people try to have their beliefs, perceptions, and behavior logically consistent. When cognitive dissonance, or lack of consistency, arises, people unconsciously seek to restore consistency by changing their behavior, beliefs, or perceptions.

Suppose Americans were aware of the limitations the framers imposed on Congress through Article I, Section 8, of the Constitution, permitting taxing and spending only for national defense, coinage of money, establishment of post offices, and a few other things? Suppose Americans knew the Tenth Amendment says, "The powers not delegated to the United States by the Constitution, nor prohibited by it to the States, are reserved to the States respectively, or to the people."

If Americans knew about these limitations, how could we possibly accept Congress's spending billions of taxpayer money on education, health care, or midnight basketball, when not even the words (education, health care, and basketball) appear in the Constitution, while at the same time profess love and respect for our Constitution? If we knew the letter and spirit of the Tenth Amendment, how could we support the growing consolidation of power in Washington? If Americans were constitutionally aware, we'd be a cognitive dissonance–suffering nation. Therefore, since we're not likely to change our behavior, we must maintain an ignorant or warped perception of the Constitution.

But let me stretch my social psychology expertise a notch further for my conspiracy-oriented friends. Suppose I was a tyrant seeking to control a constitutionally dedicated people, what might be my strategy? I'd know it's hard to teach an old dog new tricks, so I'd focus my energies on the young. I'd start out in elementary school teaching kids that the federal government's duty is to make sure income is distributed "fairly," take care of the poor and aged, and do anything that a majority of Congress decides is good for us. To protect my strategy from scrutiny, I'd hide the Constitution from the kids and keep it hidden throughout high school and college. If some wise-cracking youngster raised a question about constitutional authority for this or that, I'd say, "It's covered under the 'general welfare' clause."

My grandmother had it right when she said ignorance is bliss but she forgot to point out that it is also a way around cognitive dissonance. It took studies in psychobabble for me to discover that.

Education

At higher levels of education, namely, graduate and professional schools, American education is unmatched anywhere. All over the world, people seeking high-quality advanced degrees want to attend American universities. But at lower levels of education, primary and secondary education and increasingly undergraduate college education, America lags far behind most developed countries. In primary and secondary education, our students rank at or near the bottom. We've seen this decline become progressively worse over the past four decades while politicians and the education establishment manufacture one excuse after another to explain the disaster.

Education received by white Americans is nothing to write home about, but that received by black Americans borders on criminal fraud. We find instances of black youngsters graduating from high school with nearly a 4.0 (A) grade-point average who cannot read and compute at the eighth-grade level or achieve a combined score of 600 (out of a possible 1,600) on the Scholastic Aptitude Test (SAT). Although the education establishment can make a case that they cannot be held responsible for environmental factors that negatively affect education, such as hostile student attitudes, poor parental support, broken homes, and neighborhood violence, the grades they give and the diplomas they issue are fully under their control.

The education establishment and politicians have successfully

argued that our education problems can be solved by greater ex-
penditures of taxpayer dollars. Despite unprecedented education
expenditures, which top those of any other nation in the world,
educational outcomes are far worse than they were when we were
spending far less money. In fact, several studies demonstrate an
inverse relationship between education expenditures and educa-
tion achievement. Casual observation demonstrates this as well.
For example, Washington, D.C., New York, Detroit, and Philadel-
phia schools are among the worst in the nation in terms of student
achievement; however, in terms of per capita student spending,
they rank near the top in the nation.

Some black politicians and civil rights organizations blame the
poor quality of education received by blacks on racial discrimi-
nation. That argument doesn't hold water because the worst ed-
ucations that black youngsters receive are in cities where the
mayor is black, the superintendent of schools is black, the city
council is dominated by blacks, and most of the school principals
and teachers are black. What's more, these are the very cities
where education expenditures rank at or near the top nationally.
Moreover, education expenditures are even higher when we take
into account school-related services that don't show up in the
education budget, such as police and social services.

The columns that follow discuss just how bad education has
become; they also include some education success stories and
suggestions on how to duplicate those successes, namely, by in-
troducing competition into our education system through school
vouchers or tuition tax credits.

The Myth of Failed Policies

September 27, 1995

For years I've railed against failed government policies like public education, welfare, and foreign aid. According to Professor Robert Higgs, writing in *The Free Market*, a publication of the Ludwig von Mises Institute, labeling these government programs a failure is a mistake. One must look beyond stated intentions.

We all know that public education has been a national disgrace marked by three decades of declining test scores and students who perform well below those in other industrial nations. But, according to Higgs, calling these dismal results a public policy failure just won't wash. After all, why would politicians responsible for funding schools and administrators responsible for operating schools tolerate a failing system for decades?

Public education has been a success—not for parents and students but for teachers, administrators, support staff, and politicians. Adjusted for inflation, per-pupil spending has risen from $2,000 in 1960 to $5,200 in 1990. As a result teacher, administrator, and support staff salaries have significantly increased. The payoff to politicians, who bilk the general public to channel billions of dollars each year to the education establishment, comes in the form of the votes and support of a well organized, well-heeled, politically savvy education lobby.

Welfare is another national disgrace I've called a failure. While it would take a little more than $50 billion to raise every poor American above the official poverty line, annual welfare spending is over four times that amount. Welfare has been a success for the pocketbooks of planners, researchers, social workers, administrators, and other assorted poverty pimps. As in the case of education, the payoff to politicians who tax-gouge the public to fund these parasites is the welfare lobby's organized political muscle to get out the vote and their media clout. Any politician proposing cuts in welfare feels that media clout, as he is portrayed as wanting to starve children and abandon old people.

Conservatives also have their favorite parasites. Try proposing privatizing the Veterans Health Administration (VHA) or closing down some of its facilities. You'll be charged with betrayal of all the brave men who fought the nation's wars. VHA operates 171 hospitals, 362 clinics, 128 nursing homes, and 35 residential facilities. With 240,000 employees and a $16 billion budget, the VHA provides some of the worst health care in America. Ninety percent of eligible veterans take their health-care problems elsewhere. Most of the 10 percent of veterans who use VHA qualify by virtue of low incomes, not service-related disabilities. Nonetheless, VHA is a success to its employees and suppliers; seven thousand of those employees get salaries over $100,000.

Foreign aid, contrary to Senator Jesse Helms's argument, is not a failure. It has been a success to Third World dictatorships that have managed to pocket billions of dollars in Swiss bank accounts while their people starve. Foreign aid has also been a success for American banks like Citibank and exporters like Bechtel Corp. The scam is that Congress fleeces taxpayers. The money goes to international lending organizations like the World Bank and IMF; with strings attached it goes to foreign countries who are obliged to pay out most of it to U.S. banks and corporations. The payoff to politicians comes in the forms of corporate campaign contributions, private airplane rides, and honoraria.

Professor Higgs's bottom line lesson is: When the political process is taken into account, government policies any reasonable person would call a failure are nearly always a spectacular success.

Miseducation of Americans

October 4, 1995

Kids from poor countries like Ireland and Slovenia beat the day-lights out of our kids in math. On international surveys, French kids come in second in reading ability while our kids come in sixth. Might money explain the difference? The answer is a big fat no. We spend more money per pupil on education than any other country—$6,000 on the average while the French spend $4,600.

Paul Klebnikov wrote an article titled "What Are Condoms Made Of?" for *Forbes* magazine (9/11/95) where he sought answers for France's superior performance by visiting Clarkstown High School, in an affluent suburb of New York City, and Lycee Jean de La Fountaine in Paris, both government-owned schools. La Fontaine classes average thirty-five students; Clarkstown averages twenty-one. Clarkstown has one hundred computers and a TV studio; La Fontaine has twelve computers tucked away in a back room. Clarkstown's facility is state of the art; La Fontaine has peeling paint and rickety wooden desks.

Klebnikov figured peeling paint and rickety desks couldn't explain La Fontaine's superior academic performance so he checked it out. At Clarkstown, he visited a class called Sex Respect. The topic of the day was supposed to be sexual abstinence but in the typical "bait and switch" tactic of educationists the teacher was talking about condoms. He informed the 15- and 16-year-olds that "within a year you will no longer be able to call them rubbers. They're going to be made out of polyurethane. They'll be much thinner and more effective, like Saran Wrap."

Klebnikov visited another class called Humankind, a replacement for an old civics class, where kids discussed an assigned three-page article about the Mafia and had split into six groups to draw pictures illustrating the point of the article.

In France's La Fontaine, it was a different story. When Mme. Thomazeau entered her seventh-grade French class, the class stood briskly to greet her. After saying, "Please be seated," she grilled the class on a medieval fable: "How is the text organized? Where does the introduction end? Where is the moral?" She wasn't into self-esteem. When the class was slow in answering, she thundered, "Half a year and you haven't learned anything." "Speak up! State your argument," as she glowered through her spectacles at one student who finally raised her hand, "Don't paraphrase the text. Synthesize!"

At Clarkstown's Global Studies class, the teacher talks about U.S. support of dictator Ferdinand Marcos and Imelda Marcos's shoes. In an advanced-placement American History class, one student said that society needs more values. The teacher replied, "It's not that simple. In a free society it's very difficult to say, This is right and this is not." That's what educationists might call "values clarification." I call it undermining traditional values.

In a typical French school, there's lots of homework, emphasis on fact and formal logic, a right and wrong answer for almost everything, and a teacher lecturing to a class. The French system is less interested in making excuses for children and more concerned with making demands upon them. In American schools, it's lazy thinking, dumb-downed standards, self-expression, and feeling good about oneself. Americans fifty years or older would recognize today's typical French school as the kind they attended.

As a result of parental apathy and a predatory education establishment, we Americans have been taken to the cleaners. What I find incomprehensible is how we look to a gouging education establishment for solutions to our education problems in face of the fact that they, assisted by the U.S. Department of Education, delivered one educational disaster after another.

Save the Children

March 8, 1995

While hosting for the vacationing Rush Limbaugh in December, I interviewed several distinguished guests; one of them was Nobel laureate Milton Friedman. Friedman reminded us that one of the most serious problems confronting Americans is the disgraceful state of government education, particularly that received by black youths. The only way out, Friedman argued, is privatization.

Professor Friedman, one of history's greatest economists, has a way with examples that makes his arguments stand out in stark relief. He asked Rush's millions of listeners to compare services delivered by the U.S. Postal Service to those delivered by Federal Express and United Parcel Service. The conclusion: We're far more pleased with services provided by FedEx and United Parcel Service. Plus, it's cheaper and better. Of course, the Postal Service will argue they can deliver first-class mail cheaper than anyone else. But just ask them, if that's the case, why is it necessary for them to have a law prohibiting others from competing with them?

The reason why private carriers do a more pleasing job isn't because Federal Express and United Parcel workers are inherently better and more caring than government postal workers. It's all in the incentives. If Federal Express doesn't please enough of us, it's out of business. If U.S. Postal Service workers don't please us, they get higher budgets, higher pay, and easier working conditions, and we pay higher postage.

Identical analysis is applicable to private schools versus government schools. Private black-owned and -operated schools such as Ivy Leaf (Philadelphia), Marva Collins Preparatory School (in both Cincinnati and Chicago), and Marcus Garvey (Los Angeles) do a far superior job of educating low-income black kids than government schools in the same neighborhood. In the wake of the education establishment's many excuses for why black kids are not being taught, private schools are successfully teaching. What's more, they're doing it today while the education establishment gives promises about what we'd get tomorrow if only we'd increase its budgets and raise its pay. Its tomorrow story has played for decades with no dawn in sight.

The education white kids receive is not that great, but the average American has no idea of the disgraceful fraud perpetrated against black students. Often, black kids, with high school diploma in hand, cannot read a bus schedule, write a comprehensible paragraph, or make the simplest computations. This can't be blamed on poverty and racism unless an argument can be made on why poverty and racism exempts black kids who attend black private schools.

The answer is simple. Private schools must please parents and they have the program flexibility to do so. Like the post office, government schools stay in business and get larger budgets whether parents are pleased or not. In fact, the poorer the job they do the greater are the resources put at their disposal. Black politicians, civil rights organizations, and the education establishment have delivered black youngsters into the educational equivalent of a Jonestown massacre. Their victims have been made virtually useless for the high-tech world of the twenty-first century. The tragic history of blacks has been that of no or few opportunities.

Today, there are opportunities galore, but many black youngsters are ill-equipped to take advantage.

More black youngsters should have educational opportunities available at schools like Ivy Leaf and Marcus Garvey. That can be done by putting education resources into the hands of parents instead of the educational establishment through vouchers, tuition tax credits, or property tax rebates. The changed political scene at the state and local levels of government just may provide an opportunity to rescue black kids from the educational establishment's massacre.

Callous Conservatives vs. Caring Liberals

January 24, 1995

The Republicans want to reexamine health and safety regulations and require the Occupational Health and Safety Administration (OSHA), the Environmental Protection Agency (EPA), and other regulatory agencies to make a cost/benefit analysis prior to making regulations. Clinton and other liberals have accused Republicans of callously disregarding the health and safety of America's children. That's nonsense. It's liberal regulatory excesses that beg for relief and here's just one example why.

Mrs. Cleaster Mims is founder and director of Marva Collins Preparatory School of Cincinnati. It's a private school with a student body of 185 mostly low- and middle-income black students enrolled in grades K through eight. Virtually all of her students score at and, in some cases, two, three, and four years above grade level. The school radiates with discipline, love, and high expectations. Scores of students are on her enrollment waiting list.

To meet the demand for Marva Collins's superior, not to mention safer, education, Mrs. Mims has started a campaign to raise money to purchase a $450,000 former nursing home that will allow her a five-hundred-student capacity and provide facilities for a few boarding students. While quite a bargain, the building is in need of repairs and alterations that include mechanical-electrical modifications, teaching space renovations, painting, roofing, and exterior work that could easily run the price tag to close to $1 million. To raise that kind of money in and of itself is a daunting challenge but regulations created by "caring" liberals could easily put her mission entirely out of the question.

Because of the building's age, asbestos and lead paint are present. But according to Cincinnati architect William Miller, who made an inspection of the building, "The materials are sound and nonhazardous by prudent reasonable standards of safety." He concludes that only relatively minor repairs need to be made to address existing asbestos and lead paint hazards.

But when have you heard of OSHA and EPA being reasonable? Miller estimates the combined cost of regulatory mandates for asbestos and lead paint removal could add as much as $200,000 to the renovation. Then there're close to two hundred doors in the building. To bring them up to Americans with Disabilities Act (ADA) mandates, plus construct ramps and meet other mandates, might add another $150,000 to costs.

Mrs. Mims's plight is a result of the liberal vision of the world. Liberals see only benefits from regulations and ignore costs. Sure, it would be wonderful if the five hundred students at the new school had zero risk of asbestos and lead paint hazard. It would be wonderful if a wheelchair-bound student, who might enroll, would find no physical impediments. That's the wonderfulness of OSHA, EPA, and ADA regulations. On the other hand, the cost of those regulations, and hence their invisible victims, is the five hundred black students who might have had a better and safer education. You can bet the rent money that the hazards of government education are far greater than those posed by asbestos and lead paint in the building Mrs. Mims' wants to purchase.

All's not lost. Mrs. Mims is a woman who knows no false pride and has boundless energy. She is willing to beg, plea, and cajole these federal and state agencies who have been allowed to proliferate arbitrary, punitive, and heartless mandates. She should get our political and financial support. While we're at it, we might just ask who is more callous: politicians who support regulations that make Mrs. Mims's dream of a better education impossible or those who want to make those regulations more sensible?

Rot at the Top

April 24, 1996

For decades now, we've known about the scandalous, broad-based decline in the academic preparation of our high school students. While this has been occurring, college enrollments have skyrocketed. The question is, If more and more students are ill-prepared for college, how do we explain increased college enrollment?

The answer's easy. Colleges have dumbed-down curriculum so as to accommodate dumber students. No better evidence of collegiate dumbing-down can be found than in a report by the National Association of Scholars (NAS), based in Princeton, New Jersey, titled "The Dissolution of General Education."

The report, released last March, is a study of *U.S. News and*

World Report's annual list of "America's Best Colleges." What they find is truly remarkable. The percentage of the top colleges with English department composition requirements slipped from 98 percent in 1914 to 36 percent today. Traditional mathematics was a graduation requirement at 82 percent of the colleges in 1914; today it's 12 percent. In 1914, 86 percent of these top colleges required courses in physical and biological sciences. This requirement plummeted to 34 percent by 1993.

College administrators may protest NAS findings by saying, "We still have mathematics requirements!" But very often they're watered-down math courses such as math for sociology or education majors. Such courses teach recipe techniques where little is taught about the underlying theory. At some colleges, taking a course where essay exams are given qualifies the student as having had composition writing experiences.

Given this college rot, one should not be surprised to find companies hiring people to teach college graduates basic writing and computational skills. Neither should one be surprised to find that students earning advanced degrees in math and the sciences increasingly foreign or foreign-born. If we listen to Pat Buchanan and close our borders, Silicon Valley might become a ghost town.

In lieu of highly disciplined subjects, colleges have substituted courses with little or no academic content, such as gender (sex is the proper term) and ethnic studies. Where I teach, George Mason University, there's a new sequence of touchy-feely courses where students learn to emote about AIDS and homelessness. These courses are little more than activist propaganda and proselytization of mush-brained students.

We'd like to think that college presidents and top administrators can halt the decline in higher education, but that's whistling Dixie. They're under immense pressures by campus political forces. Boards of trustees have the ultimate responsibility for their colleges, but as I found out during my short stint as a trustee at a major university, boards of trustees are little more than yes men for the president.

The only real hope lies with parents. Parents must realize that sending their kids off to college means more than tearful goodbyes and signing tuition checks. They must read catalogs. Ask for copies of course syllabi. Find out percentages of courses taught by teaching assistants. Finally, put little confidence in statements by college admissions office personnel and official publications.

I wish the National Association of Scholars' report was exaggerated, but my almost thirty years' experience as a professor suggests otherwise. But take a wee bit of heart. There are some notable alternatives to the rot at the top where youngsters can get an excellent liberal arts education. The colleges that most readily come to mind are Grove City College in Pennsylvania, Hillsdale College in Michigan, and College of the Southwest in Hobbs, New Mexico.

Beyond Debate

July 31, 1996

Some things are beyond debate. Suppose I hire someone simply to mow my lawn. After mowing the lawn, he pulls up my rose bushes and plants azaleas in their place. Do you think I should debate with him over whether it's better to have rose bushes or azaleas in my flower bed? I think not. My response would be, "I paid you to mow my lawn, not make decisions about my flower bed. You're fired!" Let's talk about education and beyond-debate issues.

According to the *Pocono Record* in Stroudsburg, Pennsylvania

(May 15, 1996), parents of a sixth-grader are suing the East Stroudsburg Area School District for what they claim as subjecting their daughter to a compulsory strip and body cavity search. It turns out that their daughter and fifty-eight other J. T. Lambert Intermediate School girls were summoned to the infirmary. The school nurse instructed them to strip down to their underwear in preparation for a gynecological examination. Some parents said their daughters asked not to have their genitals examined, but were told they had to. Some of the girls started to cry, and at least one was denied the right to call home.

J. T. Lambert School was greeted with a storm of parental protest. Dr. Ramlah Vahanvaty, who performed the exams, explained, "What it involved is an external examination of the labia to see if there were any warts or vaginal lesions. You can't see these if you don't retract the labia." She said, "I want to do what's in the best interest of the children," adding later, "Even a parent doesn't have the right to say what's appropriate for a physician to do when they're doing an exam."

That arrogance is part and parcel of today's education. Thomas Sowell's *Inside American Education* gives numerous examples of schools usurping parental authority (i.e., doing what they, as opposed to parents, think is best for children). Often what they do is unbeknownst to parents. Fifth- and sixth-graders are shown films of childbirth. In testimony before the U.S. Department of Education, one parent told of her fifth-grade son being given a plastic model of female genitalia with a tampon inserted so the boys will know how tampons fit.

In the name of "values clarification," children are asked questions like: "What disturbs you most about your parents?" "Who's the boss in your family?" "Do you believe in God?" "Tell where you stand on the topic of masturbation." The U.S. Department of Health, Education, and Welfare produced a 1979 "health" questionnaire that included questions such as: "How often do you normally masturbate (play with yourself sexually)?" "How often do you normally engage in light petting (playing with a girl's breast)?" "How often do you normally engage in heavy petting (playing with a girl's vagina and the area around it)?" In a "values clarification" curriculum in Oregon, third-graders were asked, "How many of you ever wanted to beat up your parents?" In a Tucson high school health class, students were asked, "How many of you hate your parents?"

J. T. Lambert Intermediate School did send out notices that the school would be giving physical examinations. Like other deceptive educational practices going under euphemistic titles as "values clarification," "health education," and "gifted students" programs, the true agenda was concealed. The notice made no mention that the school physician would make a gynecological examination and "retract the labia."

We as parents pay schools to teach our kids how to read, write and do arithmetic. We don't pay them to undermine and challenge parental values and authority. It's about time we made that abundantly clear.

Educational Fraud

September 11, 1996

While there are some government schools doing a good job, by and large our education establishment is corrupt beyond repair. "There you go again, Williams," you say, "beating up on teachers." Let's look at it. Karl Zinsmeister, fellow at the American Enterprise Institute and editor in chief of its magazine *American Enterprise*, has written an article in its September/October 1996 edition titled "Doing Bad and Feeling Good."

American students rank number one in the world in how good they feel about their math skills, but a 1992 international study by the Educational Testing Service showed American students ranking last in math achievement (behind Slovenia). Research surveys show self-esteem levels at least as high among black students as white students but a majority of either are unable to write a persuasive letter, date the Civil War, or calculate simple interest.

Educationists love the humane-sounding idea of self-esteem. It gives them cover for low standards and low effort both on their part and on that of students. After all, high standards, at least in the short run, provide grief for everyone. Teachers have to threaten, cajole, and punish, and often parents have to be confronted. It's easier just to keep students feeling good about themselves—while they don't know theirs from the one in the ground—and give them social promotions.

Educationists cover up this tragedy with deceit and dishonesty. According to the College Boards, in 1972, 28 percent of college-bound seniors had an A or B high school average. By 1993, 83 percent had an A or B average. During that interval, SAT scores went south. This clearly indicates what some call grade inflation and I call educational fraud. Since SAT scores have gone permanently south, and the public is increasingly aware of that fact, the educational establishment has resorted to "renorming" the SAT so as to give the appearance of progress.

That's the subtle dishonesty but there are more blatant forms. Staten Island's Public School 5 ranked first among New York's public schools in standardized reading and math tests. One parent couldn't figure out how her daughter scored in the 99th percentile in reading, yet could not read street signs. An investigation ensued and it uncovered widespread cheating, but not by students. According to the school chancellor of New York City, the school's principal, Murray Brenner, altered answer sheets. Wrong answers were erased and punched-out overlay sheets were used to make the correct circles. One student who originally scored in the 99th percentile in math plummeted to the 18th percentile after retesting.

The half-baked, never-worked-anywhere ideas that have taken over today's education can be readily understood. First, education departments at most colleges are the academic slums of the campus. Students who become education majors have the lowest SAT sores. Students who earn education degrees have lower LSAT, GMAT, and GRE scores (tests for graduate school admission) than any other major with the exception of social work majors. People with that kind of academic grounding fall easy prey to half-baked, never-worked-anywhere schemes.

More money, smaller classes, and higher teacher pay will not cure our education problems. The long-term solution is privatization—make education subject to competitive pressure. After all, most production that pleases us is a result of ruthless competition and the profit motive. Think about it. Most of what pleases us (computers, clothing, and food) is subject to that kind of pressure and most of what displeases us is not (post office, police, and schools).

A Principled College

November 13, 1996

In 1984, Grove City College withdrew its participation in the government's Pell Grant Program. Last month, its board of trustees decided that its students will no longer participate in the government's Stafford/PLUS student loan programs. President John Moore said, "With this step, all of our student aid programs, scholarships and loans, will be financed without federal funds. Providing aid to needy students will remain a top priority."

Grove City College's decision to withdraw from the Pell Grant Program was the result of the U.S. Supreme Court ruling (*Grove City College vs. Bell*) that federal grants and loans to students constituted federal financial assistance to colleges. That meant colleges were obliged to sign a Title IX "assurance of compliance form" that it didn't engage in sex discrimination.

Grove City College has no history of sex or race discrimination. In fact, the administrative law judge in the case found that "there was not the slightest hint of any failure to comply with Title IX, save the refusal to submit an executed assurance of compliance form." Grove City College would not sign the form because it was a blank check subjecting them to Department of Education current regulations, future interpretations, and all amendments.

So Grove City College opted out of the Pell Grant Program and established its own Student Freedom Fund.

Grove City College's recent withdrawal from the federal Stafford/PLUS student loan program completely ends their involvement with government. It spares Grove City College from the seven thousand sections of intrusive regulations governing Title IV of the Higher Education Act—regulations that have cost the college two secretaries. In addition to being costly, they were intrusive, demanding information about faculty salaries, sex and ethnic data, and other questions having nothing to do with student loans. In 1997, Grove City College students will be able to borrow money through a private program established by the college and PNC bank.

Located about 60 miles north of Pittsburgh, Pennsylvania, Grove City College is a bargain. With a freshman average SAT score of 1,240, they provide an excellent liberal arts education, room and board for less than $11,000 a year. *U.S. News and World Report* named Grove City the number-one best value for "Sticker Price," second most efficient, fifth best discount price, and sixth best in academic quality among northern liberal arts schools for 1997.

Aside from being an efficient, cost-conscious operation, Grove City College promotes a moral and civil climate for its students. Alcohol is banned on campus and at college-sponsored functions. Foul language is not tolerated. There's no condom distribution. Pornographic videos and literature violate their student-conduct code. As a result, their students are honest, hardworking, courteous, and fun to be with. Their parents can be assured that they are safe, both physically and morally. There's none of the decadence, vulgarity, and violence rife at some colleges, even those where parents fork over $25,000 and more a year. These are observations gleaned over my more-than-a-decade acquaintance with Grove City College that includes team-teaching one of their courses.

There should be more principled college administrations and courageous boards of trustees willing to put their money where their mouths are and stand up to the Washington Leviathan. Among the few who do and are also tuition bargains are Hillsdale College in Michigan, the Freedom School in Hobbs, New Mexico, and the Northwood Institute in Midlands, Michigan. If any of us are in a mind to be charitable to institutions of higher education, these schools should be the targets of our generosity.

The Dumb Leading the Dumber

December 1, 1996

Employers wonder why many college graduates can't write memos, perform simple computations, or just plain think. Here's a tiny portion of the answer about what's happening to education from my university.

George Mason's Center for Service-Learning & Student Leadership sent invitations to their "Hunger Banquet." The event was billed as educating "the GMU community on the dramatic effects of world hunger. The meal dramatizes the unequal distribution of resources that can contribute to world hunger." Furthermore, the evening would contribute to student development of "critical, analytical, and imaginative thinking to make well-founded ethical decisions." Unable to attend, I asked a Ph.D. student to go and give me a report.

After donating either two cans of soup or $3, each student drew a color-coded ticket that decided their category that evening. Students who drew "First-World" tickets, sixteen of them, were escorted to their table by a well-dressed host. They ate their four-course meal on a linen-dressed table adorned with fresh-cut flowers while being entertained by a flute and oboe duet. They were told they represented wealthy Americans—15 percent of the population. Thirty students drew "Second-World" tickets. They had hamburgers, sodas, and veggies and sat at bare tables and ate with plastic utensils. They were told they were the 25 percent of our population who were just barely making it. The one hundred and forty students drawing "Third-World" tickets were handed about three ounces of water and a half a cup of rice that they ate with their hands while seated on the floor. They were the impoverished, representing 60 percent of Americans.

A speaker from the Coalition for the Homeless said hunger and homelessness were caused by: lack of affordable housing, lack of jobs paying living wages, and lack of affordable health care. He told the students that we have plenty of resources to combat poverty but choose to spend it on defense. The event was little more than propaganda, indoctrination, and lies for young minds already brimming with mush. Even more insidious, it was the kind of event that fosters class envy. To give the bulk of the students water and rice, and say they represented 60 percent of America is hideous.

The facts are that 14 percent of Americans are poor, not 60 percent. Obesity, not emaciation, is more of a nutrition problem for America's poor. America's poor have more meat and housing space than average-income Europeans. In 1993, federal, state and local poverty expenditures were $324 billion; national defense was $291 billion. Since 1965, the nation has spent $5.4 trillion on poverty. That's enough money to buy: all manufacturing equipment, every office building, the entire maritime fleet, and every airline, railroad, and trucking company, TV and radio station, power company, hotel, retail and wholesale store in the nation.

Topping off the evening's propaganda, Canada's socialized medicine was held up as a shining example of what Americans should have. Nary a mention was made of Canadian patients going to U.S. hospitals in droves, women queuing for three months for a Pap smear, and any major U.S. city having more MRI and CAT scan machines than all of Canada.

George Mason's Center for Service-Learning & Student Leadership "Hunger Banquet" is simply a small part of widespread indoctrination, propaganda, and miseducation at America's universities that misleads and confuses our young people and promotes class envy. It happens for at least two reasons: The '60s flower children are in administrative positions, and members of boards of trustees, whose duties are to direct and oversee, are derelict.

Black Education

January 22, 1997

For years I've said that if the Ku Klux Klan wanted to sabotage black academic excellence, they couldn't find a tool more effective than the public school systems in most major cities. The evidence of that tragedy continues. The latest is contained in a *Philadelphia Inquirer* story (January 9, 1997).

Tai Kwan Cureton was a student at Philadelphia's predominantly black Simon Gratz High School. An honor roll student, maintaining a 3.8 (A-minus) grade-point average, Cureton ranked 27th in his 305-student graduating class. He was president of both the student government and student peer mediation service. He did all of this while working more than thirty hours a week at a fast-food restaurant. Tai Kwan Cureton was a good kid, so what's the problem?

Cureton was a member, and captain, of Simon Gratz's renowned track team. Simon Gratz's track team's toughness dates back at least to the early 50s. My high school, Benjamin Franklin, wound up on the losing side in meets with them. Cureton was widely sought after by recruiters with scholarships in hand from top-ranking Division I schools such as Penn State, Pittsburgh, and Boston College.

That was before he received his Scholastic Achievement Test (SAT) scores. For a student to be eligible to participate in freshman athletics at Division I colleges, the NCAA rules require a minimum SAT score of 700 out of a possible 1,600. Since a person gets 400 points on the SAT for simply writing his name, a minimum of 700 means the athlete must earn 300 points out of a possible 1,200. Not meeting the NCAA requirement, Cureton said, "After I got my test scores back, they stopped recruiting me. This really hurt. It was as if my hard work, good grades, and other school activities didn't count for anything."

That's the tragedy. Cureton attended school regularly, did his school work and behaved but his high school grades were fraudulent. He and his parents were misled into believing that Simon Grant's As and Bs were equivalent to those earned elsewhere. He was academically shortchanged by his school, an outcome he did not deserve and could not have known until SAT time.

The Trial Lawyers for Public Justice has filed a class action suit on his behalf based on the Civil Rights Act of 1964 claiming the NCAA requirements to be racially discriminatory. They, along with some education "experts," allege that standardized tests are written from a white middle-class viewpoint and therefore are unfair to blacks. That allegation is nonsense. Blacks score higher on the verbal than the math portion. It's difficult to make a case for cultural bias in math. Moreover, Asians are probably the most culturally distinct group in our country. Yet they score higher than blacks and, for that matter, higher than many whites.

Low black SAT scores are simply messengers. Instead of advocates for blacks killing the messenger, they should focus their attention on the message—the fraudulent education blacks receive in our primary and secondary schools. They should consider suing the Philadelphia School Board for the issuance of fraudulent grades and diplomas. The education establishment will tell us there are many education variables beyond their control such as discipline, violence, broken homes, and poverty. But well within their control are the grades and the diplomas they give.

Tai Kwan Cureton attends college but says he longs to race against the top competition at Division I schools. His story should bring outrage to decent people, not against the NCAA standards but against an education system that systematically scuttles opportunities for our youths.

Duped Americans

April 2, 1997

For nearly four decades, the education establishment has delivered one failure and set of excuses after another. Education for blacks is nothing less than a catastrophe and education for white kids is nothing to write home about.

People can and do make mistakes, and they produce never-worked-anywhere nostrums. In most cases, we fire them or run them out of town on a rail. But educationists are immune to those corrective forces. Instead, in the wake of one education disaster after another, we call them back for more advice and yet another half-baked experiment.

Black kids are fair game for these schemes and their academic performance shows it. Higher-quality education is no mystery—let's look at some historical data from the New York Board of Education.

On achievement tests given in 1941, some elementary schools in Harlem had grade-equivalent scores in paragraph and word meaning and arithmetic reasoning and computation that were equal to or higher than those in elementary schools in predominantly white working-class schools on New York's Lower East Side.

Harlem school sixth-graders averaged a grade equivalent score of 5.5 in paragraph meaning and 5.4 in word meaning. That's to be compared to averages in Lower East Side schools of 5.1 and 4.6. The New York citywide average was 6.8 and 6.5 respectively.

In no cases were Harlem school students as much as a year below grade level. Harlem third-graders were at or above grade level and, in some subject fields, scored higher than their counterparts on the Lower East Side, including in arithmetic reasoning and computation as well.

How do we explain the fact that black kids back then were holding their own? First, let's try an explanation that's consistent with how liberals view the world: Back in the '40s, Harlem blacks faced no discrimination; school budgets must have been higher than they are now; teachers were more highly paid; classes were smaller; and Ebonics must have been the classroom language.

I'm guessing those explanations and other educationist "requirements" for improved education are balderdash. Instead, I'd put my money on differences like teachers being able to read and write themselves, school discipline, homework being assigned and done, and parental support of the school's education objectives.

White liberals, black and white politicians, and civil rights organizations have done far greater harm to black academic excellence than yesterday's racists could have ever done. They have given unquestioned support to an education establishment whose actions have condemned large numbers of black youngsters to lives of educational mediocrity, while simultaneously bleeding taxpayers to death.

But black parents cannot be held blameless. Out of a misguided sense of loyalty, they have allowed the education establishment to lead them down one blind alley after another.

Take Washington, D.C. If a Klansman was mayor, superintendent of schools, and the majority of school principals and teachers were Klansmen, it is hard for me to imagine education being any worse than it is now with a black as mayor, a black as school superintendent, and blacks as principals and teachers. The only difference would be that black parents would be up in arms about the education rot.

I think it high time that black parents—and for that matter white parents as well—stop listening to the excuses and promises of educational quacks. They ought to demand, not next year but this year, that schools cease their practice of educational fraud. If not, demand wholesale firing of administrations. And if the mayor won't fire them, fire the mayor.

Excellence in Education

April 14, 1997

"Recruiting Trends 1994–95," a study by Michigan State University professor L. Patrick Sheetz, finds that not enough college graduates have the ability to write, speak, and reason coherently in order to hold down a job.

John Leo reports in the April 21, 1997, *Newsweek* that half of college graduates cannot read a bus schedule. A recent U.S. Department of Education report said that 53 percent of college graduates could not figure out how much change they should get back after putting down $3 to pay for a 60-cent bowl of soup and a $1.95 sandwich.

There are reasons for this educational malaise. Part of it is that half-witted professors, backed by dim-witted, smooth-talking administrators, are teaching our youngsters unmitigated nonsense.

For example, Professor James Sledd, of University of Texas,

writes in *College English* that standard English is "essentially an instrument of domination." Arguing against knowledge of grammar and logic, Professor Jay Robinson of the University of Michigan says that "the myth of basic skills" helps sustain rigid and evil class structures; what college students really need is reaffirmation as "members of racial, social, and linguistic minorities."

The National Association of Scholars put out a devastating report about the dumbing-down of college curriculum that includes courses for credit like "queer theory," the works of Pee Wee Herman, and watching Oprah or Montel Williams.

Everybody has heard of these and other horror stories about the state of higher education in America. But there are forces emerging to help combat higher-education malaise.

On May 21, in the Senate Russell office building, the John Templeton Foundation kicks off a new program called Templeton Honor Rolls for Education in a Free Society. Honorees will be chosen for their commitment in teaching the interdependence of political freedom, the market economy, and the moral principles that sustain a free society.

The program is chaired by former U.S. Treasury secretary William E. Simon and administered by the Intercollegiate Studies Institute based in Wilmington, Delaware. Some 126 awards will be given to outstanding universities, departments, scholarly books, and individual professors—including a $25,000 Lifetime Achievement Award and a $25,000 Outstanding Contemporary Book Award.

William Simon says that after searching through over eight hundred nominations, "reports of academia's pending demise are both premature and exaggerated. On every college campus in America the fortunate student can still discover brilliant, inspiring, and innovative professors committed to learning, rather than indoctrination."

He's right—even at the most liberal universities. But many times these professors are isolated and under siege by their colleagues and campus administrators. National recognition for their courage, as well as emergence of organizations such as the National Association of Scholars, will help end their isolation.

In addition to honoring America's most distinguished educators, colleges, and departments, the Templeton Honor Rolls will provide guidance on colleges, universities, and departments.

For the most part, college admissions offices are simply salesmen for the college, solely interested in getting tuition-paying warm bodies. They often go to considerable lengths to conceal truth about curriculum content, freshmen SATs, graduation rates, campus crime, and other negative features about their institution.

Simon says, "Given the high cost of a college education and widespread concern about declining standards, it is more vital than ever to provide a guide that will direct parents and their children to the strongest colleges and universities and to the professors, departments and textbooks in the disciplines they wish to study."

The Intercollegiate Studies Institute makes that two-hundred-page book available free for those willing to pay the postage.

Improve Education: Fire the Experts

May 7, 1997

The best thing we can do for American education is to abolish university education departments, abolish the U.S. Department of Education, and fire education "experts."

You say, "Williams, have you gone mad?" Let's look at it.

Over the past thirty years, achievement test scores have been in free fall, as demonstrated both by SAT scores and the government's National Assessment of Educational Progress, which measures the achievement of seventeen-year-olds.

On a recent test, one-third of high school seniors couldn't identify Abraham Lincoln or the countries we fought during World War II. Only 6 percent could solve the following math problem: "Christine borrows $850 for one year and pays a simple interest rate of 12 percent. What will be the total amount of money she repays?"

A major insurance company reports that 44 percent of its applicants couldn't read at the ninth-grade level. Eighty percent of a major manufacturer's applicants flunked its fifth-grade math and seventh-grade English competency tests. Few Americans need more proof that our education system is in shambles—but why it's in shambles is important for the cure.

In the May/June issue of *American Enterprise*, in an article entitled "The 60s Rules in Public Schools," Karl Zinmeister writes that the widely used book *Secondary Math: An Integrated Approach*, features color photos and essays on the Dogon tribe of Africa and pictures of Maya Angelou and Bill Clinton. It also asks questions such as, "What role should zoos play in today's society?"

In a kindergarten class, kids spend weeks "exploring gender bias." Early education classes teach kids about a variety of family structures, emphasizing families with gay and lesbian parents. At one school, a teacher described Longfellow as British, while explaining why it wouldn't be relevant for her students to study him. Reporters from the *Los Angeles Times* visited a Northridge middle school and found classes in "baseball-card collecting, jigsaw puzzles and crocheting." A teacher at the school volunteered, "the most important job in junior high is not subject matter, but morale."

Much of the explanation for educational rot is connected to the fact that 1960s hippies have taken over colleges of education and they dominate the education establishment. Their vision is that high academic standards are elitist. To discriminate among students, based on academic excellence, risks injuring student self-esteem; failure must be defined out of existence.

For them, schooling is for building habits of social cooperation and equality rather than rigorous training of the mind. For many teachers, schooling must undermine parents and traditional values.

The liberal education agenda is no better stated than in the words of Middlebury College English professor Jay Parini: "After the Vietnam War, a lot of us didn't just crawl back into our literary cubicles; we stepped into academic positions. With the war over, our visibility was lost, and it seemed for a while—to the unobservant—that we had disappeared. Now we have tenure, and the work of reshaping the universities has begun in earnest."

Unfortunately, Professor Parini's vision of what college education should be has percolated throughout entire college curricula. Nowhere are half-witted education ideas given greater currency than in education departments, and for good reason. By and large, education departments represent the academic slums of any university. Education majors tend to have the lowest SAT scores and their professors tend to have the least academic respectability—making both easy prey to fads and half-baked ideas.

Educational reform measures that do not address methodological rot, teacher incompetency, and leftist indoctrination will bring disappointing results, regardless of the amount of money spent.

The Wrong Education Target

July 30, 1997

A July 24 *Washington Post* editorial said that had the reading portion of the Stanford Achievement Test been used as this year's criterion for promotion, 33 percent of D.C.'s third-graders and 29 percent of its eighth-graders would not have advanced. Test results in math were just as dismal: Three out of four eighth-graders and one in three third-graders scored below the norm.

At the other end of the education continuum, the President and civil rights activists are wringing their hands about the effects of California's Proposition 209 and the *University of Texas vs. Hopwood* decision outlawing racial preferences in university admission.

Noting that black admissions this year have fallen precipitously at professional schools in California and Texas, in answering a question posed by a member of the National Association of Black Journalists, Clinton said, "I don't know why the people who promoted this in California think it's a good thing to have a segregated set of professional schools."

The President's use of the word "segregation" is incredibly stupid. It makes just as much sense to call the University of California at Berkeley's Law School segregated as it is to call the NBA segregated. If whites could do 360 slam dunks in your face as well as blacks, their numbers in the NBA would be greater. By the same token, if blacks could get the same scores as whites, on the law school (LSAT) or medical school (MCAT) admissions tests, their numbers in professional schools would be greater.

The interests of most blacks are not served well by Clinton, other politicians, and civil rights activists. The fraudulent education received by blacks in D.C., and most other cities, is devastating. Blacks are not a superrace of people whose children can graduate from high school, with what might not be the equivalent of even an eighth-grade education, make up the difference in four years of college, and be admitted to professional schools on academic merit.

But where's the civil rights establishment? The Department of Education's Office of Civil Rights has launched a ludicrous investigation to determine whether refusal by the University of California to have racial preferences itself constitutes unlawful discrimination. Neither politicians, government agencies, nor civil rights organizations show much interest in stopping a callous public education establishment from making black academic excellence all but impossible.

There's no question there are many problems that plague predominantly black schools. Many of them cannot be laid at the feet of public school teachers and administrators. However, teachers and administrators are totally responsible for promoting kids who haven't mastered grade material and granting diplomas that attest that a kid has achieved a twelfth-grade level of education when in fact he may not have achieved even an eighth-grade level of education. That is no less than open, pernicious fraud.

But getting back to the decline in black enrollment at prestigious California universities, I'm not wringing my hands. More than 60 percent of blacks admitted, for example, to the University of California at Berkeley do not graduate. But there are three thousand less-prestigious colleges that blacks can attend with more compatible student bodies in terms of academic achievement, perhaps more individualized attention, and thus a greater chance for catching up.

Not getting into Berkeley is not the same as not getting into college. "But, Williams," you say, "without racial preferences there'd be far fewer blacks attending our prestigious universities." I say, graduating from a less prestigious university is better than flunking out of a prestigious one. It's better for both the student and blacks as a group.

Environment
and Health

Supreme Court Justice Louis Brandeis warned, "Experience should teach us to be most on our guard to protect liberty when the government's purposes are beneficent." Congress has taken upon itself the beneficent purpose of protecting us from the health hazards of tobacco. During the 1960s, their method was to require manufacturers to label their product with health warnings. During the next three decades, they restricted cigarette consumption in public and private places such as airports, airlines, restaurants, office buildings. None of this was completely satisfactory to what I call lifestyle Nazis. In 1998, with the help of state officials they attempted to legislate confiscatory taxes on tobacco consumption.

What has happened with tobacco regulation ought to set off panic buttons for all Americans, even among those who support what Congress is doing to cigarette smokers and the tobacco industry. The warning is that if we allow Congress to control products in the name of public health, lowering the cost of health care and protecting the nation's children, what activity can possibly escape future control? Salt consumption threatens health. So does caffeine, fatty foods, overeating, and overdrinking, not to mention a host of safety risks such as swimming, biking, skiing, and football.

There is absolutely no moral argument or constitutional authority for Congress's and state governments' war against tobacco consumption. Many might consider cigarette smoking a vice that ought to be eliminated; however, vices are not crimes. A smoker does not violate the property rights of others such as in the case of theft, rape, and murder. Vices might not be in the best interests of a person; that's a case for admonishment, cajoling, and criticism and not a case for coercion, fines, or imprisonment.

Some people argue that cigarette smoking annoys others and may even damage their health. That is a problem solved by private property rights. For example, a place of employment is private property. The owner has the right to decide whether smoking is allowed in his workplace or not. He should simply tell prospective employees that he permits (does not permit) smoking on the job. A prospective employee, so informed, has the right to decide whether he wishes to work under those conditions. Another argument is that smoking raises health care costs and some of that cost is borne by taxpayers; therefore, when people are free to smoke they impose costs on others. That is not a problem of liberty; that's a problem of socialism. No moral case can be made for the government forcing one person to pay for the health care needs of another.

There is another lesson from the antismoking campaign from which we all can benefit. Philosopher David Hume said, "It is seldom that liberty of any kind is lost all at once." When people seek to destroy a liberty, the most viable strategy is to do it piecemeal. Had the antismoking people revealed and demanded their full agenda back in the 1950s and 1960s, when they were trying to get nonsmoking sections on airplanes, they would have encountered so much resistance that they might not have gotten any of their demands. They chose the strategy of starting out with small, eminently reasonable demands. Emboldened by a succession of minor successes, they escalated their demands into the unreasonable and oppressive.

Environmentalists employ tactics similar to the antismoking crusade: exaggeration, panic, and fraudulent science. To disagree with the environmentalist agenda is not the same as calling for polluted air and water. We should apply common sense to our efforts to have less polluted air and water because to rid ourselves of any given level of pollution may not be worth what we have to sacrifice. An exaggerated example makes the point. Los Angeles has considerable pollution. If I were elected the city's mayor, and given the power, I could eliminate pollution virtually overnight. I'd simply pass laws banning all motor vehicle operation and all manufacturing activity. There would be no pollution in Los Angeles, but would the gain in cleaner air be worth the cost? Nobody recommends such a proposal, but there are EPA regulations where the costs and benefits are ignored, where the public is given frighteningly false information, and where the regulations are backed up by knowingly fraudulent science.

Health, environmental, and related issues are discussed in this section. Some of the discussion should make us pay more attention to Brandeis's warning about government doing good.

Why Do We Listen to Fools?

February 15, 1995

Jim Peron, of the Free Market Foundation of South Africa, has a book aptly titled *Exploding Population Myths*. It catalogs the lies and distortions used by the environmentalist's movement to frighten us. Fear is their tactic to get us to give them more control in the name of saving us. Let's look at it.

Paul Ehrlich wrote *The Population Bomb*, widely read on college campuses during the late sixties. Ehrlich predicted that there'd be a major food shortage in the U.S. and "in the 1970s . . . hundreds of millions of people are going to starve to death." He forecast that 65 million Americans would die of starvation between 1980 and 1989 and that by 1999 the U.S. population would have declined to 22.6 million. Ehrlich's predictions about England were worse: "If I were a gambler, I would take even money that England will not exist in the year 2000."

In 1972, a report was written for the Club of Rome warning the world would run out of gold by 1981, mercury and silver by 1985, tin by 1987, and petroleum, copper, lead, and natural gas by 1992. Gordon Taylor, in his 1970 work titled *The Doomsday Book*, said Americans were using 50 percent of the world's resources and "by 2000 they [Americans] will, if permitted, be using all of them."

It's not just these recent doomsayers who have been wrong—doomsayers have always been. In 1885, the U.S. Geological Survey announced there was "little or no chance" of oil being discovered in California and a few years later it said the same about Kansas and Texas. In 1939, the U.S. Department of the Interior said American oil supplies would last only another thirteen years. By 1949, the Secretary of the Interior said the end of U.S. oil supplies was in sight. Having learned nothing from its earlier stupid claims, in 1974 the U.S. Geological Survey advised us that the U.S. had only a ten-year supply of natural gas. The fact of the matter, according to the American Gas Association, is that there's a 1,000- to 2,500-year supply.

Idiot outfits, such as Planned Parenthood and the State Department's Agency for International Development, peddle these doomsday ideas to the world's poverty-stricken people—as they sought to do at last year's Cairo summit on population control. They say poor countries would develop if only they'd deal with their "overpopulation" problems. Nonsense! There is absolutely no relationship between high population density and poverty.

Zaire, with a population density of thirty-nine people per square mile, has to be just about the world's poorest country. Hong Kong has a population density of 247,501 people per square mile—over 6,000 times more crowded than Zaire. Yet Hong Kong's per capita income is $8,260 while Zaire's is less than $200. People are valuable. The earth is loaded with room and resources to support an even greater population. Even if the earth's entire population moved to the United States, it would make our population density 1,531 people per square mile. That's a lower density than what now exists in New York City (11,480), Los Angeles (9,126) and Houston (7,512).

What are called overpopulation problems result from socialistic government practices that reduce the capacity of people to educate, clothe, house, and feed themselves. Poor countries are rife with farm controls, export and import restrictions, restrictive licensing, price controls, and gross human-rights violations that encourage their most productive people to emigrate. The true antipoverty lesson for poor countries is the most promising route out of poverty to greater wealth is personal liberty.

America's Cigarette Tyrants

March 1, 1995

Cigarette smoke is a nuisance to some people, and there are alleged health effects from "secondhand" smoke. None of this is relevant to today's smoking regulations. It's a matter of respect for liberty and private property rights. Let's look at it.

The most rabid antismoker probably wouldn't demand laws outlawing cigarette smoking within one's own home or car. He might buy the argument that since homes and cars are private property, a person has a right to decide how they'll be used. But that points up a logical inconsistency of cigarette prohibitionists who allege a concern for health. Cigarette smoke in a house produces secondhand smoke just as it does in an office, mall, or airplane. House guests and family members of smokers breathe secondhand smoke. Therefore, if the health of others is the concern of antismokers, they ought to demand laws banning smoking even in private homes.

You say, "Williams, that's unnecessary. If I don't like being in the presence of secondhand smoke I don't have to visit your house!" You're right, but the cigarette tyrants better not make the same response. If they do, the logic of their health argument begins to crack or their totalitarian agenda to outlaw tobacco altogether is exposed.

Like a home, restaurants and airplanes are also private property. The owner has the right, at least in a free society, to decide whether smoking is allowed. He's only obliged to inform customers. Therefore, we might require him to post a sign outside his establishment saying Smoking Not Allowed or Smoking Allowed. Then people can decide whether to enter on those terms.

You say, "Williams, I'm a nonsmoker. If there weren't laws against smoking, I'd have no choice." Nonsense! There are roughly 40 million smokers, leaving well over 200 million American non-smokers. I hope you're not going to tell me that businesses have no interest in producing a satisfactory arrangement for those 200 million people. Northwest Airlines, for example, banned smoking on their flights before it was the law. Some other airlines might have followed suit.

Business executives are cowards in many respects. That's why airline executives yielded to the smoking ban on domestic flights. They would have fought had Congress extended the ban to international flights. But they should have known that cigarette prohibitionists wouldn't be satisfied. Recently, eight of the world's largest airlines joined together seeking immunity from antitrust laws in order to form a collusive arrangement to ban smoking on international flights. On January 24, 1995, Department of Transportation secretary Federico Pena granted them immunity.

Here's the story. Airline executives fear the power of the anti-smoking lobby but they also fear losing smoking customers to their competition if they individually banned smoking on their own airline. That's why they seek the collusive arrangement. But there can't be a "gentleman's agreement" to ban smoking on international flights because gentleman's agreements have a short life. They'll seek government regulations to make sure all airlines comply.

Liberty-minded people ought to find all of this not only offensive but another step toward serfdom. Many Americans think it's good to restrict smoking and applaud the intimidation tactics by the antismoking lobby. We should remember that it was decent, well-meaning Germans who help create an all-powerful government to do good things but didn't figure they were building the Trojan Horse for Adolf Hitler. Similarly, Americans are making it easy for a future tyrant.

Organs for Sale

June 12, 1995

Last week, baseball Hall of Famer Mickey Mantle, waiting just one day, moving ahead of others on the waiting list, received a liver transplant. As a result ethical hand-wringing began as to whether celebrity status played a role and whether he really deserved a liver after destroying his own through alcohol abuse. Should these be issues? Since organs are scarce, not all who want one can be served. But is there a better way of deciding who gets them? Or shall we leave the decision up to the arbitrary capriciousness of the medical profession? I say no! How about deciding the same way we decide who gets what house, car, food, or clothing—the market. The ought to be a market for buying and selling organs. Let's look at it.

Let's answer the basic question: To whom do my liver and kidneys belong? If they're mine, I have the right to sell or bequeath them to my heirs as part of my estate. That being settled, let's look at the benefits of an organ market.

When one's loved one is in the last throes of life, many of us reject requests for an organ donation out of an emotional desire not to see our loved one "cannibalized." There would be a lot of reconsideration if we knew there was $100,000 or more for some of his parts. That's the first benefit of an organ market—an increased supply of organs.

Another benefit can be appreciated if we ask questions about the optimal way to die. In financial matters, it's with a zero bank balance. But people usually die with larger balances. The reason is easy; they can bequeath it to heirs. The same principle applies to organs. The optimal way to die is go out in a big bang with all organs at failure. After all if you can't bequeath your organs, it doesn't make any more sense putting perfectly functioning organs in the ground than it makes to leave a fortune. Therefore, organs could become part of one's estate, and there'd be greater incentive to take better care of them during one's life.

"Okay, Williams," you say, "so far so good, but with a market only rich people would get organs." That makes as much sense as saying with the market only rich people will get cars, houses, and food, which we all know is nonsense. I'd much rather compete with the likes of Mickey Mantle or former Pennsylvania governor Bob Casey, who got a heart and a lung after waiting just one day, in the market than through favoritism and the medical profession's who-needs-it-the-most method.

Nonrich people have money-raising alternatives like mortgaging a home; family members and friends could do the same if necessary. They might purchase lower-quality, lower-price organs, those with fewer years of service. Plus, there would still be the option of charitable donations. These and other options available through a market exceed those available now. If a doctor says you're 230th on the waiting list, the only option you have is hope.

The medical profession wouldn't take kindly to the idea of organ markets; they'd lose their godlike power to control to say who lives and who dies. Then there are people who think selling body parts is evil. To them I say: Don't sell yours, but mine is mine so don't interfere. By the way, the most reliable test of whether a person owns something or not is whether he can sell it. If I don't own my organs, please tell me who does.

Is It Permissible?

December 27, 1995

There's widespread both medical and popular agreement that a healthy daily diet consists of fruits, vegetables, complex carbohydrates, varied proteins, six to eight glasses of water, calcium and little or no table salt. This diet, coupled with six to eight hours of daily sleep, in addition to a regimen of aerobic and resistance exercise, no smoking, and only moderate alcohol consumption, would greatly improve American health and fitness.

The problem is that not all Americans have habits and tendencies that comport themselves with such a healthy lifestyle. Thus, the question becomes, What can we do to promote the welfare of Americans and hence our nation? The answer's easy. Congress should enact a law mandating healthy diets and exercise along with the necessary and proper implementing legislation. Any congressman in opposition to this legislation could be brought into line simply by the media portraying of him as having a callous disregard for American health and fitness.

Obviously, good health and fitness are a good idea. The question is whether good ideas alone form the basis for congressional enactment of laws. The answer would be difficult if we didn't have a document laying out the rules of the game, namely, the U.S. Constitution. Since we have a constitution, the answer is easy. We see whether the constitution grants Congress the authority to mandate healthy lifestyles. According to my reading, it doesn't.

Therein lies what should be the heart of debate of congressmen who want to cut Washington down to size: What Congressional acts are impermissible under the Constitution?

The answer begins with Article I, Section 1, that says, "All legislative Powers herein granted shall be vested in a Congress of United States." The operative word is "herein." Later, in Section 8, there's specific enumeration of those powers. As it turns out, the Constitution grants no authority for at least two-thirds of congressional spending and virtually all the legislation enacted in a given year. Unfortunately, we have a kangaroo Supreme Court that sanctions the acts of a rogue Congress.

You ask, "Williams, how can Congress and the Court get away with trashing the Constitution?" Mostly, it's a result of public constitutional ignorance and contempt, but crafty congressional deception is part of the answer.

A Harvard lawyer, familiar with legalese mumble-jumble, could easily establish the constitutionality of health-and-fitness laws through the "commerce clause" that gives congress authority "to regulate commerce with foreign nations, and among the several states, and with Indian tribes." He'd simply argue that poor health and fitness has an adverse effect on individual productivity and that that, in turn, adversely impacts interstate and foreign commerce.

You say, "Williams, that argument is the height of asininity!" You're right and such asininity is the trademark of congress and the courts. For example, in 1994 Congress passed the Gun-Free School Zones Act and justified it by saying, "The occurrence of violent crimes in school zones . . . has an adverse impact on interstate commerce and foreign commerce of United States." In a narrow decision, the Supreme Court found the Act unconstitutional. Justice Souter dissented, therefore agreeing with Congress, by saying, "The only question is whether the legislative judgment is within the realm of reason."

We have an illegitimate Congress and Supreme Court. Both have massive government might to impose their will, but they have little or no moral authority. If people sworn to uphold the Constitution don't obey it, why should we the people obey their edicts? The only answers I find are ignorance and/or the fear of death.

Duped Americans

January 17, 1996

In 1993, and to the glee of tobacco prohibitionists, the Environmental Protection Agency (EPA) issued a report concluding that environmental tobacco smoke (ETS) was a Group A human carcinogen taking the lives of three thousand nonsmokers each year. These findings fueled numerous federal, state, and local regulations banning tobacco smoking in public and private places.

Last November, the Congressional Research Service (CRS), a nonpartisan, independent research arm of Congress, released its findings in a report "Environmental Tobacco Smoke and Lung Cancer Risk." Evaluating the EPA study the CRS concluded that "the results are not definitive" and that "even at the greatest [exposure] level [this is the case of a nonsmoking wife married to a smoker], the measured risks are still subject to uncertainty."

Contradicting EPA's statement of three thousand annual cancer deaths, the Congressional Research Service said that "it is possible that very few or even no deaths can be attributed to environmental tobacco smoke." In reference to EPA's manipulated statistical analysis, which would bring charges of academic dishonesty, earning dismissal, for any college student employing similar tactics, the Congressional Research Service said, "It is clear that misclassification and recall bias plague environmental tobacco smoke epidemiology studies." The Congressional Research Service concludes, "The statistical evidence does not appear to support a conclusion that there are substantial health effects of passive smoking."

While the news media devoted hours of airtime to the fraudulent EPA study, it has been completely silent about the Congressional Research Service report about the study. Tobacco prohibitionists, their allies in Congress, and "useful idiots" among the public, as well as the news media, applaud the deceitful, dishonest use of science to achieve their objectives whether it's Alar, global warming, or the number of homeless people. However, as abundant evidence makes clear, tyrants never tire of tyrannizing.

Now comes the Human Ecology Action League. They are concerned about multiple chemical sensitivity. Its spokesman said, "Perfume is going to be the tobacco smoke of tomorrow." According to a December 27, 1995, *Wall Street Journal* story by James Bovard, an adjunct scholar at the Cato Institute, Chemical Injury Litigation Project coordinator Julia Kendall said, "No one should be wearing perfume to the theater. Why should we have brain damage because people are wearing toxic chemicals?" She gave her agenda, "Basically, we want to destroy the fragrance industry." Among the targeted products of the multiple chemical sensitivity movement: scented deodorants, aftershaves, clothing softeners like Bounce, and hair sprays. If you think no one's listening to these crazies, think again. A California court recently awarded $70,000 to a woman after a coworker refused to stop wearing perfume.

Phillip Wiersch, an environmental toxicologist at George Washington University, has called multiple chemical sensitivities "a name in search of a disease." However, it will be a disease, and regulations will follow, if multiple chemical sensitivity wackos can convince the EPA, Occupational Safety and Health Administration, or agencies charged with enforcing the Americans with Disabilities Act to manufacture a fraudulent study. With such a study in hand, like the tobacco prohibitionists, they'll enlist tyrants with guns like the Food and Drug Administration's Dr. David Kessler and Representative Henry Waxman.

While it may seem far-fetched now, if the multiple chemical sensitivity people get their way we're going to have regulations banning any unnatural scent. If you think I'm an alarmist, think back to the early 60s when the tobacco prohibitionists only wanted separate airplane sections. Would anybody have believed back then we'd have today's smoking regulations?

I'm wondering how long civility can survive. I know what I'd do to one of these multiple chemical sensitivity wackos attempting to make me wash off my aftershave.

Death by Government

May 15, 1996

Development of the coronary stent, a wire-mesh tube placed in an artery to increase heart-muscle blood flow, has revolutionized treatment of certain heart conditions. The Gianturo-Roubin coronary stent reduces the need for coronary-bypass surgery and is especially valuable during angioplasty when a coronary artery collapses and prevents blood flow to the heart. According to a report, "The Human Cost of Regulation," by David C. Murray, a scholar at the Indianapolis-based Hudson Institute, the Gianturo-Roubin coronary stent was developed in 1986 but the Food and Drug Administration didn't approve its use until May 28, 1993.

We want medical device manufacturers to demonstrate safety and effectiveness. We don't want FDA arrogance, delays, and bureaucratic bungling that's responsible for the United States' lagging eleven months or more behind Europe's device-approval rate. FDA ineptitude doesn't simply impose time-wasting, costly procedures on device manufacturers; each year it kills thousands of Americans.

Approximately 15 percent of patients die undergoing emergency bypass surgery made necessary due to coronary-artery collapse during angioplasty. During clinical trials of the Gianturo-Roubin stent, far fewer patients needed bypass surgery after a collapsed coronary artery, and of those who did, only 5 percent died. Murray says roughly 1,230 American lives a year were lost in angioplasty procedures because of FDA-delayed approval of the Gianturo-Roubin stent.

If your loved one died during the early 90s during an angioplasty procedure, Dr. David Kessler, the head of the FDA, is in part responsible. The tragedy is you and your loved one are part of the many invisible victims of FDA policy. Here's the modus operandi. If FDA officials mistakenly approve a device that has unanticipated harmful effects, their necks are on the chopping block because the victims are highly visible. Career-minded FDA officials don't like that kind of exposure. They prefer the hidden mistake, erring on the side of overcaution by needlessly delaying approval. When FDA officials err on the side of overcaution, their victims are invisible. After all, you didn't know there was a device available that could have saved a loved one's life, as would have been the case had the angioplasty procedure occurred in Belgium or some other European country.

FDA delays in approval of the Omnicarbon heart valve contributed to the suffering or death of as many as eight thousand of the sixteen thousand Americans who experience either a thromboembolic event or bleeding complication with their artificial heart valves each year. Again, these people are the invisible victims of Dr. Kessler's FDA.

There are many medical devices, or improvements to existing medical devices, introduced each year and needlessly held up because of FDA self-serving Byzantine procedures. The medical profession shares some of the blame. Doctors are at least partially aware of the introduction of new tools in their profession. I think they have an ethical duty to inform patients about life-saving and suffering-sparing devices and useful drugs being needlessly held up by the FDA.

The problem is not resources. In 1988, the FDA's budget was $482 million and it was staffed by 6,869 people. That year, they approved forty-six applications for premarket approval of medical devices. By 1994, with a budget of $877 million and a staff of 8,539, they managed to approve only twenty-six applications for premarket approval of medical devices. The FDA is long overdue for overhauling. In the process, Congress should allow for private medical-device certification. After all, Underwriter's Laboratory does an excellent job assuring electrical-device safety.

Antitobacco Zealots

April 10, 1996

Tobacco executives have been accused of lying to Congress about their knowledge of tobacco's addictive nature. Scientists have been analyzing the addictive qualities of nicotine since the late 1800s. Hundreds of those medical studies have shown nicotine to be addictive. For a congressman to ask a tobacco company executive whether nicotine is addictive is just as intelligent as that congressman asking an astrophysicist whether the earth revolves around the sun. Tobacco executives fear liability suits and, therefore, deny addiction. By the way, what's so bad about lying to Congress when a list of their lies could fill volumes?

Nicotine is not cancer causing and, all by itself, poses no greater harm than caffeine, which is also an addictive substance. The health risk is associated with those 2,999 other by-products of tobacco smoke. And this is where a very important book, *For Smokers Only*, comes in.

The book was written by Dr. Brad Rodu, Professor and Chairman of Oral Pathology at the School of Dentistry at the University of Alabama in Birmingham. He has published forty articles in peer-reviewed professional journals; he has absolutely no connection with the tobacco industry; he counsels against underage tobacco use and encourages people not to begin any form of tobacco consumption. However, he urges those who smoke and have difficulty quitting to switch to smokeless tobacco and has conducted a number of studies showing the benefits of switching. Let's look at it.

If the 46 million American smokers switched to smokeless tobacco, tobacco-related deaths would plunge from 419,000 annually to 6,000 or fewer. Smoking-related heart and lung disease would disappear and so would any of the alleged effects of secondhand smoke. Oral cancer is the only significant risk of smokeless tobacco. But if every cigarette smoker switched to smokeless tobacco, there would be 50 percent fewer cases of oral cancer than there are today caused by cigarette smoking.

The smokeless tobacco Dr. Rodu has carefully researched comes in the form of a tiny tea bag that the user places inconspicuously between his gum and cheek and is manufactured under several brands. There is no spitting associated with its use. Nicotine is readily absorbed through the mucous membranes that line the cheek. The user gets his "hits" continuously with little of the adverse health effects of lighting up a cigarette.

Now you might ask: what has been Dr. Rodu's reward for showing how there could be a 98 percent reduction in tobacco-related deaths? In a word, it's persecution by the antitobacco zealots. The National Cancer Institutes attacked Dr. Rodu, not citing any errors in the study but simply for having conducted it. They conducted an investigation of him that was ultimately dropped. The American Dental Association attempted but failed to have the American Academy of Oral Pathologists, of which he is a member, condemn and censure him for doing the study.

America's tobacco prohibitionists are engaged in a systematic war of official lies to dupe us into accepting more government control over our lives. Part of these official lies can be seen by simply picking up a can of smokeless tobacco and reading its label: "Warning: This product is not a safe alternative to cigarettes." The fact of business is that smokeless tobacco is infinitely safer than cigarettes and, by the way, if we ever find a perfectly safe alternative to anything, it will be a first in the history of mankind.

Another Government-Sponsored Lie

June 5, 1996

Last November, the Congressional Research Service, a nonpartisan, independent research arm of Congress, released its findings in a report on "Environmental Tobacco Smoke and Lung Cancer Risk." In evaluating the Environmental Protection Agency's claim that environmental tobacco smoke was a class-A carcinogen, causing three thousand deaths per year, the Congressional Research Service concluded, "It is possible that very few or even no deaths can be attributed to environmental tobacco smoke. . . . The statistical evidence does not appear to support a conclusion that there are substantial health effects of passive smoking."

Now comes the revelation of more government deceit and manipulation of the American people by way of the Centers for Disease Control. In a story titled "AIDS Fight Is Skewed by Federal Campaign Exaggerating Risks" in the *Wall Street Journal* (May 1, 1996), Amanda Bennett and Anita Sharpe report a woeful tale of government deceit.

The CDC's propaganda message is that anyone could get AIDS! The fact of business is that for most heterosexuals, the risk of getting AIDS from a single act of sex is smaller than the risk of being struck by lightning. A recent major study concludes that the average risk from a onetime heterosexual encounter, with someone not in a high-risk group, is one in five million without a condom and one in 50 million for condom users. However, a single act of anal sex with an infected partner or a single injection with an AIDS-tainted needle carried a 1-in-50 chance of infection. Indeed, of all reported AIDS cases, 83 percent are homosexuals and intravenous drug users.

Why the lie? Here's what Dr. Walter Dowdle, a virologist who helped create the CDC's anti-AIDS office in the early 1980s, said: "As long as this was seen as a gay disease or, even worse, a disease of drug abusers, that pushed the disease way down the ladder (of people's priorities)." Dr. Dowdle and others thought there wouldn't be political support for AIDS prevention and research if the majority of heterosexuals believed they and their families were only minimally at risk. Thus, the CDC's public relations ploy was to deliberately create ads where the subjects wouldn't be identified as homosexual or intravenous drug users. CDC official John Ward said, "I don't see much downside in slightly exaggerating [AIDS risk]."

The CDC strategy paid off. Taxpayer funding for CDC's AIDS-related medical research soared from $341 million in 1987 to $1.65 billion today. CDC's AIDS-prevention dollars went from $136 million in 1987 to $584 million this year.

With all the lying about AIDS, we might ask questions about how the CDC is spending our money. CDC's largest prevention program is AIDS testing. In 1994, they gave 2.4 million costly AIDS tests. Only 13 percent of those tests were given to the high-risk population: homosexual or bisexual men and intravenous drug users. But Washington doesn't have a monopoly of doing things ass-backwards. A California study found that 85 percent of AIDS cases were among men who had sex with men, but that prevention programs targeting this group received only 9 percent of state AIDS prevention dollars.

There are those in the medical profession who've tried to be honest. In the 1980s, Stephen C. Joseph, former New York City commissioner of public health, blasted the notion that AIDS was making inroads into the general population. Today, Dr. Joseph, assistant secretary of defense for health affairs at the Pentagon, says, "Political correctness has prevented us from looking at the issue [AIDS] squarely in the eye and dealing with it. It is the responsibility of the public-health department to tell the truth."

Excuse Factory

August 6, 1997

I just read *Excuse Factory*, written by Walter K. Olsen, a senior fellow at the New York City–based Manhattan Institute. The book details hundreds of cases of near madness created by the Americans with Disabilities Act (ADA) and sex-harassment and labor laws. In our "enlightened" age, I could be out of touch with modernity, so let me run a few of the cases by you.

When Martin K. joined the Boston police force, he swore that he had never been admitted to a hospital. When it was discovered he'd been admitted five times for psychiatric treatment, he was fired. The Massachusetts State Court found that the city had no business taking past hospitalization into account; therefore the applicant needn't answer the question truthfully. He had a "right" to lie.

Norman Prouse, a pilot for Northwest Airlines, flew a Boeing 727 from Fargo, North Dakota, to Minneapolis with a blood alcohol level of .13 (that's about eight drinks). The two other cockpit members had alcohol levels of .06 and .08. Minnesota law defines drunk driving at .10. After spending a year in prison, Prouse's lawyer felt it would be good therapy if his client flew passengers again. In 1995, Northwest returned him to passenger service. The ADA gives alcoholism legal protection nowadays.

In 1994, near Raleigh, North Carolina, an American Eagle flight crashed, killing 13 people, due to pilot error. The National Transportation Safety Board discovered that the pilot had been dismissed from his previous job because of poor performance. American Eagle didn't know this because it didn't ask. Few airlines provide information about a former employee's performance for fear of being sued if the employee doesn't get the job.

A University of California at Los Angeles heart surgeon infected 18 patients with hepatitis B through microscopic holes in his gloves. Hospital officials knew about his condition. They explained that they kept him on the job because it was "in compliance with federal regulations." Patient interests would have made the hospital liable for charges of discrimination against people with disabilities.

The Seventh Circuit Court ordered the Environmental Protection Agency to accommodate a worker with numerous psychiatric disorders, including narcolepsy—the tendency to fall asleep at inappropriate times. The court told the EPA to tolerate an "occasional nap." That decision may have started a trend. A Michigan court found that a Detroit hospital discriminated against a surgeon with narcolepsy and awarded him $610,000 in damages.

The law recognizes other "disabilities" like "compulsive gambling." Placing of obscene phone calls is "uncontrollable impulse disorder." Failing to file income taxes is "failure-to-file syndrome"; try that next April.

Refusing to hire people with criminal backgrounds can get employers in trouble. As a result, several years ago, 10 percent of Miami's police force stood accused of major felonies. In 1993, a hundred of Washington, D.C., police officers faced charges ranging from kidnap to murder. The FBI set up a task force to watch the cops in the nation's capital.

Then there's sex harassment. According to the General Accounting Office, most sex harassment charges at military academies are filed against cadets who simply express the opinion that standards have been lowered for women's benefit. You'd expect that. In 1990, an official Committee on Women's Issues issued an edict calling for the "immediate dismissal of senior officers who question the role of women in the military."

I see no evidence of a return to sanity. But what the heck? One of the benefits of being sixty-one means that I'll be watching from above when lawyer-manufactured lunacy has taken over the country.

Environmentalists' Agenda

November 12, 1997

In December, President Clinton goes to Kyoto, Japan, to talk about warding off a predicted calamity of global warming. He's going to return and tell us that high energy taxes are necessary to reduce coal, oil, and natural gas consumption. There's no dispute that energy taxes will hurt our economy and standard of living.

Before we accept environmentalists' claims that the sky is falling, let's survey some of their past predictions. At the first Earth Day celebration, environmentalist Nigel Calder warned, "The threat of a new ice age must now stand alongside nuclear war as a likely source of wholesale death and misery for mankind." C. C. Wallen of the World Meteorological Organization said, "The cooling since 1940 has been large enough and consistent enough that it will not soon be reversed." In 1968, Paul Ehrlich, Vice President Gore's hero and mentor, predicted world famine by 1977 and the earth's 5 billion population starving back to 2 billion people by 2025. In 1975, the Environmental Fund took out full-page ads warning, "The World as we know it will likely be ruined by the year 2000. World food production cannot keep pace with the galloping population."

Environmentalists switched their prediction; now it's global warming. But is there warming? The facts are that, since 1870, the earth's temperature has risen one-half of one degree Celsius; most of this nearly imperceptible warming occurred before World War II. Study results of satellites and high-altitude balloons show that, if anything, there's slight cooling. But, if there was global warming, it might be a godsend since the average interval between ice ages is ten thousand years; we're already eleven thousand years into a warm period.

But what about man and carbon dioxide emissions? Margaret Maxey, geophysicist at Texas Tech, estimates that just three volcanic eruptions—Indonesia (1883), Alaska (1912), and Iceland (1947)—spewed more carbon dioxide and sulphur dioxides into the atmosphere than all of the activities of industrial man. According to the November 1982 issue of *Science*, termites annually generate more than twice as much carbon dioxide as mankind does burning fossil fuels. One termite species annually emits 600,000 metric tons of formic acid into the atmosphere, an amount equal to the combined contributions of automobiles, refuse combustion, and vegetation. Humans contribute only five percent of atmospheric carbon dioxide; nature does the rest.

Political satirist H. L. Mencken warned, "The whole aim of practical politics is to keep the populace alarmed, and hence clamorous to be led to safety, by menacing it with an endless series of hobgoblins, all of them imaginary." The environmentalist agenda is more sinister. While the Soviet Union has collapsed, communism is not dead. It has been repackaged under a new name: environmentalism. Communism is about extensive government regulation and control by elites and so is environmentalism.

Occasionally, environmentalists spill the beans and reveal their true agenda. Richard Allison, professor of environmental management at the University of Houston, recently said, "There is no other single force that has opened up the private sector to the public more than environmental regulations. There is no such thing as private industry anymore. It's all public."

Barry Commoner said, "Capitalism is the earth's number one enemy." Amherst College professor Leo Marx said, "On ecological grounds, the case for world government is beyond argument." Leftist Murray Bookchin said: "The immediate source of the ecological crisis is capitalism, which is a cancer in the biosphere. I believe the color of radicalism today is not red, but green."

Not all environmentalists share this anti-American, anti-capitalist agenda. They're honest, well-meaning people, but they're also useful idiots for the leftist agenda.

Decent People Helping Tyrants

July 23, 1997

In pursuit of what's deemed as worthy objectives, decent people often pave the way for tyranny.

The process usually begins by the piecemeal destruction of the foundations of liberty: private property, rule of law, voluntary exchange, and limited government. Those basic rights often stand in the way of do-gooders' objectives.

Once those foundations have become seriously eroded, it's an easy matter for egoists and tyrants to take over and produce an agenda quite different from do-gooder intentions.

The most tragic example of this process was Nazi Germany, where the seeds for Hitler's rampage were sown long before he came to power. That process, albeit at the embryonic stages, is developing in America.

What's driving the latest round of political extortion of the tobacco industry is the fact that cigarette smoking has harmful health
effects. Those health effects impose higher costs on the socialized
components of our health care system—Medicaid. Americans want
to combat those costs by supporting government measures that
trash private property rights, peaceable voluntary exchange, and
limited government in an attempt to alter personal lifestyles.

We are naive—perhaps stupid is a better word—enough to think
that lifestyle tyrants will be finished once they bring the tobacco
industry to its knees. The fact of business is that history records no
instances where a tyrant woke up one morning and said, "I'm tired
of tyrannizing, and I'm going to let people live free."

The *New England Journal of Medicine* reports that one-third of
cancer deaths and more than one-half of cardiovascular deaths
result from excess weight. Each year, over 300,000 deaths are
attributable to overweight, compared to 400,000 deaths attributable to cigarette smoking. Dr. JoAnn E. Mason of Harvard Medical
School says, "It won't be long before obesity surpasses cigarette
smoking as a cause of death in this country."

Since obesity impacts heavily on health care costs, why not do
to the food industry what government's doing to the tobacco industry? Yale University's Professor Kelley D. Brownell, director of
the Center for Eating and Weight Disorders, and others have that
agenda under way by proposing that fatty foods and those with
little nutritional content be taxed.

She suggests that the tax proceeds be used to build bike and
hiking trails. She also says that since the average child sees ten
thousand food commercials each year, 95 percent of them for junk
food and sugared cereals, Congress ought to regulate junk food
commercials. After all, the cigarette tyrants got Joe Camel banned,
why not Rice Krispies?

Dr. Ronald Griffiths at Johns Hopkins University is concerned
about coffee's addictive qualities and says, "If health risks are well-

documented, caffeine could be catapulted in public perception from a pleasant habit to a possibly harmful drug of abuse." That will become justification for FDA regulation of coffee and chocolate caffeine content.

Then there's a new bogus illness named multiple chemical sensitivity. An official in the San Francisco mayor's office predicted, "Ten years from now it will be politically incorrect to wear perfumes in public." Allergy sufferers have gotten the Albuquerque, New Mexico, city council to pass an ordinance banning the growing, selling, importing, or planting of cypress, mulberry, elm, and poplar trees, under penalty of a $500 fine.

That some people are wiser than others is the oldest idea in human history. It also accounts for most of the human misery because elitists believe that they've been ordained to forcibly impose that wisdom on others at any cost. Tragically, most Americans have bought into this vision. Maybe it's too late for a recovery. I hope not.

International

Among the international issues in this section is the ongoing tragedy in Africa. Most Americans were well aware of the injustices
of South Africa's apartheid and white rule that gave South African
blacks little participation in their country's political and economic
arena. Politicians, civil rights organizations, and assorted do-gooders made us aware of it through demonstrations and calls for
economic sanctions, boycotts, and disinvestment in American
companies doing business in South Africa.

What most people don't know, and many who do know attempt
to hide or trivialize, is that the injustices suffered by South African
blacks pale in comparison to those suffered by their fellow countrymen elsewhere on the continent. Those injustices include actual
slavery in countries like the Sudan and Mauritania and slaughter
of millions of poor souls in countries like Uganda, Rwanda, Burundi, Zaire, and Liberia. Sometimes the slaughter included unspeakable atrocities such as dismemberment and boiling in oil.
The West's open criticism of injustices by South African whites
against blacks and the deafening silence in the face of horrible
black injustices against other blacks makes one think that we only
care about black suffering when whites are the perpetrators.

I also discuss international trade issues and how political in-
dulgence of vested interests of certain businesses and labor unions
adversely affect producers and consumers. Talk about protection
is seductive, but government can't produce a special privilege for

one group of people without simultaneously creating a special disadvantage for another group. With trade restrictions, like tariffs and quotas, the disadvantage is borne by consumers of the product being protected. A clear case can be make for our asking, when the government protects one group, what other group deserves to be harmed and why?

Other columns in this section present what I believe to be a powerful argument that personal liberty, limited government, and free markets are highly correlated with growth and prosperity. By contrast, socialism and extensive government control and regulation are not only highly correlated with low growth and prosperity but also with significantly less liberty and human rights protection as well. World evidence proves that beyond a shadow of a doubt.

Visible Beneficiaries versus Invisible Victims

March 6, 1996

International trade has surfaced as an issue because of Pat Buchanan's campaign promise to protect American businesses and workers against "unfair" foreign competition. Trade issues are fertile grounds for demagoguery, so let's look at it.

Regardless of protectionist rhetoric, the bottom-line objective and result of import restrictions is to enable domestic companies to charge higher prices than they could in the presence of open competition with foreign producers. Protected companies earn higher profits. Their workers can demand higher wages and keep their jobs.

Without a doubt there are benefits to import restrictions. During the 1980's, the Reagan Administration caved in to U.S. steel industry pressure to impose import restrictions on "cheap" foreign steel. Professor Arthur T. Denzau, of St. Louis's Washington University, published a report showing that those restrictions saved seventeen thousand jobs in the steel industry. That's a blessed congressional miracle. Before you rush to endorse Pat Buchanan's ideas, you may want to check out the victim side of the equation.

Many American companies use steel. Reagan's import restrictions led to higher steel prices that raised their production costs. A minor concrete example of this is the Davis Walker Corporation of Los Angeles—once one of the largest U.S. independent steel-wire producers. After Reagan's trade restrictions, Davis Walker was forced to buy 60 percent of its steel from domestic producers at higher prices. Its foreign competitors, able to buy cheaper steel, were able to underprice Davis Walker on world markets. The company was forced to close plants in Houston, Dallas, New Orleans, Colorado, and Mississippi and eventually went bankrupt.

Companies such as Caterpillar saw their competitive position weakened by having to pay higher steel prices. That's one of the reasons we see so much foreign-produced heavy construction equipment.

Denzau says the import restrictions on steel led to a loss of 52,400 jobs in American steel-using industries. How's that for brains: for every job "saved," three were lost?

Pat Buchanan's economic advisor might say, "Williams, the problem was Reagan didn't go far enough. Pat's not going to have such half-measures!" He'd be right. Davis Walker might have survived if import restrictions had been imposed on steel-wire products entering the United States. Caterpillar wouldn't have suffered losses and layoffs if import restrictions had been imposed on foreign heavy construction equipment. But restrictions on those goods would have driven up their prices, requiring another miracle.

Steel wire and heavy construction equipment is used by American companies to produce other products. Higher prices resulting from trade restrictions will put these companies at a competitive disadvantage. Then a Buchanan administration would have to create a miracle for them. The problem facing Pat was insightfully described in Marcus Cook Connelly's play *Green Pastures*, where a frustrated God said to the Angel Gabriel, "Every time I passes a miracle, I have to pass four or five more to catch up with it."

Buchanan's right about Japan's oppressive trade restrictions. As a result, in 1993 Japanese paid $7.60 for a spark plug that Americans got for $1.69. Japanese pay four times the world price for rice and over $2,000 for a laser printer that we get for less than a $1,000.

The question for brother Pat is, How smart is it for us to get even with Japan by enacting protectionist policies that make Americans pay high prices too? Or put another way: Suppose you and I were in a row boat. If I shot a hole in my end of the boat, would you retaliate by shooting a hole in your end of the boat?

Land for Promises of Peace

October 9, 1996

Recent violence between armed Palestinian police and Israeli soldiers in Rammallah points up serious questions about the Oslo Accords, the so-called peace process between Israel and the Palestinian Liberation Organization.

This time, the violence was precipitated by Prime Minister Benjamin Netanyahu's decision to open a tunnel near holy places of both Jews and Muslims. The actual agreement to open the tunnel was reached earlier this year between Arafat and then Prime Minister Shimon Peres and Israel's Labor Party. Since Netanyahu and the Likud Party came to power, Arafat has been losing face with his followers. To bolster his tough-guy image, he has to now protest the tunnel's opening.

World leaders criticized Israel for provoking the crisis. French president Jacques Chirac counseled Israel to avoid provocations and telephoned Arafat to express his "solidarity and support" with the Palestinians. This response demonstrates western double standards. During the 1987 to 1993 Palestinian uprisings (intifada), Israel came under Western criticism for its harsh response to stone-throwing and fire-setting Palestinians. When Israel responds in kind to Arab terrorism, it also encounters criticism. But the West is relatively silent in its criticisms of the Palestinians who started the recent violence.

I am not an expert in Middle East affairs. But the way I see it is the only way there can be peace, using Arafat's 1980 words, "Peace for us means the destruction of Israel."

"Williams," you say, "Arafat has changed; he's repudiated the Palestinian Covenant calling for the destruction of Israel!" Not so. In January, speaking to Arab diplomats in Stockholm's Grand Hotel, Arafat said, "We plan to eliminate Israel and establish a Palestinian state. . . . We will make life unbearable for Jews by psychological warfare and population explosion." Arafat wants to work on "splitting Israel psychologically into two camps." A few months ago, Marwan Barguti, a top official in the Palestinian Authority in Gaza, said, "Our forces will fight the Israelis. Orders have already been given. We already have in Gaza 20,000 armed security personnel."

Like Hitler's strategy, the "peace process" is simply part of an overall Palestinian design for the ultimate destruction of Israel. British Prime Minister Neville Chamberlain, just one year before World War II began, spoke of the "desire of the German people for peace," despite evidence to the contrary and Winston Churchill's earlier 1932 warning of the "inexhaustible gullibility" of Western pacifists.

During the late 1920s and early 1930s, Hitler knew outright war was a hopeless cause. France alone could have defeated him mightily. Through talk of peace, he managed to extract concession after concession and rearm. The rest of the story is written with the blood of millions.

Similarly, the Arab states know war with Israel is their worst nightmare. Therefore, they are using the "peace process" to get Israel to give up land for nothing more than promises of peace. Again, they might heed Winston Churchill's warning to his fellow countrymen: "Every concession that has been made was followed immediately by fresh demands."

Should there be a Palestinian state, it would, like any sovereign state, have the right to have a military. Regardless of any written agreement, a Palestinian state would establish a military force that would be used, with assistance from its Arab neighbors, against Israel.

Israelis should recognize a fundamental fact of world history: Peace agreements aren't worth the paper they're written on and one concession leads to demands for another. Considerable evidence demonstrates that what holds adversaries at bay is their knowledge of a completely unacceptable cost should they attack.

Corporate Welfare

January 15, 1997

There are few instances where handouts are more flagrantly immoral than those to corporations. Corporate tax cuts don't qualify as handouts unless you believe that companies' earnings belong to the government and that it's a handout when government allows corporations to keep more of their earnings. Corporate handouts refer to the evil government practice of taking our money and handing it to corporations.

According to *Consumer Research* (November 1996), a publication of the Washington-based Consumer Research Inc., President Clinton convinced the Mexican government not to "dump" low-priced tomatoes in the U.S. market. Clinton doesn't have a monopoly on this practice. Presidents Bush and Reagan and their predecessors committed similar acts of corporate handouts. So let's look at the principle.

The government can give handouts to corporations simply by using the Internal Revenue Service to take our money and have the Commerce Department or Agriculture Department distribute it. The risk of visible handouts is that they can easily invite voter retaliation against politicians. A secretive and underhanded way is market restriction. There's little bottom-line difference between government taking $100 from me to give to XYZ Corporation and government making it possible for XYZ Corporation to charge me $100 in higher prices for what I buy.

Clinton was pressured into restricting Mexican tomato imports because of Florida tomato growers' complaints that the U.S. market has been flooded with $800 million worth of lower-priced tomatoes. One administration official said Mexico agreed to deal because of Clinton's $12.5 billion Mexico bailout. Another Clinton official said, "The math is simple. Florida has twenty-five electoral votes and Mexico doesn't."

During the winter months, Americans consume tomatoes grown mostly in Florida and Mexico. Nine wealthy Florida growers control 70 percent of the Florida market. They complain NAFTA, which lowered tariffs on Mexican tomatoes, threatens to drive them out of business. A more likely explanation for the demand for Mexican tomatoes is their taste and how they are grown. Florida tomatoes are picked green while Mexican tomatoes are vine-ripened.

There's no case for handouts to Florida tomato growers, but suppose I'm wrong. At least the handouts should be visible and require an act of Congress. Florida's congressional delegation should introduce an Aid to Dependent Florida Tomato Growers Bill for whatever millions of dollars necessary to insure the survival of Florida tomato growers. That way handout costs would be visible.

Americans could make a more informed decision about whether we want to make corporate handouts.

We'll never see such a bill and for good reasons. Most Americans would be outraged at the thought of their earnings going to wealthy corporations whining about Mexican competition. The news media would have a heyday and a congressman voting in support of such a bill would be run out of office. It's far more politically practical to give the tomato growers stealth handouts. Who's to know? Americans might grumble and groan about winter tomatoes costing a few pennies more. But it wouldn't make economic sense for consumers to organize and take action against politicians who caused the higher prices. From the growers' point of view, it's a different story. It pays them to spend resources pressuring politicians for handouts; it means millions to them. In fact, to demonstrate how much clout they have, the Clinton campaign reportedly feared Florida growers hitting them with negative ads.

Aside from the issue of evil corporate handouts is the issue of liberty. If I wish to purchase tomatoes from a Mexican producer, on mutually agreeable terms, is there a moral case for a third party preventing me from doing so?

The Road to Wealth

February 5, 1997

Why are we a rich nation? It's tempting to suggest our wealth is a result of bountiful natural resources.

However, if bountiful resources were the source of wealth, South America and Africa would be rich instead of being mired in poverty. Hong Kong, Japan and England, natural resources–poor nations, would be poor instead of rich.

Development experts and foreign aid hustlers would have us believe that past colonialism accounts for Third World poverty. That explanation ignores the fact that the United States, Canada, Australia, New Zealand, and Hong Kong have a colonial history and are rich, while Nepal, Tibet, Liberia, and Ethiopia were never colonies and are among the world's poorest nations.

Mankind's history is mostly one of grinding poverty. Poverty is no mystery. People are poor because they can't produce things highly valued by their fellow man. The real mystery is how did a tiny portion of mankind's population, for only a tiny part of his history, manage to escape poverty. We don't have all the answers but there are some useful clues.

When we see wealthy nations, what else do we see? One tendency is greater personal liberty that includes greater protection and respect for both the person and his property. The people are free to engage in peaceable voluntary exchange to a much greater extent than their poorer counterparts. There is rule of law and government plays a more limited role in the economy. As a result, these tendencies not only make for higher moral standards, they produce an important side benefit—greater wealth.

Pick up Freedom House's or Amnesty International's survey of world human rights protections. Then turn to country rankings of per capita income in the *World Almanac*. Arrange countries according to human rights protections, per capita income, and whether their system tends more towards free markets or extensive government control. A remarkable correlation emerges. Hong Kong, Switzerland, the United States, Canada, and Germany, having greater economic liberty, are at the top. Romania, Somalia, Hungary, Syria, Brazil, Zaire, and many others with highly restricted liberty are at the bottom.

The good news is that, following the collapse of the Soviet empire, many more people have a greater measure of liberty. Nonetheless, at least 25 percent of the human race continues to live under brutal authoritarian regimes and unthinkable poverty. That's the standard human condition. Little is older than the notion that some people know what's best and they've been ordained to forcibly impose that "wisdom" on others. It's a notion accounting for most human misery.

It's a notion in vogue with America's liberal elite. They differ only in degree, but not in kind, from global tyrants who show little reluctance to forcibly impose their will on others.

If you think I'm wrong, consider what would happen to anyone who declared that he is an emancipated adult and fully capable of tending to his own retirement needs. Further, he disavowed any Social Security benefit or any other government handout in his retirement years. Plus, he resolutely refused to make "contributions" into Social Security. Depending on his level of resoluteness, he could suffer fines, property confiscation, imprisonment, or death at the hands of our government.

There's no complete answer to why some nations are rich and others poor. But you can bet the rent money that a large part of the answer has to do with personal liberty and private property rights. Even if liberty and private property rights had nothing to do with wealth accumulation, we want it anyway because it's morally superior to authoritarianism.

Africa's Tragedy

June 18, 1997

In terms of natural resources, Africa is the world's richest continent. It has 50 percent of the world's gold, most of the world's diamonds and chromium, 90 percent of the cobalt, 40 percent of the world's potential hydroelectric power, 65 percent of the manganese, millions of acres of untilled farmland, as well as other natural resources.

Despite its wealth of resources, Africa is home to the world's most impoverished and abused people. Of the forty-one black African nations, only three (Senegal, Botswana, and Mauritius) allow their people the right to vote and choose their own leaders. Only two (Botswana and Senegal) permit freedom of expression and criticism of government policies. In countries like Uganda, Rwanda, Burundi, Mozambique, Sudan, Chad, and others, ethnic genocide has taken the lives of untold millions of innocent civilians. Slavery is still practiced in the Sudan and Mauritania.

African leaders are quick to blame the legacy of colonialism for their troubles. I'll never make an argument for colonialism but the fact of business is that the average African was better off under colonialism he has been under independence.

For example, when Zaire became in independent in 1960, it had 31,000 miles of main roads; today, less than 3,500 remain usable. Before independence, every African country was self-sufficient in food production; today most depend on imports, and others stand at the brink of famine. At the time of independence, the average growth rate among African countries was 3 percent. By 1980, it had fallen to 1 percent, and by 1990, to a negative 2.8 percent.

By contrast, African countries with a greater measure of freedom and stability, Botswana, Mauritius, Cameroon, and Senegal, have growth rates of 8, 4.4, 4.5, and 1 percent, respectively.

People who think more foreign aid is the solution should know that the money either winds up in the hands of the elite and deposited in Swiss bank accounts or is used to pay bribes to keep corrupt governments in power. Some African chiefs of states are among the world's richest men, such as Zaire's deposed Mobutu. If foreign aid doesn't fall into the hands of kleptocrats, it's used in ways that'd make a lunatic blush, such as status symbols, factories, and other projects of little or no use.

The legacy of colonialism, used so often by Africans, is a sham excuse that can't hold water. After all some of the world's richest countries—like the United States, Canada, Australia, New Zealand, and Hong Kong—were colonies. What's true about those ex-colonies that's untrue about Africa? The answer is a no-brainer. There's a greater measure of personal liberty, more secure private property rights, more limited and honest government, and rule of law.

These features are critical ingredients for peace and prosperity in any country but even more so for African countries, some of which have over two hundred antagonistic ethnic groups. Switzerland was a country with a history of bitter ethnic divisions whose citizens now live in peace. That achievement was made possible by developing a system of limited central government authority with most decisions made at more local government units (cantons). Just as important in conflict reduction was the development of respect for private property, rule of law, and stability in its laws.

Oppressive regimes have always exported their most talented and ambitious people to freer and richer countries. Africans who migrate to the United States do well. As an American, I love that but it's especially devastating for Africa.

Economic Freedom and Progress

July 16, 1997

"Economic Freedom of the World: 1997," written by Professors James Gwartney (Florida State University) and Robert Lawson (Capital University), uses seventeen objective factors to derive a summary economic freedom rating, from zero to ten, for 115 countries, the freest being a ten.

As has been the case for the past two decades, Hong Kong is the world's freest economy with a rating of 9.3, a full point higher than Singapore. New Zealand, the United States, and Mauritius, a tiny island nation off the coast of Africa, rounded out the top five. Switzerland, the United Kingdom, Thailand, and Costa Rica occupied spots six through nine. Four countries—Malaysia, Phillippines, Australia, and Panama—were tied for the tenth place.

At the other end of the spectrum, the least-free economies were Algeria, Croatia, Syria, Burundi, Haiti, Iran, Nigeria, Zaire, Ukraine, and Albania.

People mistakenly stress the importance of democracy as key to economic progress. While economic and political freedom are both parts of personal liberty, there are fundamental distinctions. Economic freedom refers to the rights of individuals to engage in exchange activities, decide how they'll earn a living, keep what they earn, decide what goods they will purchase, and protect private property rights. These are the core elements of economic freedom.

Political freedom refers to procedures to elect government officials, decide political issues, and whether the franchise is broadly extended. Civil liberty has to do with rights to assemble, free speech, fair trials, and religious freedom. Recognizing these distinctions, we can see how a country like Singapore can have few political and civil liberties yet have top ranking in economic freedom.

On the other hand, democracies like Israel and India have considerable political freedom and civil liberties but have high levels of government intervention and control that restrict economic freedom.

Gwartney and Lawson break the 115 countries into five groups, according to their economic freedom rating, and then look at per capita GDP and growth in GDP. For the twenty-three most-free countries, average per capita GDP was $14,829. For the next group it was $12,369. For the least-free economies average per capita GDP was $2,541.

It's the same story with growth rates. The freest economies grew at 2.9 percent while most of the countries in the least-free category experienced negative growth rates.

There is no question about a positive correlation between economic freedom and higher standards of living. Low taxes, monetary stability, free markets, and laws that protect private property are far more important ingredients for economic prosperity than a democracy.

Of course, the best of all worlds is a combination of political, civil, and economic liberty. Professors Gwartney and Lawson point out that preliminary evidence suggests that a side benefit from the greater wealth, which stems from economic freedom, is that it strengthens people's demand for political and civil liberty.

If Gwartney and Lawson are right, and all evidence suggests they are, we can easily see why four decades of foreign aid expenditures have produced little success. We can give billions to African countries, Egypt, and Israel but they'll continue to be basket cases or at best wallow in the swamp of economic mediocrity because they have not established the necessary condition for prosperity—

economic freedom. It'd be great if poor countries and our State Department discovered that simple fact.

Blacks in America versus Africa

December 3, 1997

Back in 1972, I interviewed at the University of Massachusetts. Had I known more about the university, I would have never visited in the first place.

At a reception for me, a leftist professor asked me what did I think about capitalism and slavery. I told him that slavery has existed under all systems and that black slavery is by no means unique. In fact, the word *slave* is derived from Slav—the Slavish people.

Then he insisted that I tell him my thoughts about slavery and my ancestors. I told him slavery is a horrible human rights violation; however, I have personally benefited from the horrors suffered by my ancestors.

The reason is simple: Assuming I would have been born anyway, my wealth and liberties, as well as those of my fellow American blacks, are greater as a result of being born in the United States than any country in Africa. In other words, while slavery was a brutal institution, I can be thankful for its results. Needless to say, the professor and his colleagues were horrified by my response.

What Keith B. Richbourg reports in his book, *Out of America: A Black Man Confronts Africa*, provides excellent evidence supporting my position. Richbourg is the Hong Kong bureau chief for the *Washington Post* who spent three years covering Africa. His story should make every black American thankful for being born in the United States.

Richbourg recounts standing on a Tanzanian bridge seeing one or two bodies floating down the river every minute—victims of Rwandan genocide—many dismembered. Cambodia's Khmer Rouge murdered a million in three years; the Hutu accomplished that in a few months.

The July/August 1997 *American Enterprise* adaption of Richbourg's book has a visual example of African brutality—a dismembered head sitting on a table in downtown Monrovia. In Kenya, the Masai loot, murder, and destroy Kikuyu towns. Unimaginable brutality is also the story in Nigeria, Uganda, Mozambique, Chad, Sudan, Ghana, Somalia, Central African Empire, Zaire, and most other black countries.

What have you heard black Americans saying about these gross abuses? I mean those "leaders" who picketed, condemned, and supported sanctions against South Africa for its racist apartheid policy. Richbourg asked Doug Wilder, Virginia's first black post-Reconstruction governor, about human rights violations in black Africa. Wilder replied, "We cannot and should not force them to undergo a metamorphosis in seconds. Our job is not to interfere, and to understand that there is a difference from what they are accustomed to." Can you imagine the condemnation that would have greeted a white politician saying the same thing in 1980 but about South Africa?

Wilder shouldn't be singled out as a villain. By their silence, self-appointed black leaders, civil rights organizations, and the Congressional Black Caucus feel the same way. Their position differs little from one that says blacks brutalizing other blacks is understandable but brutalization by whites is intolerable; whites are held to civilized standards of behavior. That's a position with a domestic counterpart. There's tolerance and excuse-giving for the daily slaughter and mayhem in black communities. Outrage and moral posturing is reserved for when a white cop shoots or mistreats a black.

"Africa is often held up as a black Valhalla. Sorry, but I've been there," says Richbourg. Because a person was born in, or traces ancestry to, a country doesn't mean its practices are beyond condemnation. Instead of condemnation, what we hear are praises and lies about "Mother Africa" from black leaders and Afro-centric demagogues. It's about time we heard some of the truth and Keith B. Richbourg delivers it.

Free Trade versus Fair Trade

January 7, 1998

The defeat of President Clinton's call for "fast-track" authority proves that people love monopolies in what they sell and free markets in what they buy. It means higher prices for what they sell and lower prices for what they buy. Businessmen and union leaders concoct all manner of myth-making to achieve monopoly power and international trade is no exception. Let's examine some of it.

There's the bugaboo about trade deficits, as in complaints that we buy more from Japan or Mexico than they buy from us. That's not only mythology, but it's not true. Let me use domestic trade to make my point. I buy more from my grocer than he buys from me, but is there a "trade deficit?" When I buy $100 worth of groceries, the value of my current account (goods) rises by $100 but the value of my capital account (money) goes down by $100. By the same token, the grocer's current account (goods) goes down by $100 and his capital account (money) rises by $100. There's no trade imbalance whatsoever; I've given him $100 worth of value and he's given me $100 worth of value. Similarly, when a Japanese automaker sells us a $15,000 car, his current account goes down by $15,000, and ours goes up. He might purchase $15,000 worth of AT&T stock instead of buying California oranges. But just as in the grocer example, his capital account rose by $15,000, and ours goes down.

Protectionists (seekers of monopoly) sometimes argue that American workers can't compete with low-wage foreign workers. On its face, this argument is ludicrous. If true, we would export almost nothing; American wages are about the highest in the world, yet we are the world's major exporter. Wages alone explain virtually nothing about trade patterns. It's wages relative to productivity. For example, the fact that a Mexican road construction worker might earn just $3 an hour, while his American counterpart earns $25 an hour, doesn't mean Americans can't compete. The reason is simple. American workers have more capital (modern heavy equipment) working with them, making the output of a day's work much greater.

How about tariffs saving jobs? That's kind of true, but they're saved at the expense of other jobs. Steel-tariff restrictions might save jobs for steelworkers, but they destroy other jobs. Steel tariffs raise steel prices. Thus, steel-using companies—like tractor, refrigerator, and car manufacturers—face higher production costs. Higher costs weaken their ability to compete both domestically and internationally. Politicians love this. Steelworker beneficiaries of tariffs will be eternally grateful and know whom to vote for. The invisible victims in steel-using industries won't know why they are unemployed. Politicians can blame their plight on anything from Reaganomics, the UPS strike, or global warming.

There is no intellectually respectable argument against free trade. The thousands of pages found in GATT and NAFTA are not about free trade, but they are for side deals and giveaways. Thousands of pages are not necessary free trade. At one time there wasn't free trade within our borders; here's what our Founders wrote to promote free trade: "No Tax or Duty shall be laid on Articles exported from any State. No Preference shall be given by any Regulation of Commerce or Revenue to the Ports of one State over those of another; nor shall Vessels bound to, or from, one State, be obliged to enter, clear, or pay Duties in another." That North American Free Trade Agreement is found in Article I, Section 9, of our Constitution. With a word change here and there, it could just as easily serve us internationally.

Law and Society

For the most part, laws that are consistent with personal liberty are those laws that prevent one person, or the state, from encroaching on the rights to life, liberty, and property of another. Most of what constitutes America's legal structure today violates at least the liberty and property of another. Supreme Court Justice William O. Douglas said, "The right to work, I had assumed, was the most precious liberty that a man possesses." That opinion was also held by Justice Joseph P. Bradley, who viewed occupational freedom as an "inalienable right." And Justice Rufus W. Peckman said, "The liberty mentioned in that Amendment [Fourteenth] means . . . [a person has the right] to earn his livelihood by any lawful calling; to pursue any livelihood or avocation." That was the thinking of earlier Supreme Court justices. Looking at today's laws, one would think that the right to work is a privilege conferred by the state to particular individuals. Several columns in this section speak to that point, showing how licensing laws and minimum wage laws have deprived people of their right to work in their chosen field.

Of course, as my grandmother used to say, if you are doing something you are not supposed to be doing, you cannot do what you are supposed to do. Government should not be in the business of parceling out favors and privileges to particular Americans, but it is supposed to protect us from criminals who would murder, rape, and rob us. It is doing a poor job in that area. Twenty thousand Americans are murdered each year; many hundreds of thousands more are raped, robbed, and burglarized. Statistical crime reports give unambiguous evidence on how poor a job government is doing to protect us against societal parasites. However, there is good news: Some crimes are falling. It does not take rocket science to discover why. The nation has been building more prisons; in some states early releases, pardons, and paroles have been restricted. States like California have enacted "three strikes and you're out" legislation calling for mandatory long sentences for repeat offenders. In roughly thirty-seven states, concealed-carry laws permit law-abiding citizens to carry concealed weapons. According to some estimates, millions of crimes have been prevented by armed citizens simply brandishing their weapon to would-be attackers and criminals.

The high rates of crimes are merely symptomatic of widespread moral decadence in our country. Some of the decadence is represented by unprecedented rates of illegitimacy, daytime trash television shows, lack of respect for teachers, and other forms of behavior that would not have been dreamed of fifty years ago. The columns in this section discuss these and other issues.

Thou Shalt Not Covet

June 28, 1995

As a Sunday school kid, I never quite understood the significance of the commandment, "Thou shalt not covet thy neighbor's house, thou shalt not covet thy neighbor's wife, or his manservant, or his maidservant, or his ox, or his ass, or any thing that is thy neighbor's." It was easy to understand why you shouldn't covet your neighbor's wife. After all, that could lead to adultery—but what's wrong about being jealous about your neighbor's other possessions? Liberals have helped me see the light: Jealousy is a precursor to evil. It causes otherwise decent people to fall easy prey to scummy charlatans.

Look at the debate surrounding the Republican-proposed tax cuts. Liberals protest it isn't fair to cut taxes of those earning over $200,000. Liberals make the incredibly thoughtless argument that since the wealthy have benefitted the most from society they also owe the most. Higher taxes are a way to make them "give something back." Liberals' agenda is to make us jealous and make us think that one person has more because another has less so they can succeed in their redistributionist agenda.

But how do people earn money in a free society? Let's take the extreme example of billionaire Bill Gates, founder of Microsoft. There is no evidence that Gates enslaved or robbed anyone. There's a lot of evidence that millions of common people like you and me voluntarily gave him money for software programs that make life easier and more pleasurable, like Windows, DOS, and other products. Gates served us well and he's rich because millions upon millions of independent decision makers agreed that his products were superior to the next-best alternative.

Liberals make the nonsense argument that people like Gates owe society something. If anything society benefited far more from Gates's activities than Gates himself. That's nearly always the case. People who invented products like MRIs, miracle drugs, and laser machines or services like overnight mail, e-mail, and hotels benefited society much more than anything they themselves might have received. Just ask yourself: Who received the greatest benefit from the antibiotic that may have saved your loved one's life—the inventor who got profits from sale of the medicine to you or you and your loved one?

How appropriate is it to hold people who serve us so well up to scorn, abuse, and ridicule? We might also ask, How appropriate is it for us to make social mascots out of society's leeches, vermin, and parasites? How much sense does it make to confiscate the wealth of those who serve us and reward those who seek to live off and prey on others?

Liberals are about control. Jealousy is their powerful instrument for the politics of envy. By getting us to covet that which belongs to our neighbor, we in turn give them the power to confiscate what are perceived as ill-gotten gains of others and pass it around. In the process we all wind up being less free, less prosperous, and less moral and become a nation of thieves engaged in the futile attempt to live at each other's expense.

You'd think at least the church would be in the forefront in preaching against envy. But one of the greatest successes of liberals is their co-optation of America's church leaders into their evil agenda. Today's church leaders, along with members of Congress, have forgotten God's commandment against coveting and probably interpret the commandment "Thou shalt not steal" as God really meaning "Thou shalt not steal, unless there's a majority vote."

America's Liberal Cancer

November 29, 1995

Ideas of the liberal media and academic elite, supported by liberal politicians, have delivered one disaster after another. Their agenda has featured attacks on shame, traditional values, and civilized standards of conduct.

Take the afternoon television sleaze shows where hosts have guests ranging from those who've slept with their daughters' boyfriends or teenage male and female prostitutes to gang bangers and other lowlife. Viewers are supposed to believe that these lifestyles are morally equivalent to any other lifestyle. I'm not calling for censorship or even tuning out because there's a bit of voyeurism in all of us. Just recognize these people are America's human debris.

The so-called spouse abuse crisis is a modern liberal cause and part of a devious agenda. According to U.S. Department of Justice statistics, the 1992 rates of assaults per thousand of the population by marital status were never married (males, twenty-three; females, twelve); divorced or separated (males, fourteen; females, nine); married (males, six; females, three). Clearly, both men and women are safer when married. The least likely assault victim is a wife. What the liberals call wife-beating is more accurately labeled girlfriend or partner beating.

Male-female relationships within marriage are far more stable than partnerships—in my day called shacking up. Reduced assault rates are just one benefit. Children raised in a traditional family have higher cognitive skills and lower delinquency rates. The poverty rate for traditional families is lower; in the case of blacks, it's around 7 percent, compared with 34 percent for blacks in general. Married men not only earn higher incomes, but they're healthier and live longer as well. Despite these benefits, liberals demean, attack, and undermine what they trivialize as the "Ozzie and Harriet" family. The reason is simple: Liberals have an agenda incompatible with the traditional family.

Friedrich Engels's first draft of the *Communist Manifesto* called for deliberate undermining of the family as a means to accomplish the Marxist agenda. Like Marxists, liberals want people to be loyal and obedient clients of the state. Strong families undermine that agenda. Liberals want to determine when sex and what moral values are taught children. They want minor children to have abortions. Judges who rule that children can get abortions with neither parental knowledge or consent help undermine family authority. Hillary Clinton and her pals advocate children's rights. Getting their hands on our children at early ages gives liberals more time to undermine family values; that's why they attack home schooling.

Who are the heroes of liberals and targets of their endless compassion? It's easy: bums and vagrants. The ACLU will go miles to make sure a foul-smelling, nuisance-making vagrant can enter a library but not an inch for a law-abiding person who's been mugged. Its endless compassion extends to barbaric criminals. It has helped set criminals free to prey on us and led the fight to make us defenseless by its gun control efforts.

Also included among liberal hero/mascots are disease carriers. Liberals seek early parole for AIDS-infected prisoners and call for anonymity laws that enable AIDS-infected people to spread their deadly disease to others. The medical profession participates in the dishonesty about AIDS by having us believe that AIDS can't be acquired through casual contact, as they did some years ago when a San Francisco hospital punished nurses who used masks and gloves while handling AIDS patients.

If our country is to survive and prosper, we must summon the courage to condemn and reject the liberal agenda, and we had better do it soon.

Constitutional Corruption

October 18, 1995

Let's ponder these questions: Why did Congress amend the Constitution in 1916, giving it the power to collect taxes on any source? Why was the Seventeenth Amendment enacted in 1913 to select Senators by popular vote rather than, as originally designed, by state legislatures? Finally, why did Congress pass the Eighteenth Amendment in 1919, outlawing alcohol sales?

To really get into these questions and gain an appreciation for today's rogue Congress and Supreme Court, let's not get bogged down on the merits of these amendments. Let's simply look at the Constitution's restrictions. In Article I, Section 8, of the Constitution, the Framers enumerated eighteen functions of the federal government. Nowhere among those functions was Congress given the power to prohibit alcohol sales. Article I, Section 2, of the Constitution expressly states that "direct taxes shall be apportioned among the several states" and forbids direct taxes on individuals. Then there's Article I, Section 3, that requires state legislatures to appoint Senators.

During earlier periods, Congress and the Supreme Court had far greater respect for the Constitution. They understood that if the federal government was to have a power not delegated, or expressly forbidden, by the Constitution, they had to use the provisions of Article V to gain that power by amendment. They knew, for example, that Congress had not delegated power to prohibit alcohol sales. They couldn't find that power by manipulating the "commerce clause" or going penumbra hunting.

Today, it's an entirely different story. Congress, the White House, and the Supreme Court have abiding contempt for the Constitution, and we Americans are left with a constitutional carcass. Take just a tiny comparison of today with yesteryear. Yesteryear, there were alcohol prohibitionists; today, we have tobacco prohibitionists. No matter what we think about the alcohol prohibitionists, we can have a bit of admiration for them because they used the constitutional route to get their agenda across. Tobacco prohibitionists employ constitutional stealth: taxes, majority votes, and the totalitarian tactics of the Environmental Protection Agency and the Food and Drug Administration.

In 1787, the Constitution would have never been ratified without both the Ninth and Tenth Amendments. "The enumeration in the Constitution, of certain rights, shall not be construed to deny or disparage others retained by the people" is the Ninth Amendment, and "Powers not delegated to the United States by the Constitution, nor prohibited by it to the states, are reserved to the states respectively, or the people" is the Tenth. The Framers justifiably feared concentration of power in Washington. Today, the Ninth and Tenth Amendments have been completely trashed, and Congress is well on the way to finally trashing the Second and Fifth Amendments.

When and how we developed today's constitutional contempt is debatable. The federally caused Great Depression played a role but the education establishment has played a greater role through the dumbing-down of Americans. The resulting ignorance has allowed us to let charlatans and quacks in the legal profession tell us what the Constitution means. The Constitution was not written for intellectual elites; it was understandable to a nation of mostly farmers at the time it was written.

So where do we go and what do we do? Each of us is duty-bound to read and understand our Constitution. If we do that, we'll realize Washington has little or no moral authority. Its authority rests mostly on intimidation and force of arms. And like the Founders, we should adopt the attitude that "there is one thing in the world more wicked than the desire to command, and that is the will to obey."

Poor People Are Poor
But Not Stupid

November 22, 1995

Writing for the Washington-based Heritage Foundation, Robert Rector and William Lauber, in their aptly titled study "America's Failed $5.4 Trillion War on Poverty," report the 1993 tab for federal, state, and local poverty programs was $324 billion.

Between 1965 and 1994 poverty programs have cost taxpayers $5.4 trillion in inflation-adjusted dollars. That's a lot.

With $5.4 trillion you could purchase every U.S. factory, all manufacturing equipment, and every office building. With what's left over, one could buy every airline, trucking company, and our commercial maritime fleet. If you're still in the shopping mood, you could also buy every television, radio, and power company, plus every retail and wholesale store in the entire nation. There wouldn't be enough money to buy our fishing, agricultural, and forestry industries, but just wait—projected welfare spending over the next five years is $2.8 trillion.

Do poor people get all this money? Figure it out for yourself. In 1993, there were forty million poor people and $324 billion spent on poverty programs. Dividing that money up and simply giving it to the poor would yield $8,100 a person or $32,400 for a family of four. A lot of the money goes to the poverty industry's double parasites—people who suck the blood of the affluent and fester the sores of the poor.

Welfare advocates, experts, and congressmen try to convince us that people don't join the welfare class just to receive a measly $400 monthly check. They are right but for the wrong reason; welfare benefits are much higher. The Washington-based Cato Institute published a study, "Work vs. Welfare Trade-off." Authors Michael Tanner, Stephen Moore, and David Hartman compare welfare benefits to the salary a person might get by working before taxes were taken out. There are 77 different welfare programs, but the authors based their calculations on the six most common: Aid to Families with Dependent Children, food stamps, Medicaid, housing, nutrition assistance, and energy assistance.

In Oregon, that welfare package for a single mother with two young children is worth $16,959. To net $16,959 by working, that mother would have to be able earn a $19,000 pretax yearly salary, or $9.23 an hour. In Hawaii, that mother's welfare package would come to $27,736. That means she'd have to earn a $36,000 pretax salary or $17.50 per hour to break even with what she gets on welfare. The pretax hourly wage equivalent of welfare benefits in New York City is $14.75, Philadelphia, $12.45, Baltimore, $11.35, and Detroit, $10.90.

Many welfare recipients don't have skills to earn those hourly wages. From a short-run economic point of view, it may not make much sense to give up welfare benefits, worth $12 or $14 an hour, in exchange for a $5 or $6 an hour job, plus the drudgery of getting up in the morning, traveling, and taking orders all day. Surveys show that nearly 70 percent of welfare recipients are not looking for work. Not working may be a rational short-run decision but it has devastating long-run consequences.

To finance the welfare agenda Congress forces each taxpaying household to be a slave to the tune of $3,400 a year in taxes. A person may object to my reference to slavery. Slavery is the appropriate generic term, considering the essence of slavery is one person being forcibly used to serve the purposes of another. That's why I stand so steadfastly against poverty and corporate handouts. It must be my roots that makes me a latter-day abolitionist.

Today and Yesteryear

March 20, 1996

To gain a fuller appreciation of where we are, we should pay some attention to where we've been. Education is in shambles, but how bad is it compared to yesteryear? In the past, in order to enter public high school in Jersey City, New Jersey, students had to pass an entrance exam. In 1885, test questions included: Name the states on the west bank of the Mississippi River and the capital of each. What is the distance from the equator to either pole in degrees and in miles? Write a homogeneous quadrinomial of the third degree.

Today, few of those entering high school, few who are graduating, or few teachers have even the slightest inkling of the correct answers. Spring those questions on them, and see for yourself. I doubt whether yesteryear's students knew more because they were genetically superior to today's. I also doubt their better basic education can be explained by higher educational expenditures. The answer lies in the deliberate dumbing-down of education standards, half-baked, failed education theories, school time wasted on fads like AIDS awareness, homelessness, environmentalism, sex indoctrination, and endangered species, learning how to feel good about yourself even if you're an academic idiot, and, finally, teachers and administrators who, for the most part, represent the very bottom of the intellectual/academic barrel.

How about today's illegitimacy compared to yesteryear's? Nationwide illegitimacy stands at 31 percent and growing. At its current growth rate, we risk becoming a nation of bastards well before the end of the next century. Today's illegitimacy is new. In 1940, the illegitimacy rate was 3.5 percent nationwide. How do we explain this? If we believed the preachments of former Surgeon General Jocelyn Elders and her fellow travelers, in 1940, there must have been greater high school condom distribution and more birth control clinics as well as more sex education classes and more abortions.

That's nonsense. Having been a teenager during the 40s, I can personally testify that young people's hormones were in an uproar back then just as they are today. The difference is they weren't indulged. There were values as to appropriate dating age and respectable hours to return from a date. Suggestive talk to a girl might win you a slap in the face, perhaps a boot to the butt if her brothers and father found out. For boys, sexual exploits were mostly confined to fantasies and lies.

During the 60s, the liberal vision saw the traditional values constraining sex impulses to be old-fashioned and needlessly impeding fun. Let-it-all-hang-out values took over. Illegitimacy doubled that decade and has been growing ever since. Social sanctions like shame and disgrace went by the wayside, and welfare took care of the effects of personal indiscretions. It's nothing in today's air or water that explains today's skyrocketing rate of illegitimacy; it's today's values and social policy.

But there's a lot of good news between yesterday and today. Despite what the pundits preach, Americans are materially better off than we've ever been. The first measure is life itself. In 1970, life expectancy at birth was seventy-one years; today it's more than seventy-five years. In 1970, 30 percent of households had two or more cars; today, it's 54 percent. Fewer than 100,000 people used computers in 1970; today there are 76 million users. Since 1970, the accidental death rate per 100,000 of the population has fallen from 56 to 35. By any measurement standard the American standard of living has risen phenomenally. We all live in and benefit from an age of unprecedented wealth and it's our values that are preventing us from being even wealthier.

Coming to Our Senses

May 22, 1996

The Federal Bureau of Investigation released its 1995 preliminary crime statistics earlier this month. Nationally, serious crime dropped by 2 percent. The violent crime category showing the steepest decline, 8 percent, was murder. Decreases in other violent offenses were 7 percent for robbery, 6 percent for forcible rape, and 3 percent for assault. Property crimes were down, too: Car theft and burglary, down 6 and 5 percent, respectively.

For decades now, we've listened to judges, social workers, and psychobabblers who've counseled us that the way to deal with crime is to find the original causes of crime and then have government programs to eliminate those causes. As the elite went about this fool's errand, from the safety of their high-rent neighborhoods, fear became the order of the day. Sales of protective devices such as bars for our windows, car alarms, and pepper gas sprays skyrocketed. Now that we're finally beginning to turn the corner on crime, we might ask: Did judges, welfare workers, and psychobabblers discover crime's original causes unbeknownst to us?

I think not. What has happened is we've become more sensible about crime and criminals. What Texans are doing is just one example of our increasing sensibility. Earlier this year Texas A&M economics professor Morgan Reynolds wrote a report titled "Crime and Punishment in Texas" that was published by the Dallas-based National Center for Policy Analysis.

Texas experienced a 29 percent increase in serious crime during the 1980s. However, since the beginning of the 1990s, Texas's overall rate of serious crime has been cut by 35 percent—the lowest since 1973. Burglary is the lowest since 1968. The murder rate is the lowest since 1966. Compared to 1991, this lower crime rate means that 1,140 fewer Texans will be murdered in 1996 and there'll be 450,000 fewer crimes reported to the police.

I searched through Professor Reynolds' report with a fine-tooth comb, looking to see whether Texans had discovered the original causes of crime. My search was in vain. All I found was that Texans have implemented some old-fashioned, archaic notions about criminals and crime. Over the last four years, Texas has increased its prison capacity from 49,000 to 150,000. Its prisoners per 100,000 of the population has increased from close to the national average to 64 percent above the national average, giving it the highest incarceration rate in the nation. The average time convicts spend behind bars for serious crimes was 1.9 years in 1990; today, it's three years.

One of the reasons convicts are spending more time in jail is that fewer are paroled. In 1990, 80 percent of prisoners who petitioned for parole received approval; in 1994, only 22 percent of those petitioning received approval. The fact that prisoners are spending more time in jail has raised what statisticians call the expected punishment for crimes. During the 1980s, if you murdered someone in Texas, the odds were that you could expect to be in jail two years; today, it's over nine years. For rape, the expected punishment was five months; today, it's nineteen months.

More than 250,000 Texans are still victims of violent crimes each year, and more than 2 million are victims of property crimes. While we can be proud of Texans for having led the nation away from the reckless ideas about criminals, they have a long way to go. I'd like to see the Texas legislature pass a law whereby any law-abiding adult has the right to walk into a sheriff's office and be sworn in as a deputy and issued a permit to carry a deadly concealed weapon.

Political Extremism

June 26, 1996

Congressional Democrats and the news media love to label certain Americans as extremists. Usually, the victim of their appellation is the American who demands that government respect both the letter and spirit of the United States Constitution.

The Gun Owners of America and the National Rifle Association are extremists because they fight government encroachments on our Second Amendment guarantee to bear arms. In that regard, there are some other extremists who should be identified. Patrick Henry warned, "The militia, sir, is our ultimate safety.... The great object is that every man be armed . . . everyone who is able may have a gun." Richard Henry Lee said, "To preserve liberty, it is essential that the whole body of the people always possess arms and be taught alike, especially when young, how to use them."

The Framers gave us the Second Amendment not so we could go deer or duck hunting but to give us a modicum of protection against congressional tyranny.

The Fifth Amendment says "[N]or shall private property be taken for public use without just compensation." There's nothing complicated about those twelve words. You tell me: Which of those words permits the Fish and Wildlife Service to come upon your property, find a red-cockaded woodpecker, and then prohibit you from using 1,000 acres resulting in a $1.8 million loss of value, as in the case of a North Carolina farmer?

Americans shouldn't passively comply with tyrannical acts like this. Of course, politicians and the news media would label me an extremist. But I'm proud to be in good company. Thomas Jefferson's seal said, "Rebellion to tyrants is obedience to God." And, if you're like many and think I'm too critical and suspicious of government, there's another with similar suspicions. George Washington said, "Government is not reason, it is not eloquence. It is force. Like fire, it is a dangerous servant and a fearsome master."

Liberals and the news media are constitutional extremists in one way. They revere the First Amendment that says "Congress shall make no law . . . abridging the freedom of speech, or of the press." If you don't believe they have an "extremist" vision of the First Amendment, ask them what ways should Congress regulate the press "in the public interest?" They'll say none. Try to tell them that freedom of the press is an anachronistic, simplistic idea inconsistent with a complex, dynamic society. They still won't accept any government regulation of what they print and broadcast.

Why is it that news media people and liberals are so "extremist" when it comes to First Amendment guarantees and can easily find justification for government restrictions on other liberties? The simple answer is that people love freedom for themselves but not for others. But of greater explanatory worth is the fact that free speech is critical to a tyrant's pursuit of tyranny. Once they've accomplished that goal, free speech becomes a thing of the past as well. That was surely the pattern of twentieth-century tyrants like Hitler, Stalin, Castro, and Mao.

An extremist like Thomas Paine warned, "Those who expect to reap the blessings of freedom must, like men, undergo the fatigue of supporting it." We can't rest on the fact that the Framers gave us the world's greatest Constitution. In 1789, Benjamin Franklin admonished, "Our new Constitution is now established, and has an appearance that promises permanency; but in this world nothing can be said to be certain, except death and taxes."

Do you think Clinton should enact an executive order banning Fourth of July celebrations? After all why honor a bunch of anti-government extremists?

Partial Birth Abortions

September 23, 1996

I've been wondering about the partial-birth abortion bill, vetoed by President Clinton in April and overridden by the House last week. The mystery to me was how anybody can be partially born. It raises the same dilemma as saying someone was partially exterminated, partially dead, or partially raped. It seems to me these physical states are binary, like on or off. So I investigated the partial-birth procedure that President Clinton wants to preserve.

First, what is a partial-birth abortion procedure? It's a simple technique medically known as dilation and extraction. The abortion specialist pulls the baby out of the birth canal feet first until all but the skull is exposed. Scissors are used to puncture the skull, and in the words of Dr. Martin Haskell, a famous Dayton, Ohio, abortionist, "the surgeon removes the scissors and introduces a suction catheter (tube) into this hole and evacuates the skull contents. With the catheter still in place, he applies traction to the fetus, removing it completely from the patient."

According to anesthesiologists, while the mother is under a local anesthesia, there is no relief for the baby who "is more sensitive to pain than a full-term infant would be if subjected to the same procedures," says Dr. Jean A. Wright, associate professor of pediatrics and anesthesia at Atlanta's Emory University School of Medicine.

Why the procedure? It turns out that the U.S. Supreme Court ruled that Fourteenth Amendment protections apply only to persons, not the unborn. However, a living, just-delivered baby, no matter how premature, feeble, and tenuous, is constitutionally a person. Legally a baby is not born, and hence not a person, until the head passes through the birth canal. Therefore, when an abortionist leaves the head in the birth canal, he is free to kill the baby and escape murder charges. It's a matter of three or four inches that makes the legal difference between murder and abortion.

Now you may wonder why the procedure is used at all. Dr. Martin Haskell, who reportedly has performed more than a thousand dilation-and-extraction procedures, says, "Among its advantages are that it is a quick, surgical outpatient method that can be performed on a scheduled basis under local anesthesia," adding that he "routinely performs this procedure on all patients twenty through twenty-four weeks from LMP (last menstrual period) with certain exceptions." Haskell sometimes uses this mostly elective procedure as late as six months into a pregnancy, while other doctors have used it as late as nine months.

Americans will never agree on every aspect of the abortion controversy, but this kind of abortion, having little or no medical justification, has to be disgusting even to many proabortionists. It is a practice that comes just short—3 inches—of infanticide.

Under immense pressure from proabortion groups, President Clinton vetoed the Partial-Birth Abortion Ban Act (HR 1833) that would have prohibited the procedure except if necessary to save the life of the mother. Most Americans (71 percent) see the partial-birth ban as a reasonable measure. But many abortion activists see the ban as that important camel's nose into the abortion tent and they must fight the nose, lest the entire beast enter.

The historical evidence of other "reasonable" measures suggests proabortionists have adopted the right strategy. After all, who would have thought, at the time, a "reasonable" measure like banning fully automatic weapons would have led to today's gun-control laws? Who would have thought yesterday's "reasonable" measure requiring smoking and no-smoking sections on airplanes would have led to today's restrictions?

Hurting Others

November 20, 1996

Let's ask a question: Do we help others with meager choices by eliminating their best-known choice? While you ponder that, how about an example? If there's a person with only one slice of bread, and we all think he should really have five, do we improve his situation by taking that one slice? "Williams," you say, "you've got to be crazy; nobody's that stupid!" If we accept the idea that we shouldn't destroy a person's best choice, let's talk about actions of the U.S. Department of Labor.

The *Cleveland Plain Dealer* (October 20, 1996) carried a story, "Halt to Screw Work Sad." R.P. Coating Corporation of Cuyahoga Heights, Ohio, had been paying inner-city Cleveland residents a piecework rate of about $1.50 for every thousand screws and washers they assembled in their homes. Some screw workers used that meager pay for beer and bingo money, while others depended on it to live. Most of the workers were elderly, disabled, or welfare recipients. It was attractive work to homebound people, especially single mothers, many of whom had their children helping out.

In September, the Labor Department investigated R.P. Coating for possible violations of minimum-wage and child-labor laws. Dave Elsila, spokesman for the United Auto Workers (UAW), said, "We've been following for years the movement of work outsourced to parts plants in the Third World and Mexico, and to find the same kind of work going on in our own back yard is shocking to us." As a result of the investigation, R.P. Coating has stopped their home-work screw-assembly operation.

Cheryl Hall, a single welfare parent of four, said, "We felt cheated, but it was a chance to make money." She and her sister, also a single parent, earned $120 a month assembling screws. Now without any work, Hall said, "I'm not doing much of nothing now but staying home with four kids. I really don't know what I'm going to do yet." Others among the fifty households doing assembly work expressed similar regrets about the cessation of their chances to earn extra money.

Here's our question: If these people had superior alternatives, why in the world would they be doing the tedious, monotonous, and hand-aching work of assembling screws? Obviously, they saw it as their best alternative. In comes the Labor Department to destroy their best alternative without offering them something superior.

The liberal mentality would say, "Williams, if they need more money, we ought to increase welfare!" Is that really a superior alternative? Let's look at it. The children who were helping their parents were learning discipline, responsibility, and cooperation rather than being out on the streets doing mischief, drugs, and crime. The adults were exercising the correct moral initiative— trying to be at least partially financially independent. How decent is it to destroy these benefits, as humble as they are? Is handout money a superior alternative to honest work and family cooperation?

The Labor Department actions are in part a result of misguided good intentions. But a more important motivation is that it's protecting the interests of labor unions who'd rather see contract work go to its members at much higher pay. Government-backed job destruction helps explain why there is so much spiritual poverty where it did not exist yesteryear. Years ago, the values held by blacks were expressed by what my stepfather used to say, "Any kind of job is better than begging and stealing." That's a message roundly denounced by the actions of black politicians and white liberals.

Extortion or Voluntary Exchange

August 13, 1997

Last month, Autumn Jackson was convicted of extortion, conspiracy, and crossing state lines to commit a crime. When sentenced in October, she faces up to twelve years in prison and a fine up to $750,000. Jackson is in hot water because she demanded $40 million from Bill Cosby in exchange for her silence about being his illegitimate daughter. We don't know whether Jackson is telling the truth or not, but how just is the law she violated?

Imagine you catch me leaving a hotel with a young lady who's obviously not Mrs. Williams. You proposition, "Williams, rights guaranteed me under the First Amendment to the United States Constitution allow me to tell the world about your affair, eliminating any chance you have to become the nation's first black President." Let's stop here and ask: Have you done anything immoral or wicked? I think not. You are simply stating a human right protected by our Constitution.

Then you say, "I'll tell you what. If you give me $10,000, I will not exercise that right."

Now the ball is in my court. I must decide whether to forgo any presidential aspirations, plus risk Mrs. Williams going upside my head. Or, I could fork over $10,000 for your not exercising your God-given right to spill the beans. It's simply a choice where I decide which is more valuable: giving up $10,000 and retaining my presidential chances and no attacks from Mrs. Williams or keeping my $10,000 and suffering the consequences.

Let's stop again. Has there been any coercion or violence involved? It's simply a take-it-or-leave-it proposition, not unlike others we make every day. You promise to do something good for me (not tell) if I do something good for you (fork over ten grand).

It's just like my human rights, protected by the Constitution, to sleep and watch television all day. George Mason University's president in effect says, "Williams, if you don't exercise your right to sleep and watch television all day, and teach instead, I will give you so-many thousands of dollars each year." Would you call that extortion? Of course not; he's simply offering to do something good for me if I do something good for him.

I am hoping that Autumn Jackson's lawyers appeal the decision and make the argument that she was exercising her First Amendment rights in offering the $40 million deal and Bill Cosby was exercising his rights by not accepting it. Whether we like the proposed deal or not, applying the notion of extortion to the Jackson/Cosby case is unjust.

You say, "She might be lying and Cosby's reputation will suffer." That's a nonissue for at least two reasons. Whether she's lying or not, if people believe her, Cosby's reputation suffers. But more importantly, reputations consist entirely of what others think of you. Bill Cosby does not own his reputation unless you're willing to argue that my thoughts and opinions about Cosby are his property. Jackson has the right to influence my opinion of Cosby.

We should worry about extortion when physical threats are involved. If we did, our attention would shift to the U.S. Congress. Think about their retirement and health care programs. They tell us: Either you "contribute" to Social Security and Medicare or we'll take your property, put you in jail, and, if you resist, we've authorized our agents to use violence.

If Autumn Jackson had offered Bill Cosby such a proposition, I'd be the first to say, "Jail her for life!"

Private Interest, Public Good

July 9, 1997

Adam Smith, author of *The Wealth of Nations* and father of modern economics, said about people in general and businessmen in particular, "By pursuing his own interest, he frequently promotes that of society more effectually than when he really intends to promote it." That's a lesson lost in today's rhetoric of "giving something back," "feeling another's pain," and caring.

High-schoolers and college students are routinely fed leftist propaganda about businessmen's greed. Quite often, the lesson begins with one of the "robber barons" such as John D. Rockefeller. But Rockefeller should be celebrated, at least by the farthest left of the left, animal rights wackos. Here's the story.

America was the world's leading whaling nation. According to James S. Robbin's article, "How Capitalism Saved the Whales," appearing in the October 1992 issue of *The Freeman*, we had 735 whaling ships in 1846, doing 80 percent of the world's whaling.

In the first two decades of the nineteenth century, whalers killed an average of fifteen thousand whales annually to produce 4 million to 5 million gallons of sperm whale oil, 6 million to 10 million gallons of train oil, and 1.6 million to 5.6 million pounds of bone. These products lighted lamps and provided soaps, paint, lubrication, candles, perfume, corset stays, buggy whips, and other useful products.

When whaling finally stopped at the turn of the twentieth century, there were an estimated fifty thousand whales left. Surely, if an average annual kill of fifteen thousand whales a year continued, whales would now be extinct.

What saved the whales? Was it a triumph by Greenpeace or early animal rights wackos? If you say yes, put on the dunce cap.

Whales were saved by the self-interested motives of the much-maligned "robber baron" J. D. Rockefeller. The first step was made by Abraham Gesner, a Canadian geologist. In 1849, he devised a method whereby kerosene could be distilled from petroleum, but it took Rockefeller to make kerosene production a commercial success. With his partner, Samuel Adams, Rockefeller set up a network of kerosene distilleries that would later become known as Standard Oil.

As kerosene became cheaper and available throughout the nation, our whaling fleet fell from 735 in 1846 to 39 in 1876. The last American whaling ship left port in 1924 and grounded on Cuttyhunk Island the next day. Spring steel came to replace whalebone in corsets, automobiles replaced carriages, and the demand for whalebone buggy whips and wagon suspensions collapsed.

In 1879, Edison began marketing the incandescent bulb. As our country became electrified, both whale oil and kerosene were driven from the illumination market.

Whales were not the only beneficiaries of Rockefeller's activities. The Galapagos turtle was nearly driven to extinction as sailors on whaling ships killed them for fresh meat. With the decline in whaling, the turtles were able to survive. Oil drilling in Pennsylvania helped restore lakes that had become contaminated by natural petroleum leakages.

You might say, "Rockefeller didn't mean to confer these benefits, so it doesn't count!" If one takes that position, nothing counts. After all, we all have cars, houses, and food, which I think is wonderful. But I doubt whether producers of these goods labored for our benefit because they cared about us.

That brings up another Adam Smith quotation, "I have never known much good done by those who affected to trade for the public good." In other words, most good done in the world is done by people pursuing their own narrow selfish interests. Ironically, most world evil is done in the name of good.

Moral Decadence

November 5, 1997

Our moral standards are in steep decline. What's worse is that, as older generations of Americans pass away, fewer and fewer Americans are even aware of the decline. Younger Americans probably think today's standards have always been so, but I know differently because I'm old-fashioned beyond redemption.

Channel surfing sometimes brings me to shows like *Jerry Springer, Jenny Jones, Ricki Lake*, and *Montel Williams*. These shows feature guests telling detailed stories of behavioral rot, such as mothers sleeping with their daughters' boyfriends, kids who curse and threaten their parents, parents who teach their kids how to shoplift, and proud welfare recipients. It seems as though acceptance or rejection of their deviant behavior is measured by the applause of a voyeuristic audience.

Deviancy and immorality are not new in human history. What's new is the willingness of people to put bizarre lifestyles on display to millions of strangers. Even worse is the relative absence of social sanction against these lifestyles. Years ago, people would have been personally ashamed if others knew about their corrupt lifestyles. They'd try to hide it rather than go on national television or radio to broadcast it.

That says a lot about today's America. People show little hesitance to condemn smokers—behavior acceptable yesteryear—and are nonjudgmental about behavior long considered disgraceful and immoral.

Then there are television advertisements featuring female personal hygiene products, with pictures and descriptions that leave little room for the imagination. Discretion is a thing of the past. Years ago, for example, sanitary napkins were discreetly sold and wrapped in plain brown paper. Condoms were sold with similar discretion. You say, "Williams, you're a prude!"

I confess—kind of. Selling sanitary napkins in plain brown wrappers and condoms from under the counter might be prudish; but it seems to me that to openly advertise certain personal hygiene products is a bit much. If you disagree with me about all this, let me ask: If female personal hygiene items are socially appropriate for TV advertisement, is it also appropriate for a man to discuss the pros and cons of these items with his female coworkers? I suspect he'd risk charges of sexual harassment.

What about personal character? We have a president who has dodged the draft, openly cheated on his wife, and has lawyers seeking an out-of-court settlement on charges of indecent exposure, not to mention presiding over a scandal-a-day administration. Yet Clinton receives high approval ratings from the general population.

Clinton's moral lapses say little about the man himself. He's just one among thousands of men who've dodged the draft, cheated on their wives, or been charged with indecent exposure. The fact that he became president, was reelected, and retains a high approval rating does say something about the new standards Americans have for what's acceptable conduct. This is the first time in our history that a draft dodger and open womanizer could have been elected and reelected president and, in the face of one scandal after another, get high public-approval ratings.

Most of human behavior cannot and should not be regulated by law. Informal codes of conduct and moral standards provide the glue that holds society together. When these codes and standards, sometimes called traditional values, are ignored, trivialized, or forgotten, we take another step towards barbarism and incivility.

It Didn't Turn Out That Way

December 10, 1997

American faith in crusaders, and other do-gooders, is a direct result of the fact that we don't bother to look back at their last promises and predictions. Let's resurrect a few.

Since 1987, twenty-four states have enacted laws requiring local authorities to issue concealed-weapon permits to law-abiding citizens. When these measures were debated, opponents predicted that America's streets would turn into "Dodge Cities" and that "blood would run in the streets."

Enough time has transpired to examine their predictions. According to Jeffrey R. Snyder's report "Fighting Back," published by the Washington-based Cato Institute, counties where shall-issue gun-licensing laws went into effect, murders fell by 7.65 percent, rapes by 5.2 percent, robberies by 2.2 percent, and aggravated assaults by 7 percent. While researchers dispute the causal connection between concealed-carry laws and the drop in violent crime, the fact is our streets didn't turn into "Dodge Cities." If anything, they're more civilized.

What did the do-gooders say about the Republican-controlled Congress's repeal of the 55-mph speed limit? Ralph Nader said, "History will never forgive Congress for this assault on the sanctity of human life." Judith Stone, president of Advocates for Highway Safety, predicted "6,400 added highway fatalities a year and millions of more injuries." Former head of the National Highway Traffic Safety Administration Joan Claybrook said that Republicans "buried leadership in the rich opportunities afforded by political power." That's the Claybrook who said that air bags were safe and would provide protection for people whether they are seated properly or not.

According to recently released data by the NHTSA, speed-related deaths didn't rise by 6,400, but fell by 258. According to a MediaNomics editorial by Stephen Moore: "In the 27 states where higher speed limits had been in effect for at least six months, highway fatalities were virtually unchanged. California raised its speed limit to 70 mph and fatalities fell to their lowest level since 1961." Safety experts debate about the effects of repealing the national speed limit. One thing for sure is that the crusader prediction of 6,400 additional fatalities was dead wrong.

How about predictions of deadly global warming? The facts are that, if anything, the earth is cooling. We need not fear deadly global warming as much as the deadly public policy based on the false predictions. Federal Corporate Average Fuel Economy (CAFE) standards, initially justified to save oil but now justified to "protect the environment," kill thousands of people each year.

Since CAFE standards have been in effect, auto manufacturers have reduced the weight of their cars by an average of 1,000 pounds. According to a report by Julie C. DeFalco, "CAFE's Smashing Success," all auto crash studies show that smaller cars are less safe than larger cars. Applying those research findings to traffic fatality figures for 1996, DeFalco concludes that of the 22,000 passenger car deaths, 2,700 to 4,700 were the result of CAFE's downsizing effect.

Congress is well aware of the deadliness of CAFE standards, but they are captives of the Naderites, Claybrooks, and the lunatic environmentalist fringe. People who die or suffer needless injuries because of CAFE standards don't know the cause of their plight, plus, they don't have a strong Washington lobby. Politicians love situations where they can appease one group and not have to worry about the victims of that appeasement.

The most amazing thing about all this is not that people make mistakes. What's truly amazing is how the media presents these people over and over and how we listen to their foolish predictions time after time.

Thinking about Issues

November 6, 1996

Making our value premises explicit and clear can help untangle contentious public policy issues, or at least let us know where people stand. Let's state my personal value premise. I cherish private property rights. "OK," you say, "but what are private property rights?" Private property rights refer to an owner's right to acquire, keep, use, and dispose of property in ways that do not violate property rights of others. If that's a shared value, there's little debate on a whole class of public policy issues. Let's see.

I am the property of Walter Williams. Among other things, that means I have the right to take chances with my own life but not that of others. Mandating that I wear a seat belt violates my rights, whereas drunk-driving laws and vehicle safety inspection laws don't. Choosing not to wear a seat belt raises my risk of death. That's my right. Driving drunk or driving an unsafe car raises the risk of harming others. That's not my right. "Williams," you say, "we gotcha this time. If you don't wear a seat belt and wind up a vegetable, you burden society, which has to take care of you." That's not a problem of private property rights; it's a problem of socialism (weakened private property rights). People's money belongs to them. They shouldn't be forced to take care of me.

This term the U.S. Supreme Court is taking up the "right-to-die" issue. Private property rights can illuminate. Pretend it's *United States vs. Williams*. First, the Court should determine just who owns Williams. The evidence will show that while some of my ancestors were owned, my mother and father were not. Having attained twenty-one years of age, it would seem that he owns himself. That finding of self-ownership would make the Court's task easy. Their 9–0 decision would read: Though the thought of Williams ending his precious life is distasteful and while the loss of his insightful weekly columns will be a great loss to society, nonetheless, we find he owns himself and has the right to dispose of his life in any manner consistent with the safety of others.

There'd be a different decision if I didn't own myself. The first complexity would be to find out just who owns Williams. But let's fudge that complexity by saying Congress owns him. That being the case, I wouldn't have the right to take chances with my life. Congress would have every right to force me to use a seat belt. Moreover, they'd have the right to force me to stop smoking, exercise, get a plenty of rest, and restrict my dietary intake of salt, cholesterol, and alcohol. In *United States vs. Williams*, the Court would rightfully decree that I had no right to dispose of Williams. After all, that would be destroying government property.

I disagree with the ways some people "unwisely" use their property. Many drink and smoke too much, wear gaudy attire, become couch potatoes, and don't buckle up when they drive. But the true test of one's commitment to liberty and private property rights doesn't come when we permit people to be free to do those voluntary things with which we agree. The true test comes when we permit people to be free to do those voluntary things with which we disagree.

Undoubtedly, my position is offensive to many, and mankind's history is on their side. Private property rights and self-determination have always received a hostile reception. People have always had what they consider to be good reasons for restricting the liberties of others.

Government against the Poor

October 30, 1996

Those intricate hair-braiding styles sported by black girls, and sadly enough by some black guys, can fetch a price as high as $200. But most of the hair-braiding industry is underground. In New York state, to practice hair braiding legally, one must attend no less than 900 hours of costly cosmetology classes. In California, North Carolina and Massachusetts, it's 1,600, 1,500, and 1,000 hours, respectively. What's taught in these classes has little or nothing to do with braiding.

In order to operate a taxi in New York, you need a chauffeur's license ($20 annually) and successful completion of classes ranging from fourteen hours to eighty hours, depending on proficiency in English and map reading. That's the easy part. If you want to own your taxi, you must buy a medallion (license) that costs $175,000. If you can't afford that, you can lease a vehicle from someone who has a medallion for $450 to $650 per week.

Let's do one more. New York's Metropolitan Transportation Authority (MTA) runs a bus service that not only provides poor service, but runs at a loss as high as $3.94 per passenger. Enterprising black residents of Brooklyn, Queens and Harlem have gotten permits to purchase and operate "dollar" vans to pick up passengers along fixed routes such as a shopping plaza to a train or bus stop. In one 18-month period, eighteen thousand citations were issued to vans for offenses such as picking up or discharging passengers at or near bus stops.

In these cases, and many others, entrepreneurial people try to start a business and state and local governments throttle their efforts. Why? Incumbent cosmetologists don't want competition from hair braiders. A neat way to forestall that competition is to get politicians to write laws that make legal entry costly. It's the same with taxi medallion holders. If the license to own a taxi costs $175,000, there will be fewer owners. Those who are already in can charge higher prices and render shoddier services. The MTA and the bus drivers' unions don't want to face the customer losses if vans are free to provide more flexible services. Union drivers earn $25 an hour in pay and fringes, and van drivers threaten that income.

I don't know how you feel but I think this is a rotten, mean-spirited, despicable use of government. Some people want to start a business and others use state police powers to thwart their hopes and dreams.

Poor people, who want to get into these and other businesses ideal for those with modest means, have an advocate. It's not the NAACP, Jesse Jackson, or Ted Kennedy; it's the Washington, D.C.–based Institute for Justice. They have already broken up taxi monopolies in Denver, Indianapolis, Cincinnati, and deregulated hair braiding in Washington.

They're about to take on the Big Apple. Their recent report, "Is New York Killing Entrepreneurship," by William H. Mellor details other regulatory targets such as child care—a child care center director must have a master's degree or be enrolled in a master's program to get a license. You need a license to repair video cassette players, to be an usher, or sell tickets at wrestling matches. I hope the Institute for Justice is successful in tearing down these barriers, but in the meanwhile, I applaud the courage of those New Yorkers earning an honest, albeit illegal, living.

Poor people don't need welfare. They need government to leave them alone to find their own solutions. After all, that's how millions of other poor people made it before the advent of the welfare state.

Potpourri

Quite a few columns defy assembly into a particular category. Some of them represent the economist's tendency toward "intellectual imperialism," that is, applying economic theory to areas not traditionally thought of as economics. Some of these areas include marriage, sex, animal rights, morality, and the law. Economists show little hesitation delving into these matters since economic theory has something to say about whether there are benefits or costs associated with doing it. Plus, it's fun to show people that economic theory is a powerful tool of analysis. I also include a few short articles that were not published as columns.

Rights versus Wishes

June 7, 1995

Congress's budget debate would be much more honest, and perhaps more fruitful, if we cleaned up some of our thinking about what is a right and what isn't. People say they have rights to medical care, decent housing and food, even if they can't pay for it. If these goodies aren't forthcoming, somehow, their rights have been violated. Let's discuss rights.

Imagine that I meet an attractive young lady. I ask her to marry me. Suppose she says no. Have my rights been violated? Or suppose I ask to live in your house, and you say no. Have you violated my rights to decent housing? Finally, suppose I ask you for a job, and you say, "No! I refuse to hire you because you're too tall, and I don't like tall people." Have you violated my rights? In any meaningful sense of the term *rights*, none of these acts constitutes a violation of my rights.

True rights, such as those in our Constitution, exist simultaneously among people. The exercise of a right by one person does not diminish those held by another and imposes no obligations on others except those of noninterference. If I ask for a job, a person is no more obliged to enter into a work contract with me than she would be obliged to enter a marriage contract with me. By contrast, if you and I enter into a work contract, or if a young lady agrees to marry me, and a third party initiates force to prevent the transaction, my rights have been violated.

To say people have rights to housing, medical care, and jobs is an absurd concept. Those "rights" can be realized only by governmental imposition of burdens on others. For government to guarantee a "right" to housing, it must diminish other people's rights to their earnings. This modern vision of rights, if applied to my right to speech, worship, and travel, would require government to force (tax) others to provide me with an auditorium, church, and airfare.

If, instead, we called these newfangled rights *wishes*, I'd be in agreement with most other Americans. I also wish everyone had decent housing, nutritious meals, and good medical care. However, if we called them wishes, there'd be cognitive dissonance problems among people making the pretense of morality. The average American would cringe at the thought of government punishing one person because he refused to make someone else's wish come true.

If I simply had a wish for a five-bedroom house, and Congress told its agents at the IRS to take other people's money to make my wish come true, you wouldn't think much of Congress. Americans find it easier to live with their consciences, and find congressional initiation of force against others more palatable, if it were said I have a "right" to a five-bedroom house. After all, it's Congress's job to protect rights.

We can compare rights versus wishes another way. Suppose someone initiated force to prevent another from speaking, and Williams privately stepped in to protect that person's right to speak. Would I be declared a hero or villain? Then suppose I saw a homeless person and did privately exactly what government does—initiate force to take someone's money to guarantee that homeless person's "right" to housing. What would you call me? In the first case, most would probably call me a hero, and in the second, I'd rightfully be called a despicable thief.

Separating wishes from rights has great relevance to today's federal budget debate. After all, Congress's making wishes come true constitutes two-thirds of federal spending. The nation's problem is there's not a single member of Congress who has the courage to point out that the moral route to a balanced budget is for Congress to protect rights, not guarantee wishes.

Crazy Money

July 12, 1995

In order to fully appreciate this column, you just have to get your pay stub and see how much of your earnings was taken out for Social Security. Lake Providence, Louisiana, is probably the poorest town in the country. But one of its citizens does quite well. According to *Reader's Digest* (May 1995), Rosie Watson goes to the post office each month to pick up nine federal welfare checks totaling $3,893 worth of tax-free income that adds up to $46,716 a year.

Miss Watson, 44, gets $343.50 in disability payments because a Social Security judge found her too stressed out to work. Weighing 386 pounds, her common-law husband also gets a disability check for the same amount. Rosie has seven children ranging in ages from thirteen to twenty-two. They've all scored poorly on psychological tests and lagged behind in school. Under government welfare rules, her kids are eligible to receive $458 each for failing to demonstrate "age-appropriate behavior." These welfare payments in Lake Providence and other communities are so widespread that they are popularly known as "crazy checks."

According to the *Reader's Digest* story, Rosie's handouts haven't contributed much for civilized living standards. "The screen door hangs open. Soaps blare from the television. Roaches crawl the walls in the living room; the kitchen is caked with dirt. The house lacks a telephone, but Rosie does have two scanners to monitor police calls." Rosie explains her scanners, saying, "That's so I know what's going on."

Willie Bell, a black, is the principal of Southside Elementary School across the street from Rosie's house. Bell complained, while appearing before the National Commission on Childhood Disability, that "SSI is having an impact on my students' academic performances because I have honor roll students who are no longer trying because of the need to substantiate their claims for disability benefits." Bell and his staff say parents are encouraging, or coaching, their children to perform poorly and misbehave in school to get the SSI checks. "The children don't want to fail." Mr. Bell says, "They are doing what Mama wants."

Ray Owens, school psychologist from Moorehouse Parish, said, "Many parents don't spend the money (crazy money) on the child." One father's boy, Owens recalls, was bleeding from the gums but one dentist wouldn't treat the boy because he didn't accept Medicaid. The father responded, when asked why he didn't spend some of the $458 on a private dentist, "That's my money."

If I didn't know better I'd swear the "crazy money" scheme was part of an insidious Ku Klux Klan plot to sabotage black education. However, this program and others that produce similar bizarre disincentives have the support of "caring" white liberals, black politicians, and civil rights activists. If the Republican Congress ever got around to ending the crazy money program, rest assured we'd hear choruses of liberal howls of protest just as we heard when changes were being made in the school lunch program. They'd accuse the Republicans of abandoning the nation's children, with the media buying into the charge.

History is not going to be kind to liberals. With their mindless programs, they've managed to do to black Americans what slavery, Reconstruction, and rank racism found impossible: destroy families and the work ethic. Liberals share Rosie Watson's vision of a compassionate society. Rosie says, "I've got nothing to hide. SSI has done a lot for our family. We're not able to work, and it's the best income."

Unappreciated Miracles

September 13, 1995

Think about shopping for food. In effect each of us tells our supermarket: "I'm not going to tell you when I'm coming to shop. I'm not going to tell you how much and what I'm going to buy. When I do shop, you'd better have what I want, or I'm going to fire you by taking my business elsewhere." That's a tall, uncompromising order, but it's filled so routinely that we think it nothing. If you think it's nothing, contemplate shopping in the former Soviet Union, a nation with the genius to compete with us in space and weaponry but a nation that couldn't hold a candle to our supermarkets.

The average American supermarket stocks over twenty thousand different items. Who arranges all that? What's necessary to have those items on the shelves? Who and how many people are involved? The answer's easy: Nobody knows. The process defies comprehension. "C'mon, Williams," you say, "it's easy. The manager goes to a wholesaler and buys what he needs." If you think that's all there is, you trivialize the miracle.

Pretend Congress appointed you U.S. Supermarket Czar charged with making all the arrangements for Americans to have just one of those twenty thousand items—bananas. How will you get people in Costa Rica, some of whom may not like Americans, to work hard to grow, harvest, and ship bananas? What are all the arrangements necessary for the shipping crates? Do you know how to make a chain saw or axe to chop down trees for the wood to build crates? What's necessary to mine iron ore so as to make nails and wires for the crate? Then we have to keep in mind that the bananas have to get from Costa Rica to the supermarket. That means ships and trucks are needed. What do you know about truck and ship building and navigation?

There are literally millions upon millions of inputs and people cooperating with one another to get just one of those twenty thousand items to your supermarket. Somehow these inputs show up to do their job at the right time and right place, as if, to use Adam Smith's phrase, they are "guided by an invisible hand." All that good effort occurs without love and caring. The Costa Rican farmer, the crate manufacturer, and the ship captain don't give a hoot about you but you have the bananas as if they did.

The coordination that makes all those other items available at your supermarket is nothing short of a miracle. To think that one human being, or a group of humans, can possess the knowledge and information to accomplish the task is the height of human arrogance and conceit. That knowledge and information is widely dispersed across society in bits and pieces. That's why top-down central planning always produces disappointments, shortages, and bottlenecks. The banana czar might have remembered everything except a compass and the banana boat is lost at sea. Think back to the 70s during our government-sponsored energy crisis. Our energy czar had some parts of our country awash with gasoline and home heating oil while other parts were dry. Better yet, how would we like our groceries to be delivered by the same people who deliver our mail?

The forces behind all that coordination and cooperation that put those twenty thousand items in your supermarket are three simple things: prices, private property, and human lust for more. That's the beauty and simple magic of markets.

Myths, Lies, and Propaganda

December 13, 1995

Thomas Sowell's new book, *The Vision of the Anointed*, has numerous tidbits that are helpful in the understanding of the political demagoguery and deliberate media lies about budgets and other social issues.

Take the charges of Republican tax cuts for the "rich." Is a person rich if his income puts him in the top 20 percent of income earners, or is it the top 5 percent? That's for you to answer, but here are the facts: In 1992, a $60,000 a year salary qualified you for the top 20 percent of income earners and $100,000 a year qualified you for the top 5 percent. There are truly rich people in our country but ask a person earning $100,000 a year, with two children in college, a mortgage, and almost half his income taken in taxes, whether he feels rich like ABC's Peter Jennings or Senator Ted Kennedy. But according to the political rhetoric, and media lies, a tax cut for such a person is equated with undeserved tax cuts for the rich. Clinton and his media allies deliberately mislead us about richness in order to foment class envy as a means to greater power and control.

How about the "glass ceiling" lies where occupational and income disparities between college-educated women and blacks on the one hand and white men on the other are portrayed as a crisis requiring government intervention. Sowell points out that men with master's degrees outnumber women with master's degrees two to one. Men with Ph.D.'s outnumber women by 59 percent. Although women earn 37 percent of Ph.D.'s, they earn almost half of them in social sciences and more than half in education. Men earn more than 80 percent of natural sciences Ph.D.'s and 90 percent of engineering Ph.D.'s. Ph.D.'s earned by blacks exhibit a pattern similar to women. Should anybody be surprised by people holding more advanced degrees, and in the hard sciences, earning more than those with touchy-feely degrees?

What about media stories charging banks with mortgage discrimination against blacks? The media presented the Boston Federal Reserve study as controlled and definitive. A follow-up study took into account significant differences in black/white net worth, credit histories, existing debts, and the size of the loan sought as a percentage of the value of the property. When these factors were taken into consideration, the racial difference in mortgage approvals virtually disappeared. When Alicia Munnell, author of the flawed, media-hyped story, was approach by a *Forbes* magazine writer, and confronted with her study's deficiencies, she responded, "I do not have evidence [of mortgage lending discrimination]. . . . No one has evidence." Did you hear the media report that?

Washington Post writer Haynes Johnson is just one of those to spread the claim that half of all marriages end in divorce. That's unforgivable ignorance. Sowell says that in a particular year the number of divorces may well be half the number of marriages; however, the marriages counted took place that year while divorces being counted are from marriages that took place over decades. If the same reasoning was applied to deaths and births, and if deaths were half the number of births in a given year, Haynes Johnson might report that half the population died that year. The fact of business is only 11 percent of all adults who were ever married are now in divorced status. Married people outnumber divorced people by 54 million to 3 million.

Sowell's *The Vision of the Anointed* exposes one media lie and invented crisis after another. It's a book well worth its price for some informative Christmas reading.

When Should Violence Be Initiated?

January 3, 1995

I've always argued immorality is the root cause of most of our great social and economic problems. Let's put my argument in another light by going to first principles and asking: What's the moral basis for initiation of violence by either a person or government?

Part of the answer is simple and has a broad consensus: A person is morally justified to use violence when another initiates violence against his person or his property. Self-defense is one of those "unalienable rights." Governments represent people's efforts to collectively provide self-defense. We authorize governments to carry out our natural right of self-defense. The only legitimate purpose for government initiation of violence and threats is to prevent or punish those who'd use it against others. By granting government a near monopoly on the use of violence, more order is created and there's less preying upon the weak by the strong. The bottom line is moral government use of force cannot have a purpose exceeding private use of force.

Let's examine this generality and ask: Do people have the right to rape, murder, or steal? Fortunately, most Americans would answer no; but the next question poses a problem. Is there a moral basis for granting government officials the right to rape, murder, or steal? Most Americans would give a no answer for rape, but they'd be speaking with a forked-tongue if they said they were against government murder or theft.

"Doggone it, Williams," you say. "You've just insulted the entire nation." Let's look at it. Do people have a moral right to take someone else's money, by threats or force, for themselves or to give to someone else? If they don't have the moral right to do so privately, how can they grant government that right?

You say, "Government programs like welfare, Medicare and farm handouts aren't the same as theft; they're a result of a democratic process." Such a position differs little from saying that acts, clearly immoral when done privately, become moral and perhaps even laudatory when done by government.

The moral bankruptcy of that position becomes clear if we applied it to rape. Some might object to my calling welfare, Medicare and farm handouts theft and prefer to delude themselves, calling them income redistribution. That being the case, might we give sanction to government-sponsored rape by renaming it "compassion" redistribution?

Next: Suppose I want to manage my own retirement needs and resolutely refuse to pay into Social Security. The first moral question you might ask is: Have I initiated violence or the threat of violence toward anyone? The answer is a clear no.

Then, if I have not initiated violence and threats toward anyone, what is the moral basis for threats and violence being initiated against me? Plus, if I resolutely refuse to obey Social Security mandates, and refuse to submit to fines, property confiscation, and arrests, the ultimate penalty will be death at the hands of government. Some might argue that government initiation of violence is just desserts for disobedience; however, laws do not necessarily establish morality as clearly demonstrated by the Fugitive Slave Act, Nazi anti-Semitic laws, and South Africa's former apartheid laws.

The founders of our nation, clinging to the self-evidence of "certain unalienable rights," risked execution for treason and went to war with Britain for tyrannical acts of Parliament and King George that pale in comparison to today's tyrannical acts of Congress. Today's tolerance of tyranny highlights a danger of democracy, namely, tyrannical acts assume an aura of moral legitimacy when there's a majoritarian process.

Economics 101

January 30, 1996

Economists haven't done a good job of making economic theory accessible to the ordinary person. If we did a better job, there'd be fewer Americans falling prey to promises of free lunches, equating profits to evil, or seeing capital gains tax cuts as handouts to the rich. Economic theory is simple and fun, and it has tremendous explanatory power.

The first postulate of economics is that humans prefer more of those things that give them satisfaction. It might be more homes, more cars, more love and peace, more charity, or more war. The limits to human wants seldom reveal themselves. This postulate yields at least two important behavioral predictions: People will seek the cheapest way to achieve a particular goal; and as the cost of something rises, they'll take less; as it falls, they'll take more. Then there's that unpleasantness associated with the human condition: Every benefit has a cost.

Let's try out these ideas, keeping in mind that we're explaining human behavior, not saintly behavior. Suppose I placed a higher value, and was willing and able to pay $200, on a service you provided. Another person was willing and able to pay only $25. Assuming you prefer more to less, I'd be your customer. However, buyers have a way of concealing the value they put on services; therefore, sellers face the challenge of discovering who places higher values on their service. Airlines, for example, get a handle on this by a person's length-of-stay on a trip and whether there's a weekend included. Businessmen have fewer travel-day options, are more likely to travel on short notice, and are willing to pay higher prices than tourists.

Lest you conclude airline price discrimination is evil, needing congressional attention, consider the following: Suppose you saw a beautiful young lady married to a fat, old, ugly, cigar-smoking man, what prediction would you make about that man's income? If you're like most, you'd predict it's pretty high. That beautiful young lady, like airline executives, is practicing price discrimination. She knows he has fewer choices just by looking at him.

How about the hoopla accompanying the lifting of the federally mandated 55-mph speed limit? Opponents claimed "55 saved lives." I'm sure that if 55 saved lives, 35 would save even more lives, and highway fatalities would be unimaginable if the mandated speed limit was 5 mph. Surely, there'd be an enormous benefit to a 5-mph speed limit; the problem is, there'd be an even more enormous cost. Saving all those lives wouldn't be worth that cost in time and inconvenience. If we only look at benefits, and ignore costs, a 5-mph speed limit or any other decision is wonderful.

American workers earn more than Chinese workers. It's not because we have caring employers, wonderful labor laws, and wonderful unions. We earn higher wages because we're more productive. We're more productive because we have more capital (machines, tools, and education) working alongside us. The reason why workers building roads using earthmovers and bulldozers earn higher wages than workers using shovels and wheelbarrows is because they have more capital working with them. Increases in the rate of capital formation leads to increases in productivity and, hence, wages. Capital gains taxes and other harebrained tax laws raise the cost of capital; less is formed, and wages are lower than otherwise.

Economics is easy, fun, and important to understand. If you come across a person who says he took an economics class and found it boring and complicated, he had a bad teacher. He should have taken Williams's class.

Animal or Human Compassion

February 14, 1996

America is a rich nation with seemingly limitless compassion, partially evidenced by our $5 trillion failed effort to eliminate poverty and dependence. After thirty years of failure, we might start asking some questions about the nature of our compassion toward the poor. The most important questions are: Should we show animal or human compassion toward the poor, and which is better?

Compassion toward animals includes making sure the animal has adequate food and water, medical attention when needed, suitable shelter, and a toy or two for entertainment. In addition, that compassion must be extended to the animal's offspring.

A zookeeper or pet shop owner could supply us with a list of other necessary provisions. Animal compassion bears none of the hardships and complexities of human compassion. You don't have to instill lessons of independence. In fact, independence is a negative. What zookeeper or pet owner wants his animal getting up one day and saying, "The hell with you and your paternalism; I'm leaving!" With animal compassion, you don't have to worry about teaching the difficult and often heart-wrenching lessons of deferred gratification, planning for the future, and bearing the burdens of unwise decisions.

Human compassion goes beyond animal compassion. Provision of physical needs alone is insufficient. Moreover, behavior that's compassionate toward humans may qualify as cruelty to animals. For example, if you were to supply a human with a week's supply of food, and he ate it in a day, letting him do without for the remainder of the week would be a good lesson as well as just desserts for his lack of foresight. Expecting an animal to defer gratification, plan for the future, and bear the burden of unwise decisions is cruelty. Animals live day to day.

What would we think of a parent who provided incentives for his child to focus his attention on today's gratification to the exclusion of the future and let the child know that if he dropped out of school and couldn't provide for himself the parent would care for all his needs? Or what if the parent told a daughter who's made the mistake of having an illegitimate child, "Here's $500. Come back next month and there'll be another $500. And if you have another illegitimate baby, you get $600." I doubt whether there are many people who would see that parent's behavior as responsible, much less compassionate—but it's precisely what we do to the poor.

Today's welfare debate should focus on our pretense of human compassion. How compassionate is it for us to let people know they can disregard education and be virtually useless to employers and still be fed, housed, and clothed? How compassionate is it for us to let young men know they can make a girl pregnant and walk away from their responsibilities? What kind of incentives do we create for illegitimacy when young ladies know they can become pregnant with impunity? When we create these incentives for one generation, what's the message sent to the next?

Human compassion toward the poor cannot be engineered in Washington—it's even doubtful at the state level. The job of helping poor people to become accountable, independent, and successful can only happen at the local level through charities, civic organizations, community, and families. Also, it will take a willingness for us too see some people in some pain.

After all, forcing people to bear the burden of unwise decisions is part of the lesson not to make unwise decisions. The most important component of human compassion is forcing, demanding, and helping people to learn they can be better than animals.

Income Lies and Propaganda

March 27, 1996

The rich are getting richer. The poor are getting poorer. The middle class is disappearing. That's the litany of political hacks, quacks, and scum who seek control over our lives in the name of fairness. People making those claims about income in America are misguided, foolish, or sinister manipulators. Let's look at the facts.

The Minneapolis-based Center of the American Experiment just released a report by John Hineraker and Scott Johnson titled "The Truth about Income Inequality." Yes, leftists on college campuses, in Congress and the news media are right. There has been a net decline in the number of middle-class Americans—families earning between $15,000 and $50,000. But all of this decline is a result of families moving into a higher income category, above $50,000 in inflation-adjusted dollars. The number of families earning more than $50,000 grew from 24 percent of the population in 1970 to 32 percent in 1990.

Representative Richard Gephart whines that high-income earners are "winners" in "the lottery of life." Robert Reich, secretary of labor, calls high-income earners the "fortunate fifth." These statements reflect resolute, incurable stupidity. If your annual family income is $100,000, you're in the top 20 percent of earners and $50,000 qualifies you for the next 20 percent. We might just ask all those Americans in those income categories whether they think their income is a result of winning a lottery. I'm betting they're going to say, "Hell no, we work our butts off."

Statistics confirm their story. In 1990, of the families that comprised the lowest 20 percent in income, only 45 percent worked at all, and of those working, only 24 percent worked full time. By contrast, of families in the top 20 percent, 93 percent had two or more members working, and amazingly, 11 percent of those families had four or more workers. Hineraker and Johnson reached the sensible, though boring, conclusion: The reason upper-income families earn more is because they "simply work more jobs and longer hours" than families with lower income.

What about the massive economic expansion of the 80's that led to the creation of 19 million new jobs? Liberal liars tell us these were mostly low-paying, hamburger-flipping jobs, but here's the distribution of jobs created by type and percentage according to Bureau of Labor Statistics: managerial/professional (33 percent), production (19 percent), technical (22 percent), operators (8 percent), services (17 percent). The average pay for those new jobs was $23,000.

There's considerable income mobility in our country as seen by a Treasury Department tax returns study. Of those in the bottom 20 percent of income, in 1979, 86 percent moved to a higher income class by 1988. And how about this: Fifteen percent of those who were poor in 1979 went all the way to the top income category by 1988. Mobility is a two-way street. The Treasury Department study found that of those taxpayers ranking in the top 1 percent in 1979, 58 percent fell to a lower category by 1988. You tell me how these facts gibe with the liberal claim that the rich get richer and the poor get poorer?

Differences in income are mostly explained by people's differences in skills, discipline, drive, and productivity. James Madison said the "first object of government" is that of protecting the "different and unequal faculties of acquiring property" that naturally result in the possession of different degrees and kinds of property, in a word—income inequality. Contrast Madison's vision with today's Congress, which sees high skills and productivity as characteristics they should punish and penalize.

Adjustment Problems

June 19, 1996

Being sixty years old means a lot of things, notwithstanding pending expiration. For one thing, being of a different generation means adjustment problems associated with modern life. This is not an era when common sense and personal responsibility are taken for granted.

A few weeks ago, my wife purchased an unpainted cabinet to help give my office the appearance of greater orderliness. As any reasonable person would do, I read the instructions on the can of Minwax Polycrylic stain. The label also contained the following warning: "Do not take internally." I wondered: Is there a person who'd turn a can of stain up to his lips to take a swig? If you think about it, the warning is useless. A person stupid enough to drink stain is also probably too stupid to read. So why the warning? My guess is the Minwax lawyers. Someone might drink Minwax stain, sue the company, and win a large settlement because an enlightened judge sees the company as being responsible for a person's stupid act.

Then there's America's children. I've spent a life loving children, not all, but most. Now, children are becoming my enemy. Children allow themselves to be used as tools for intrusive government. As soon as somebody mentions less government spending for school lunch programs, somebody else marches a child across the stage and accuses, "You want to starve this child!" When welfare reformers talk about forcing able-bodied people off welfare, the first thing you hear is, "You want to starve children!" When congressional tyrants want to restrict what we see on television, read on the information superhighway, or they want to stop adults from smoking, once again, children are used as tools. If America's children want to win back my love and faith in them, they must stop being used as tools for scoundrels. Children should call a press conference to tell the nation that if anybody wants to know what children want and think, ask children, not their unappointed spokesmen.

There's another adjustment problem for older men. I can't find it in me to treat ladies like men. When traveling on a public conveyance, I offer my seat to a lady if no other seats are available. When walking with a lady, I assume the curb position, not to mention holding doors open. Some see these acts as gentlemanly respect, others see them as contemptible, chauvinist pig insults. How does one tell, beforehand, a lady from a woman?

Then there's race. Today's race experts say that the pathology of many black lives is the result of a legacy of slavery, segregation, and racism. For these reasons, many black youngsters are illiterate, less than 40 percent of black children are raised in two-parent families, and black crime is rampant. But in 1950, when I attended North Philadelphia's Benjamin Franklin High School, we never heard of a kid who couldn't read. As early as 1870, in most major cities, close to 80 percent of black kids lived in two-parent families.

Black neighborhoods, even the housing project where I lived, were safe enough to sleep outside on those hot, humid summer nights. How do you square the race experts' claim that slavery and racism are responsible for today's problems with the facts of yesteryear? All I come up with is that slavery and racism can have delayed effects, skipping entire generations before their effects are manifested. But that doesn't seem plausible.

There's a light at the end of the tunnel to my adjustment to newfangled ideas and practices. The problems won't be with me as long as they have been already.

Trusting Experts

July 24, 1996

Some people wonder why I'm suspicious of experts. People might think, "Williams is too cynical." Let's investigate a few experts and their monumental predictive blunders. In 1949, *Popular Mechanics* opined, "Computers in the future may weigh no more than 1.5 tons."

With my IBM Thinkpad weighing about 4 pounds, *Popular Mechanics* was at least technically right. But how about Thomas Watson, the chairman of IBM? In 1943, he predicted, "I think there is a world market for maybe five computers." Then there was Ken Olsen, chairman and founder of Digital Equipment Corporation, who said, "There is no reason anyone would want a computer in their home."

Computer experts don't have a monopoly on wrong predictions. In 1899, Charles H. Duell, commissioner of the U.S. Office of Patents, proposed closing the agency because "Everything that can be invented has been invented."

Duell knew for sure airplanes would not be invented, because, in 1895, Lord Kelvin, noted physicist and president of the prestigious Royal Society, said, "Heavier-than-air flying machines are impossible." After airplanes were finally invented, Marechal Ferdinand Foch, Professor of Strategy at Ecole Superieure de Guerre, said "Airplanes are interesting toys but of no military value."

A 1921 *New York Times* editorial had a great prediction about Goddard's research on rocketry: "Professor Goddard does not know the relation between action and reaction and the need to have something better than a vacuum against which to react. He seems to lack the basic knowledge ladled out daily in high schools." The *New York Times* editor might have been influenced by another expert, Lee De Forest, inventor of the vacuum tube and father of television, who said, "Man will never reach the moon regardless of all future scientific advances."

No socioeconomic class has a monopoly on bad predictions. "This fellow Charles Lindbergh will never make it. He's doomed." That was millionaire aviation enthusiast Harry Guggenheim's prediction about Lindbergh's chances for success in man's first solo trans-Atlantic flight.

Back in 1859, when Edwin Drake was trying to enlist drillers to his oil-drilling project, some of them said, "Drill for oil? You mean drill into the ground to try and find oil? You're crazy." In 1876, a Western Union internal memo said, "This 'telephone' has too many shortcomings to be seriously considered as a means of communication. The device is inherently of no value to us." Then there are economists. In 1929, Irving Fisher, professor of economics at Yale University, said, "Stocks have reached what looks like a permanently high plateau."

"I'm just glad it'll be Clark Gable who's falling on his face and not Gary Cooper." That's what Gary Cooper said when he decided not to accept the leading role in "Gone with the Wind." In 1962, there was another entertainment industry rejection: "We don't like their sound, and guitar music is on the way out." That was Decca Recording Company turning down the Beatles.

History has shown that mankind makes grossly erroneous predictions, but to err is human. Mankind tends to survive errors and erroneous predictions, as history has aptly demonstrated. We have home computers, we have telephones, and we enjoy Beatles' music.

We survived because the "experts" making false predictions had no power to impose their vision of the future on others. Those who had another vision of the future were free to go about their business of inventing the "uninventable" and developing the "undevelopable."

For this reason alone we should not allow experts, no matter how smart they are—or think they are—to control any aspect of our lives.

Corporate Downsizing

August 14, 1996

One strategy of those who seek increased control over our lives is to manufacture a crisis. Corporate downsizing stories on the presidential campaign trail and in the national press are an example of that strategy. Let's put downsizing in perspective by asking whether it's bad for the country and something government should prevent. But first a brief history of downsizing.

At our nation's birth, 95 percent of the population was one way or another engaged in agriculture. Today, only 2 percent of Americans farm. In anybody's book, that's some heavyweight downsizing. Was it bad for our country? Should earlier Congresses have taken legislative action to prevent losses of agricultural jobs? Years ago heavy construction—building railroads, roads, dams, and tunnels—involved teams of men laying track and wielding sledgehammers, picks, and axes. Today, there are highly paid guys pushing buttons and pulling levers on huge pieces of construction equipment. They do in a day what hundreds of men couldn't do yesterday. Construction downsizing destroyed thousands of jobs. What should Congress have done to save those jobs?

Downsizing is mostly a process where companies find cheaper production methods. Labor tends to be the costliest input; therefore, companies have profit incentives to seek methods to save on labor. When they use less labor, that labor is freed up to be used elsewhere in the economy. If labor-saving methods had not been found to free up that 95 percent of early Americans engaged in farming, where would we have gotten workers to produce other goods that contributed to our wealth? Also, if people weren't freed from farming, where would they have gotten the time to be educated and become more productive?

We don't have to go back to our early history to make these points. Last year, according to a forthcoming article in *Policy Review*, Wal-Mart added forty-one thousand new jobs, Motorola added five thousand, and Intel added nearly ten thousand. In fact, there were 9.5 million new jobs created in the last four years. If AT&T, IBM, and others weren't finding ways to use less labor (downsizing), where in the world would Motorola, Wal-Mart, and Intel have gotten their new workers? The alternatives would have been to bid up wages and hence the price of the product, wait for new workers to be born, or get more foreigners.

In a dynamic, robust, and growing economy, there are always going to be changes in the use of labor. Some jobs will be eliminated while others are "born." Using government to prevent this process will make the nation poorer. We'd be far less wealthy had an earlier Congress saved the stagecoach driver's or the ice man's job. In India, weavers and spinners had considerable political clout. They used that clout to save their jobs by preventing greater mechanization of the textile industry. Until quite recently, India's textile industry was like ours was in 1920. India's job-saving restrictions imposed high costs on its population in terms of higher textile prices.

None of all this is to deny there are hardships faced by displaced workers, particularly those up in years who have children to raise and mortgages to pay. They may be forced to retrain or accept lower-paying jobs. A robust, growing economy facilitates their transition, not one crippled by various "job-saving" laws and regulations. At any given time, most people are employed (94 percent). Should we accept crippling the economy by stifling innovation for the benefit of a tiny percentage of American workers who find themselves unemployed as a result of changes in labor use? I think not.

The Broken Window Fallacy

August 28, 1996

With each reading of the late Henry Hazlitt's *Economics in One Lesson*, I'm impressed by how clearly this economist/columnist understood basic economics and how much better off we'd be with one iota of his insight.

In Hazlitt's broken window story, a hoodlum tosses a brick

through a baker's window and flees. The baker is furious, but a person in the crowd that gathers reminds the baker that his misfortune has a bright side. The $250 it takes to replace his plateglass window will create work for the glazier. And, after all, if windows were never broken, what would happen to the glass business? The baker was also reminded of the multiplier effects. The glazier will have $250 to spend with other merchants, who in turn will have $250 to spend with still other merchants and so on. One just might conclude that the brick-throwing hoodlum, far from being a public menace, was a public benefactor.

Hazlitt says that the first conclusion is correct: More business for the glazier. The glazier will be no more unhappy to learn about the vandalism than an undertaker is to learn of a death. The baker, however, will be out $250 that he planned to pay the tailor to make him a new suit. Because he has to replace the window, he has to do without the suit. So, instead of having a window and a suit, he has to make do with just a window. The glazier's gain in business is the tailor's loss of business. From the community's point of view, it's poorer by one suit that would have come into being. It's easy to see the hoodlum's act as stimulating employment because the new window will be visible. Since the baker can't buy a new suit, the unemployment for the tailor is invisible.

"Williams," you say, "what's the big deal about that story?" There're many examples of how we buy into various versions of the "broken window" fallacy. Some history professors teach that, while World War II was a terrible thing, it brought us out of the Great Depression—no such thing. Yes, there was an increased demand for guns, tanks, and bombs. Neither Santa Claus nor future generations gave us resources to fight World War II. America had the resources at the time of World War II to make war equipment. Those same resources could have gone into houses, cars, and refrigerators.

A variant of the broken window fallacy is when mayors, labor bosses, and the chambers of commerce tell us we need to use tax money or float a bond to construct a convention center, new sports arena, or a bridge because of all the jobs that will be created. Taxpayer money comes from taxpayers. If taxpayers kept their money, they would have spent it on cars, home remodeling, and other things that also would have created jobs. So like Hazlitt's broken window story, certain jobs are created while others are reduced or don't come into being. The advantage for politicians pushing government spending is that the created jobs are visible, but the jobs that are eliminated or don't come into being are invisible.

Social Security is another variant of the broken window fallacy. People who support the program marvel at its benefits. They have no idea of what there'd be if the same money were put in private retirement plans. Among those benefits would be a higher national savings rate, a greater investment rate and a higher gross national product, which, according to some estimates, would be 18 percent higher. All that is invisible while Social Security checks are visible.

Reading Hazlitt will make you more informed than most economists.

Private Virtue, Public Vice

December 18, 1996

Several years ago, Mrs. Williams and I purchased a condo for my eighty-five-year-old mother because, among other things, we were concerned about her safety going up and down stairs in her three-story home—not to mention neighborhood safety. For a number of years, we've sponsored several scholarships to enable black students to attend private schools. We've also given financial assistance to various family members who have needed it.

"OK, OK, Williams," you say, "don't think you're the Lone Ranger, I help others out too—what's the point?" Helping others by digging in one's own pockets is a laudable private virtue. Generosity has always been a key distinguishing feature of American people. We do about 85 percent of all world giving.

Some people say there's not enough generosity to take care of all needs; therefore, we need government. That proposition differs little from saying that if people do not give enough voluntarily, then government intimidation, threats, and coercion should be used to take their money. Good people must ask if that proposition should serve as the foundation for a moral society.

Let's go back to my story. Suppose my wife and I couldn't afford a condo for my mom, give scholarships, or help family members. Suppose further you agreed with me that my mom should have safer surroundings, that black youngsters should have an alternative to rotten government schools, and that our family members should be helped. Would that consensus justify my private use of intimidation, threats, and coercion to take another person's money to finance those worthy goals? "Williams," you say, "that'd be theft and you should go to jail." I agree.

Here's my question: Would your conclusion change if I managed to get one other person to agree to take someone else's money to finance those worthy goals? What if ten other people went along with me, a hundred, a million, or 269 million other people? From a moral point of view, your conclusion that it'd be theft shouldn't change. The only differences would be technique and the number of people involved.

There are many Americans who believe that a majority consensus and legality establish morality. They see private confiscation of property as theft but public confiscation as a virtue, a sign of caring, and accepting social responsibilities. Americans who make the pretense of Christian faith act as though God's law to Moses, "Thou shalt not steal," really means "Thou shalt not steal unless you do it legally through a majority vote."

Private efforts to help our fellow man, aside from being moral and praiseworthy, are far more effective. The giver is more likely to become a monitor and part of the solution. Very few of us would, year after year, voluntarily give to people who lay around watching TV all day, engaging in self-destructive behavior, and making no effort to get a job or educate themselves. We would scold, threaten, help, and encourage that person to get their act together. That kind of involvement with solutions is virtually impossible through today's government handout system.

I am optimistic. Americans are coming to recognize that a private virtue can easily be a public vice. I'd be even more optimistic if church leaders began to teach their congregations that God did not put any escape clause in his commandment "Thou shalt not steal."

Freeloaders

March 5, 1997

John Stossel's ABC special "Freeloaders," which aired last week, showed just how far we've come to being a nation of parasites. It featured people (thieves) who'd go to a restaurant, eat half their meal, and then place an insect in the remaining food in order to get the meal without charge.

Stossel interviewed bums holding signs "Will work for food" who refused any job offered. Rich sports team owners used politicians to gouge taxpayers for subsidized stadiums. Then there was the king of corporate parasites, Dwayne Andreas, CEO of Archer Daniel Midlands (ADM), the so-called supermarket to the world.

There have always been parasites and thieves—but let me speculate on why so many otherwise decent and honest Americans are caught up in an attempt to live at the expense of others.

Mrs. Williams and I paid tens of thousands of dollars in taxes last year. We know some people who paid less than $3,000. Our question is: What did we get from government that others who paid much less didn't get? We figure nothing. What's more, Congress gave most of our tax money to other Americans who hadn't earned it.

We didn't have to take this lying down. We could have tried to recoup some of our money by getting a federal grant to pay our daughter's college tuition, organizing our neighbors to get a HUD grant to build a tennis court nearby, or get some other middle-class handout.

We did none of that. Not all people accept tax gouging lying down. When legalized theft begins, it pays for everybody to get in on the action. Those who don't are left holding the bag.

Another part of Stossel's show featured taxpayer money sponsoring overseas advertisements for McDonald's and Campbell Soup. In these cases, I could make myself whole and avoid using Congress as a middleman. On my next McDonald's visit, I could pay for one soda and drink two. Or, I could eat most of my hamburger, put a bug in the other part, and demand my money back. You say, "Williams, that's dishonest!" I ask, "Is it dishonesty when you try to recoup what was stolen, even if it was stolen legally?"

The most outrageous show segment featured Andreas, who's given politicians millions of dollars to help him enrich himself at our expense. For that money, congressmen voted to restrict sugar imports that, in turn, drove up sugar prices. Higher sugar prices benefit Archer Daniels, which produces corn syrup—a sugar substitute. When sugar prices are high, sugar users (soda, candy, and food processors) turn to corn syrup as a sweetener, and we pay higher food prices.

Archer Daniels also manufactures 50 percent of the nation's gasohol, a grain-based gasoline additive. Led by former Senator Bob Dole, the company's man in Washington, Congress changed the tax code to give write-offs to oil corporations that add gasohol to their products, further enriching Andreas's company.

What we saw on "Freeloaders" was morally wrong and has devastating implications for liberty. No one has the right to take or receive what someone else has earned unless it is given to them. After all, if one American is "entitled" to live at the expense of another or receive a special privilege, what principle of justice allows us to deny those entitlements and special privileges to other Americans?

It's tempting to blame politicians for turning us into a nation of thieves, but you'd be wrong. Politicians are just the pimps trying to make a sale—you and I are their anxious customers.

Petty Annoyances

October 1, 1997

People think runaway government is the only thing that bothers me, but there are some minor nuisances that bother me as well.

Chief among them are people's seeming inability to differentiate between the number zero and the letter *O* in conversation—even telephone operators. An information operator might say, Dial 3 1*O*-3zero55.

I'd ask, "If I follow your instructions, entering the letter *O* instead of the number zero, will I reach my party?" They always say no. Then I ask them, "Why do you say dial *O* when you should say zero?" Our chit-chat usually degrades after that. I'm guessing the confusion is because both *O*s and zeroes are round.

I make errors of grammar and syntax now and then that I attribute to an advanced age. But you'll never hear me say, "Loan me some money." Mrs. Viola Meekins, and Dr. Martin Rosenberg, my junior high and high school English teachers, would go ape, saying, "Sentences need verbs!"

Loan is a noun; the verb lend is required. Not every sentence has an explicit verb, which brings up my next annoyance. How many times have you heard a person say, "He is not as tall as me" or "They are not as fast as us"? Every time I hear errors like these, I visualize Dr. Rosenberg's twisted, sarcastic expression as he's about to verbally pounce on a student. "Are you saying, 'He is not as tall as me am' or 'They are not as fast as us are'?"

That's nonsense, he'd explain; the words *am* and *are* are elliptical (missing, but understood) verbs, and their subjects must be in the nominative case (I and we). By the way, this grammar instruction occurred at North Philly's Benjamin Franklin High School in the early 50s before black kids were seen as victims and teachers worried about self-esteem.

Another petty annoyance is when a person knocks on my office door and asks, "May I disturb you?" Depending on my mood at the time, I might reply, "You've already disturbed me; what do you want?" I wonder why people don't use the more sensible alternative: "Excuse me for disturbing you."

Then there's the grocery store checkout line. Sometimes a person with just one item to purchase asks, "Do you mind if I go in front of you?" Once in a while, I'll experiment and courteously answer, "Yes, I do mind." Most often the person looks at me in shock, slowly turning into mild anger. I wonder why. If a question is asked that can have a yes or no answer, why get miffed if a no answer comes? Sometimes I ask people, "Do you mind if I smoke?" A lot of times, I get a yes-I-do-mind answer, but I don't get miffed.

Speaking of smoking . . . Sometimes I'm invited to an event—it could be a boring meeting, conference, or lecture—where a flat no response is probably not appropriate. I'll ask whether smoking is permitted. Most times, the answer is no. Then I tell the person, "Sorry, I can't come because I just have to smoke." I tell them, "You have your rules, but I have mine."

Then there's the airplane pilot. I'm sound asleep. The pilot comes on the public address system to announce, "Those seated on the right side of the aircraft can see the Grand Canyon." Sometimes I wonder whether there's a person on the ground saying, "Those looking up can see an airplane."

Despite these petty annoyances, I generally make it through the day not losing focus on my big job of trying to save our country.

Economics 101

May 21, 1997

Many people think economics is about businesses and financial institutions but economics is much broader than that. Economic theory makes a valuable contribution whenever there are costs and benefits of any human action.

Take dating. Suppose you see a fat, old, ugly, cigar-smoking man dating a beautiful young lady. What prediction would you make about that man's income? I'd guess that you'd say it's pretty high. Why? Essentially, what the man tells the beautiful young lady is, "Look, I can't compete for your hand on the basis of a guy like Williams; so I'm going to offset my disadvantages by offering you greater splendor."

That's what economists call a "compensating difference." Suppose do-gooders come along and claim that it is unfair for beautiful young ladies to charge fat, old, ugly, cigar-smoking men higher prices than handsome men. They get a law passed forbidding beautiful young ladies from demanding more from fat, old, ugly, cigar-smoking men than handsome men. What then happens to the probability of fat, old, ugly, cigar-smoking men dating beautiful young ladies? If you said zilch, go to the head of the class. Such a law would deny them their most effective means of competing with handsome men, namely, offering a higher price.

The same principle applies to any less-preferred person or good. Most people prefer filet mignon to chuck steak. The reason chuck steak sells is because it offers a "compensating difference"—it sells for a lower price. If we made a law saying that chuck steak had to be sold for the same price as filet mignon, chuck steak wouldn't sell. It couldn't offset its perceived quality differences by offering a lower price.

I do speaking engagements, for which I am paid. So does Nobel laureate Milton Friedman, for handsome fees as high as $30,000, which I don't get. In the interest of fairness, suppose a law is passed saying that people had to pay me the same as they paid Friedman. What do you think would happen to the probability of my being hired? Right. It's just like the fat, old, ugly, cigar-smoking man; it would go to zilch. The reason I have speaking engagements is because I am free to say, "I'm not as good as Friedman, but I'm not as expensive either."

What about the minimum wage? That's a law that says no matter whom you hire, you must pay them a minimum of $5.15 an hour. That produces effects not dissimilar from any of the above examples. A person perceived to be worth only $3, in terms of productive output, just won't be hired though he would be hired if it were legal for him to offer a compensating difference as I do when competing with Friedman. Thus, one of the effects of the minimum wage, though not its intention, is to reduce employment opportunities for low-skilled people.

The lesson here is that economic theory, like any other good theory, such as Galileo's law of falling objects, is perfectly general. Some people may object, saying, "Williams, we're dealing with humans not inanimate objects!"

No problem. The law of gravity says that the independent influence of gravity is to cause a falling body to accelerate at 32 feet per second per second. It matters none whether that falling object is a brick or a human. It's the same with economic theory—whether we're talking about fat, old, ugly, cigar-smoking men, chuck steak, speaking honoraria, or a low-skilled worker. When prices are controlled, the less-preferred are always handicapped.

Capitalism and the Common Man

September 17, 1997

There are some arguments so illogical that only an intellectual or politician can believe them. One of those arguments is that capitalism benefits the rich more than it benefits the common man. Let's look at it.

The rich have always had access to entertainment—sometimes in the comfort of their palaces and mansions. The rich have never had to experience the drudgery of having to beat out carpets, iron their clothing, or slave over a hot stove all day in order to have a decent dinner; they could afford to hire people. Today, the common man has the power to enjoy much of what only the rich could yesteryear. Capitalism's mass production has made radios and televisions, vacuum cleaners, wash-and-wear clothing, and microwave ovens available and well within the reach of the common man, sparing him the drudgery of the past.

What about those who became wealthy making comforts available to the common man? Henry Ford benefited immensely from mass producing automobiles, but the benefit for the common man, from being able to buy a car, dwarfs anything Ford received. Individual discoverers and companies who produced penicillin, polio, and typhoid vaccines may have become wealthy, but again it was the common man who was the major beneficiary. In more recent times, computers and software products have affected our health, safety, and life quality in ways that dwarf the wealth received by their creators.

Here's a little test. Stand on the corner and watch people walk or drive by. Then, based on their appearances, identify which persons are wealthy. Years ago, it wouldn't have been that hard. The ordinary person wouldn't be dressed as well—surely not wearing designer clothing—nor would they have nice-looking jewelry or be driving by. Compare the income status of today's airline passengers with those of yesterday. You'll find a greater percentage of ordinary people.

That's one of the great benefits of capitalism: It has made it possible for common people to enjoy at least some of what wealthy people enjoy. You say, "Williams, common people don't have access to Rolls Royces and yachts!" You're wrong. Microsoft's Bill Gates is superrich and can afford to ride in a Rolls Royce and go yachting. So can Williams—just not as long. I can rent a Rolls or a yacht for a day, half-day, or an hour.

Capitalism is relatively new in human history. Prior to capitalism, the way people amassed great wealth was by looting, plundering, and enslaving their fellow man. Capitalism made it possible to become wealthy by serving your fellow man. Capitalists seek to find what people want and produce and market it as efficiently as possible.

Here's a question for us: Are people who by their actions create unprecedented convenience, longer life expectancy, and more fun available to the ordinary person—becoming wealthy in the process—deserving of all the scorn and ridicule heaped upon them by intellectuals and politicians? Are the wealthy obliged to "give something back?" For example, what more do the wealthy discoverers and producers of life-saving antibiotics owe us? They've already saved lives and made us healthier.

Despite the miracles of capitalism, it doesn't do well in popularity polls. One of the reasons is that capitalism is always evaluated against the nonexistent utopias of socialism or communism. Any earthly system pales in comparison to utopias. But for the ordinary person, capitalism, with all of its warts, is superior to any system yet devised to deal with our everyday needs and desires.

Economics of Unionism

August 20, 1997

The Teamsters' strike against United Parcel Service (UPS) gives us a chance to think about unions and labor issues. In a free society, people have the right to form voluntary associations. Therefore, any impediment, including so-called right-to-work laws, to people joining and forming labor unions is offensive. On the other hand, when union membership or dues payment is made mandatory as a condition of employment, that is equally offensive.

Union leaders argue that collective bargaining benefits all workers, even those who aren't members. They should not be allowed to "free ride"; thus, compulsory dues are justified. That's a little more complex argument, but the fact that one person benefits from the activities of another doesn't necessarily make the case for compulsory payments. For example, if I catch my neighbor enjoying my beautiful rhododendrons, should she be forced to pay part of their costs rather than "free-riding"?

Union leaders argue that their struggle for higher wages is against the employer and that their major weapon in that struggle is the strike. They're wrong on both counts. By itself, the strike is not much of a weapon. Instead, union power lies in its ability to prevent employers from hiring other workers in their places. They can achieve this through either labor laws or violence. Otherwise, a strike is little more than a mass resignation. That's why the 1981 air traffic controllers' union strike was a disaster; they could not prevent the Federal Aviation Administration (FAA) from hiring other workers. The real struggle of labor unions is against other workers. Their ability to demand wages that may exceed their productivity depends on their ability to prevent employers from hiring replacements.

Competition is always between either seller and seller or buyer and buyer—not buyer and seller. If Wal-Mart wanted to rig the game in order to charge higher prices, it would try to get K-Mart and Sears (other sellers) out of the market, not you and me (buyers). Unions represent sellers—in this case, sellers of labor services. They benefit from restricting entry by other sellers (workers) and having more buyers (employers). This aspect of the conflict between unions and other workers is seen by the fact that when there's a strike involving violence, it is workers who disagree with the union who are most likely to be assaulted, injured, or killed by union members, not employers.

Higher wages are not caused by unionism. If unionization was the route to higher wages and living standards, poverty could be wiped out instantly in countries like Haiti, Zaire, and Romania simply by unionization.

High wages are related to worker productivity. The challenge is to make people more productive. One way is through what economists call investment in human capital (i.e., education and skills training). Another is through greater formation of physical capital—machinery, tools, and equipment. When we see highway construction around the world, workers using a lot of heavy equipment receive higher wages than those using picks and shovels. Heavy equipment operators are more productive because they're working with more capital. Therefore, rising wages are tied to increased capital formation. One way to increase capital formation is to change our tax policy that makes capital formation more costly—eliminate capital gains and corporate profit taxes.

The bottom-line protection for today's workers is rising worker productivity and many employers' competing for their services. After all, the bulk of our labor force is not unionized and for the most part doing quite well.

Visible Outputs, Invisible Input

March 26, 1997

How about a mini-Williams autobiography? From exceedingly humble beginnings, I am now in the top one percent of income-earners. How did that come about? Maybe someone saw me walking around North Philadelphia and said, "Williams, I'm going to make you well off." That would have been nice, but it didn't happen that way.

In 1960, stationed in Korea, twenty-four years old, it dawned on me that if I didn't get started soon, I'd never get anywhere. My wife and I agreed that when my army tour was over, and we had saved $700, we'd move to California and I'd go to college. Discharged on July 2, 1961, I got my job back with Yellow Cab. After Thanksgiving with Mom, we were on the road to California in my 1951 Mercury, towing our worldly possessions in a 4′ × 6′ trailer.

Connie landed a $65-a-week job; I started at California State College that February. My wife's meager earnings meant powdered milk and "checks and dirties" eggs. Butter was out of the question except for holidays. Shopping was an excursion that might include seven stores in one evening, purchasing only those items on sale. Ten and a half years later, going to school year round, including summers, I was awarded a Ph.D. in economics from the University of California at Los Angeles.

Our story of sacrifice and hard work is a story millions of Americans can tell. The story's point is quite different. People can easily see the fruits of others' efforts (big houses, fancy cars, and money) but they usually don't see the effort that produced these fruits. As a result they conclude that it's not fair for some people to have much more than others. Envy sets in. They fall easy prey to demagogues and charlatans, who convince them there's something unjust when some earn higher income than others. Justice requires that Congress step in to take away "ill-gotten" gains and return them to their "rightful" owners.

It's understandable that people see things this way. The results of hard work, sacrifice, and risk taking are visible. The actual hard work, sacrifice, and risk taking are not visible. They might conclude, "I'm a decent, hardworking guy just like Bill Gates, Sam Walton, or Fred Smith. For them to have all that money, they must have done something nonkosher."

The fact of business is there are only a few wealthy or well-off people who are where they are because of inheritance or pure luck. Most high-income people achieve that status through hard work, sacrifice, and risk taking. In fact, if you survey Fortune 500's periodic listing of America's wealthiest men, it's not old money like the Vanderbilts, Rockefellers, and Morgans. It's mostly first-generation rich people like the Fred Smiths, Bill Gates, and the late Sam Walton. For the most part, they are people who had modest starts but a vision of how to please their fellow man.

Instead of being held up to ridicule and scorn, these people ought to be America's heroes. Fred Smith, who produced a way to guarantee next-day mail delivery to most any place on the globe, shouldn't be portrayed as the enemy of the common man. Sam Walton, who beat his competitors' prices, shouldn't be put in the scorn category.

If there are any who should be held up to scorn and ridicule, it's societal parasites—people who forcibly take from others giving nothing in return. That category includes thieves, robbers, and con artists. It also includes otherwise honest people who use Congress to do the looting for them, for example, welfare recipients and corporate CEOs of companies like Archer Daniels Midland, Gallo, and McDonalds.

The Welfare Debate

1996

There is no getting around the fact that the erosion of spontaneously evolved traditional value lies at the heart of our most intractable socioeconomic problems. "Tradition," as Friedrich A. Hayek points out, "is not something constant but the product of a process of selection guided not by reason but by success."[1] It is no historical accident that certain forms of behavior such as teen sexual abstinence, education, marriage, and work evolved as an integral part of our shared values. Those values maximize the potential for human success while their refutation leads to today's growing social pathology.

Traditional values have been under siege for several decades exemplified by the teachings of the intellectual elite such as Professor Andrew Cherlin, a sociologist at the Johns Hopkins University who, according to Professor Andrew Hacker, is an authority on marriage and divorce. Cherlin says it has yet to be shown that "absence of a father was directly responsible for any of the supposed deficiencies of broken homes."[2] The real issue, Cherlin continues, "is not the lack of male presence but the lack of male income."[3] That vision differs little from that which says a father and husband can be replaced by a welfare check. It is a vision adopted

---

1. Friedrich A. Hayek, *Law, Legislation and Liberty*, vol. 3 (Chicago: University of Chicago Press, 1973), p. 166.
2. Cited in Andrew Hacker, *Two Nations: Black and White, Separate, Hostile, Unequal* (New York: Charles Scribner's Sons, 1992), p. 73.
3. Ibid.

by many and has produced unprecedented chaos, most notably among a large sector of the black population.

Contrary to the confident pronouncements of the intellectual elite, a "legacy of slavery" cannot explain the social chaos seen today among a large section of the black community. A hundred years ago, with blacks being one generation out of slavery, a slightly higher percentage of black adults married compared to white adults. This remained true in every census from 1890 to 1940. As of 1950, 72 percent of black men and 81 percent of black women had been married.[4] As of 1940, among black females who headed households, 52 percent were forty-five years and older; only 14 percent of black children were born to unmarried women.[5] One study of nineteenth-century slave families found that in up to three-fourths of the families, all the children had the same biological mother and father.[6] In New York City, in 1925, 85 percent of kin-related black households were double-headed.[7] In fact, "Five in six children [in New York City] under the age of six lived with both parents."[8] Both during slavery and as late as 1920, a teenage girl raising a child without a man present was rare among blacks.[9]

In marked contrast with the past, in 1992, a majority of black children—54 percent—resided in female-headed households.[10] Il-

4. Thomas Sowell, *Vision of the Anointed: Self-Congratulation as a Basis for Social Policy* (New York: Basic Books, 1995), p. 81.

5. Ibid.

6. Herbert Gutman, *The Black Family in Slavery and Freedom: 1750–1925* (New York: Pantheon Books, 1976), p. 10ff.

7. Ibid., p. xix.

8. Ibid.

9. Ibid., p. 455.

10. Arlene Skolnick, "The American Family," in *Focus on Children: The Beat of the Future*, Report of the 1992 Media Conference at the Columbia University Graduate School of Journalism, p. 60. Cited in Thomas Sowell, *Vision of the Anointed: Self-Congratulation as a Basis for Social Policy* (New York: Basic Books, 1995), p. 273.

legitimacy has become an accepted way of life when nationally 66 percent of black babies are born out of wedlock and, in some poor inner-city neighborhoods, the illegitimacy rate is over 80 percent.[11] Children are raising children and the black marriage rate has plummeted.

Although the social impact of welfare has been particularly devastating to black families, it has by no means spared white families. In 1965, when now Senator Daniel Patrick Moynihan wrote the controversial *The Negro Family*, black family illegitimacy stood at 25 percent compared to 66 percent today. Today, the illegitimate birthrate for the nation as a whole is 30 percent. The nation as a whole is now further down the road to family disintegration than black families were in 1965. Illegitimacy among white high school dropouts is 48 percent.[12]

Widespread family breakdown or, what is more descriptive— families not forming in the first place—has produced the pathology that is an integral part of today's urban landscape. No one should be the least surprised by high crime rates and atmosphere of violence where young men are being raised without fathers and with often incompetent mothers. The cultural values of many urban communities have become young male adolescent values: violence, predatory sex, and instant gratification or what Charles Murray has characterized as *Lord of the Flies* writ large.

Without families there is precious little that can be done to enrich a youngster's life and raise his potential for future success. Consider the question: What are some simple threshold basics necessary for a youngster to get a good education? Someone must make sure homework is done. Someone must ensure that the youngster goes to bed early enough to get a good night's rest. Someone must make him obey the schoolteacher. It is not likely that *any* of these

11. U.S. Bureau of the Census, *Current Population Reports*, Series P-60, 1994.
12. Ibid., p. 3.

threshold requirements can be accomplished by a politician, social worker, teacher, or consultant. If they are not met, the quantity of public expenditures on education is immaterial; education will not occur.

Evidence that government "solutions" do little to solve social pathology is seen by the fact that the nation has spent $5.4 trillion, in constant 1993 dollars, on poverty programs since 1965 and that the problems of dependency they sought to address are worse now than in 1965.[13] Although government cannot solve the problems of pathology and dependency, it should not create the "moral hazard" where poor people are rewarded for self-destructive behavior that brings them welfare benefits.

Charles Murray is right in pointing out that whether reform should be tough on the parents or compassionate toward their children is a false political choice. Suffering and destruction of children are already with us despite today's massive welfare. We have had thirty years to find out what does not work. If we are serious about welfare reform, different approaches must be tried and we must be willing to see pain. Our thinking about the cure for the pathology created by welfare dependency must embody at least some of what we think would help a heroin addict. If the addict and those who propose to help him are unwilling to see him in pain, then neither he nor they are serious about being cured.

As with heroin addiction treatment, there may be something said for going "cold turkey." If welfare were ended or greatly reduced, one doubts that men, women, and children would starve. After all, there were poor Americans long before the welfare state and there is little evidence of starvation. If welfare were eliminated, coupled with commensurate tax reductions, charity would play a greater role. Communities and neighbors helping would not pres-

13. Robert Rector and William Lauber, *America's Failed $5.4 Trillion War on Poverty* (Washington, D.C.: Heritage Foundation, 1995).

ent the destructive moral hazard of government entitlement programs where simply meeting a means-test qualifies one for welfare without any obligation to make those future enhancing self-improvements such as work, education, care of children. Moreover, the specter of starvation is a strong inducement for one to seek work. Work alone is the most effective antipoverty tool. Work coupled with marriage, and postponing starting a family, is almost a guarantee of not living in poverty since a married couple working, even at minimum wage jobs, would earn $17,000 and the poverty income for a family of four is $14,763.

Crime and Business

1997

In most discussions about economic development in black neighborhoods, a critical group of questions are left unasked, the most important of which is: To what extent are black neighborhoods hospitable to economic activity? This is a question that must be faced honestly. If it is faced honestly, one cannot escape the conclusion that crime imposes high costs on black neighborhoods and as such is a strong impediment to economic growth. The magnitude of that crime can be demonstrated by a few statistics.

In absolute numbers, blacks commit most of the crime in the United States. Blacks account for half of all the arrests for assault and rape and two-thirds of arrests for robbery. Blacks are disproportionately more represented in all categories of felonies, except those requiring access to large sums of money such as embezzlement and stock fraud. Criminologist Marvin Wolfgang said, "For

four violent offenses—homicide, rape, robbery and aggravated assault—the crime rates for blacks are at least 10 times as high as
they are for whites." Close to 90 percent of the victims of black
criminals are black. These and other statistics make it clear that
most crime occurs mainly *within* black communities.

Regardless of any argument about just what might explain the
high crime rate in black neighborhoods, a fact that is beyond debate is that criminal activity imposes a very high cost. A considerable burden of that cost is borne by the overwhelmingly law-abiding, often poor black citizens who can least afford it. Indeed, poor
people are most dependent on law and order for their safety and
welfare. Wealthier people have the financial resources to defend
themselves by purchasing alarms, hiring private guards, and, if it
gets too bad, migrating out of high-crime neighborhoods. Those
options are less available to poorer citizens.

High crime rates impose not only personal safety costs but economic costs as well. In the wake of the 1992 Los Angeles riots, a
frequent complaint heard from black residents was the relative
absence of supermarkets and banks in their neighborhoods. They
complained that they had to either shop at higher-priced "Ma &
Pa" stores in their neighborhoods or bear the expense and inconvenience of traveling to faraway supermarkets or shopping malls.
They also complained that the absence of banks make it necessary
for them to cash checks at costly check-cashing establishments
within their neighborhoods. Occasionally, we hear complaints that
fast-food delivery establishments refuse to deliver merchandise to
customers in certain areas. None of these actions can be explained
by a racial discrimination argument that white merchants do not
want the dollars, and subsequent profits, that come through black
hands. A more satisfactory explanation has to do with the costs of
doing business in high-crime neighborhoods as opposed to that of
doing business elsewhere.

Consider for a moment how crime affects the operation of a

supermarket. One of the methods supermarket managers use to maximize profits is to maximize the quantity of merchandise turnover per square foot of floor space. In pursuit of that goal, supermarkets place items in spaces beyond the cash register and often outside on the sidewalk adjacent to the store. In some cases, some of the items are left there overnight. Such a sales strategy is far more feasible in an environment where crime—in this case shoplifting—is low.

In higher-crime areas, supermarkets eschew this sales strategy. They cannot place items near store entrances. They cannot place items outside the store unless there is a security guard or store employee there to police them. All this means that a supermarket manager in higher-crime areas must pay for a given amount of square footage but cannot use as much of it as his counterpart in a lower-crime area. As such it raises the cost of business.

Other more visible costs of doing business in higher-crime areas are the widespread use of iron gates to cover store windows and fewer hours of operation. These additional costs are coupled with higher fire and burglary insurance, if available in the first place. None of this is to say that stores in lower-crime areas do not experience crime costs. However, the magnitude of these costs is smaller, particularly when they are considered as a percentage of total sales. In other words, $10,000 worth of shoplifting has a smaller impact on profitability when total sales are $100,000. In the former case, the shoplifting might be a minor nuisance to be written off against taxes, where in the latter case that same $10,000 might mean the same difference between being in business or out of business.

High crime not only lowers the profitability of business but lowers the value of anything located in the area. The value of property is related to the certainty that the owner has the right to decide how the property is used. Arson and wanton property destruction negatively affect ownership rights. Consider the case of ordinary housing. In black neighborhoods, houses or other buildings, were they located somewhere with a greater overall respect for property rights, would fetch multiples of what they currently fetch in areas with weak respect for property. A virtual laboratory experiment tends to confirm this. When black neighborhoods are "gentrified," that is, middle-income people come in and virtually buy up whole rundown neighborhoods and make improvements, thereafter property prices skyrocket.

Another, somewhat unnoticed, cost of crime is that it tends to change other elements of the character of a neighborhood. When there is high crime, poor schools, and unkept streets, the people who have the means and care the most about school security and neighborhood amenities are the first to leave. They are replaced by people who do not care as much or do not have other alternatives. All this tends to reduce the social leavening that makes for vital and stable communities.

A first-order condition for economic growth in black communities and, for that matter, any other community is law and order. Unless the issue of crime is adequately addressed other efforts to promote economic growth are for nought.

Drugs, Economics, and Liberty

1998

No one disputes that narcotics do harm to people. However, there is not nearly as much consensus as to what is the correct public response to narcotics use and sales. Let's start by acknowledging that there is no question whatsoever that narcotic use and sales in our country can be virtually eliminated. It can be accomplished at a monetary cost far less than the tens of billions spent so far in the nation's "war on drugs." We could suspend habeas corpus and constitutional guarantees against unreasonable search to more easily gather evidence on people who use or sell drugs. We can make those arrested bear the burden of proof of innocence and, on conviction, summarily execute them. Countries with far less wealth and police resources than ours have used that strategy and so could we. I think most Americans would, and should, recoil at that kind of drug war strategy. So we have to examine less draconian alternatives. A few thoughts on the economics of drug trade might give us guidance.

There's no mystery why people use mind-altering drugs. It makes them feel good, at least temporarily. That's not only true about cocaine, heroin, and marijuana use; it's also true about mind-altering products like cigarettes, cigars, coffee, tea, wine, and whiskey. There's considerable evidence that people prefer their vices in diluted form, hence, the popularity of filtered cigarettes, light beer, wine coolers, and mixed drinks. The same seems to be true, at least to some extent, about illicit drugs.

When vices are legally prohibited, some supply responses change people's behavior. Imagine there's a supplier of illegal marijuana. Government steps up its efforts to stop his supply by increasing interdiction efforts, along with stiffer fines and prison sentences. Which is easier to conceal and transport—a million dollars' worth of marijuana or a million dollars' worth of cocaine? Obviously, it's cocaine because there is far less bulk per dollar of value. Thus, one effect of prohibition is the tendency toward increased sales and use of more concentrated forms of vice such as crack cocaine and ice.

Prohibition also has an impact on prices. To supply the addiction needs of those who are not able to pay the prohibition-induced higher prices of cocaine, producers will seek to find cheaper substitutes such as crack. This is borne out by the fact that crack is far more popular among poorer addicts than wealthier ones.

Another effect of illegality, high prices, and high profits, coupled with greater government drug interdiction efforts, is that it encourages entry by suppliers who are more ruthless, innovative, and have a lower regard for civility and the law. Pantywaist, petty, otherwise law-abiding practitioners are ousted. In addition, since the courts are unavailable to enforce agreements made among traders, as in the case of legal transactions, disputes are more likely to be settled through violence.

Another supply response to prohibition, largely ignored in the drug debate, is the inevitable tendency toward corruption of government officials. Today's level of drug trade, and for that matter the 1920s prohibited liquor trade, could not flourish without official corruption. It's not difficult to see how police officers, customs inspectors, and other law enforcement officers, earning $30,000 or $40,000 a year, can succumb to the temptation of thousand-dollar bribes to look the other way. No doubt there are politicians, who oversee lawmen, who are also tempted by bribes. Even otherwise law-abiding parents are quieted by money and expensive gifts from their children who are involved in some aspect of the drug-dealing trade.

The "war on drugs" restricts supply and raises prices. When we bust up one drug operation, another one emerges virtually overnight to take its place. When drug warriors make a big drug bust, law-abiding citizens shouldn't be that jubilant. Instead, we should expect higher prices, more ruthless participants, more crime, corruption, and greater social costs.

Another dangerous cost of the war on drugs is that it has given respectability to the violation of our constitutional guarantees. Civil forfeiture laws have been enacted where property can be confiscated without due process in clear violation of the Fifth Amendment. A parent can have his automobile or home confiscated if, unbeknownst to the parent, his offspring is involved in drug usage or sales in the same. Anti-money-laundering laws violate our rights to privacy in our transactions. Murderers and rapists have been freed from prison to make room for nonviolent drug users.

From the demand, or personal use, side of the drug issue, what should we do? Lysander Spooner (1808–1897), one of the great American thinkers of the nineteenth century, suggests that while vices may be self-destructive or offensive, like all peaceful, voluntary activities they should remain outside the province of law and government. The vices Spooner referred to include "gluttony, drunkenness, prostitution, gambling, prize-fighting, tobacco-chewing, smoking, and snuffing, opium-eating, corset-wearing, idleness, waste of property, avarice, hypocrisy, etc., etc." Spooner added that if practitioners of these and other vices cannot be reformed voluntarily, if they go on to what other men call destruction, then they must be permitted to do so. He reminds us that the maxim of law is there can be no crime without criminal intent to invade the property or person of another. People practice vices for what they perceive as their own happiness—not to violate the rights of another. In other words, in a free society, people have the right to destroy their own lives but not those of others. When government coercion is used to promote virtue, there cannot be liberty. However, there is conduct that people might engage in under the influence of narcotics such as impaired driving, robbery and burglary to fund their habit, and other acts that threaten the rights of others. Such acts are criminal and should be punished.

We Americans have to ask ourselves if there is a better way to fight the drug scourge. I think we need to focus more on the demand side of the drug problem. After all, most people don't use marijuana, cocaine, and heroin. The reason they don't has nothing to do with its price or the fact that it's illegal. Their decision has much more to do with their values and common sense. Rather than near-exclusive reliance on the law and government, I believe greater and longer-lasting gains can be made through civil society where we cajole, admonish, teach, and ostracize people about the use and destructive effects of narcotics. It is foolhardy to have public policy that forces people who are hell-bent on destroying themselves to become violent criminals and destroy innocent people in the process. It is also foolhardy for society to create circumstances where we compromise official integrity and personal liberties in the name of a war on drugs that has been increasingly shown to be a failure.